HUNTING
CHE

HUNTING CHE

How a U.S. Special Forces Team
Helped Capture the World's
Most Famous Revolutionary

Mitch Weiss
and Kevin Maurer

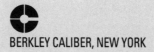

BERKLEY CALIBER, NEW YORK

THE BERKLEY PUBLISHING GROUP
Published by the Penguin Group
Penguin Group (USA) Inc.
375 Hudson Street, New York, New York 10014, USA

USA I Canada I UK I Ireland I Australia I New Zealand I India I South Africa I China

Penguin Books Ltd., Registered Offices: 80 Strand, London WC2R 0RL, England
For more information about the Penguin Group, visit penguin.com.

This book is an original publication of The Berkley Publishing Group.

Library of Congress Cataloging-in-Publication Data

Weiss, Mitch.
Hunting Che : how a U.S. special forces team helped capture the world's most famous revolutionary / by Mitch Weiss & Kevin Maurer.—First edition.
pages cm
Includes bibliographical references.
ISBN 978-0-425-25746-3
1. Guevara, Che, 1928–1967—Death and burial.   2. Special forces (Military science)—United States—History—20th century.   3. Bolivia. Ejército—Commando troops—History—20th century.   4. Revolutionaries—Bolivia—History—20th century.   5. Guerrillas—Bolivia—History—20th century.   6. Bolivia—History, Military—20th century.   7. Bolivia—History—1938–1982.   8. Shelton, Ralph, 1929–2010.   9. Prado Salmón, Gary.   10. Rodriguez, Felix I.   I. Maurer, Kevin.   II. Title.
F2849.22.G85W45 2013
980.03'5092—dc23
2013003086

First Edition: July 2013

PRINTED IN THE UNITED STATES OF AMERICA

10 9 8 7 6 5 4 3 2 1

Jacket design by D. Abbiate
Jacket photos: book cover © Shutterstock; Landscape © Irene Lamprakou / Trevillions Images
Book design by Laura K. Corless
Interior maps copyright © 2013 by Travis Rightmeyer

ALWAYS LEARNING

PEARSON

To Ralph "Pappy" Shelton, a true patriot

The green beret is again becoming a symbol of excellence, a badge of courage, a mark of distinction in the fight for freedom.

John F. Kennedy, 1962 letter to the United States Army supporting Special Forces

CAST OF CHARACTERS

U.S. SPECIAL FORCES

Major Ralph "Pappy" Shelton: Leader of the Green Beret team that trained the Second Ranger Battalion in La Esperanza, Bolivia. Born in Corinth, Mississippi, he dropped out of school in the tenth grade to pick cotton and do odd jobs to help support his mother. Shelton joined the military as a private and worked his way up to major. He fought in Korea and was deployed to Laos and the Dominican Republic. The mission to Bolivia was his last.

KEY MEMBERS OF HIS TEAM

Captain Edmond Fricke: Executive Officer/S-3
Captain LeRoy Mitchell: Executive Officer/S-3
Captain Margarito Cruz: S-2
First Lieutenant Harvey Wallender: S-2
Master Sergeant Oliverio Gomez: Team Sergeant
Master Sergeant Roland Milliard: Intelligence Sergeant
Sergeant First Class Daniel Chapa: Light Weapons Sergeant
Sergeant First Class Hector Rivera-Colon: Heavy Weapons Sergeant
Staff Sergeant Jerald Peterson: Medical Specialist
Staff Sergeant James Hapka: Medical Specialist
Staff Sergeant Wendell Thompson Jr.: Radio Operator
Sergeant Alvin Graham III: Radio Operator

THE GUERRILLAS

Ernesto "Che" Guevara: An Argentinian doctor, he abandoned his profession to help Fidel Castro overthrow Cuban dictator Fulgencio Batista. Che was the charismatic, iconic symbol of the Cuban Revolution.

With his long hair and scraggly beard, green fatigues and beret, he preached a simple message: The duty of a revolutionary was to make revolution. He eventually left Cuba to spread revolution—first in Africa, then Bolivia.

KEY MEMBERS OF CHE'S GUERRILLAS
(The first name is the guerrilla's alias, followed by his or her real name.)

Joaquin (Acuna Nunez Juan Vitalio): A Cuban-born officer who was a member of the Central Committee of the Cuban Communist Party. He was the rear guard commander.

Tania (Tamara Bunke Bide): Born in Argentina to German parents, she was sent to Bolivia in 1961 to facilitate the arrival of the guerrillas and set up an urban support structure.

Paco (Castillo Chavez): A Bolivian Communist recruited to the party with promises of going to the university in Havana or Moscow. Instead, he was drafted into Che's guerrilla band. After his unit was ambushed, he provided key information and details that allowed the Bolivians to find Che.

Inti (Guido Peredo): A Bolivian guerrilla, he was one of Che's most tactically proficient and capable fighters. He worked with Peruvian guerrilla fighters before joining Che's force.

Camba (Orlando Jimenez Bazan): A Bolivian guerrilla trained in Cuba.

Antonio (Orlando Pantoja): Che's lieutenant in the Sierra Maestra, he was the head of Cuba's Coast and Harbor Surveillance.

Arturo (Rene Martinez Tamayo): A captain in the Cuban Army Department of Investigation.

Moises (Moises Guevara Rodriguez): A Bolivian Communist and union mining leader.

Ernesto (Freddy Maymura): A Bolivian who was a medical student on scholarship in Cuba.

Braulio (Israel Reyes Zayas): A Cuban veteran of the Sierra Maestra and the Second Front of the Escambray.

Miguel (Manuel Hernandez): A veteran of the Sierra Maestra campaign with Che.

Chino (Juan Pablo Chang Navarro): A Peruvian Communist Party leader.

Coco (Robert Peredo Leigue): A Bolivian who bought the Nancahuazu farm property.

Julio (Mario Gutirrez Ardaya): A Bolivian medical student on scholarship in Cuba.

Pacho (Alberto Fernandez Montes de Oca): A longtime Che friend and Cuban director of mines. He entered Bolivia with a Uruguayan passport and alias: Antonio Garrido.

Willy (Simon Cuba): A Bolivian guerrilla who was captured with Che near La Higuera.

Jules Regis Debray: A French Communist, he was famous for writing a book about revolutions. He was arrested in April 1967 after leaving Che's camp. He later confirmed Che's presence in Bolivia. His arrest kicked off the manhunt that eventually led to the death of the guerrilla leader.

Ciro Roberto Bustos: An Argentinian painter and a salesman, he was with Che and arrested with Debray. Like the Frenchman, he eventually revealed Che's involvement with the guerrillas and provided the Bolivian government with sketches of the guerrilla fighters.

George Andrew Roth: An Anglo-Chilean journalist who was arrested with Bustos and Debray after leaving Che's camp.

CIA OPERATIVES

Félix Rodríguez: A member of the Cuban exile community, he was part of a clandestine unit that had taken part in the Bay of Pigs invasion. Rodríguez worked with the CIA on numerous anti-Castro plots and raids before being selected to hunt Che in Bolivia.

Gustavo Villoldo: Another Cuban exile, Villoldo fought in the Bay of Pigs invasion and was a veteran of numerous raids into Cuba. He volunteered to hunt for Che in the Congo and was urged to "volunteer" for the Bolivian mission.

Larry Sternfield: The CIA officer who recruited Rodríguez and Villoldo for the Che mission.

John Tilton: The head of the CIA in La Paz.

THE AMERICANS

Douglas Henderson: A career diplomat, Henderson served as the U.S. ambassador to Bolivia during the guerrilla insurgency led by Che.

Walt Whitman Rostow: A staunch anti-Communist, Rostow served as a national security advisor in the Kennedy and Johnson administrations.

Dean Rusk: The secretary of state under Kennedy and Johnson, he wanted to keep U.S. forces out of Bolivia.

Richard Helms: The CIA director, he was highly critical of Barrientos and wondered if the Bolivian president could survive the Che crisis.

Robert Porter: The commander of United States Southern Force (SOUTH-COM), the general sent a Special Forces unit to Bolivia to train the Rangers.

William Tope: A brigadier general on Porter's staff, he went on a fact-finding mission in Bolivia to gauge the rebel threat.

Magnus Smith: The Eighth Special Forces Group commander, the colonel assigned Shelton to Bolivia.

Harry Singh: An American with the U.S. Agency for International Development, he provided Shelton with the materials and machinery to help build a school in the village.

BOLIVIAN HIGH COMMAND

René Barrientos Ortuno: A dashing air force general elected Bolivian president in 1966. A charismatic leader, he was pro-American and had strong ties to the peasants, who supported his administration.

Alfredo Ovando Candía: A general who seized power with Barrientos in a 1964 military coup. They ruled together until January 1966, when Barrientos resigned to run for president. After Barrientos's victory, Ovando took over the military.

Luis Adolfo Siles Salinas: A close friend of Barrientos who was elected vice president in 1966.

Jorge Belmonte Ardile: An air force general, he was a member of Barrientos's inner circle.

BOLIVIAN COMMANDERS

Gary Prado Salmon: A captain in the Bolivian Army, he became a commander of one of the Bolivian Ranger companies trained by Shelton's team.

Joaquin Zenteno Anaya: A colonel in the Eighth Division, his unit worked with the Rangers to trap the guerrillas.

Arnaldo Saucedo: An Eighth Division intelligence officer, the major worked closely with the CIA's Félix Rodríguez to track down Che Guevara.

Andres Selich: A lieutenant colonel who was one of the first Bolivian officers to interrogate Che.

Jose Gallardo: A colonel who was placed in charge of the new regiment and training camp in La Esperanza.

Miguel Ayoroa Montano: A major, he was appointed the Rangers' battalion commander.

Mario Vargas Salinas: A captain who was in charge of an ambush that wiped out Che's lost contingent at Yado del Yeso.

Jaime Nin de Guzman: A helicopter pilot who shuttled Bolivian officers from Vallegrande to La Higuera after Che was captured.

BOLIVIAN SOLDIERS

Augusto Silva Bogado: A captain with the army's Fourth Division in Camiri, his unit was on patrol when the guerrillas ambushed in March 1967.

Hernan Plata: A major who was among the Bolivian soldiers captured in the same ambush.

Ruben Amezaga: A second lieutenant and friend of Prado, he was killed during the ambush.

Mario Salazar: Trained by the Special Forces, he joined the army to hunt down and destroy Che's guerrilla force.

Ruben Sanchez: A major whose unit was ambushed on patrol in the Nancahuazu River valley in April 1967. He was captured in the ambush.

Luis Saavedra Arambel: A lieutenant, he was fatally shot during the same patrol.

Jorge Ayala: A second lieutenant who helped reorganize troops during the April ambush.

Carlos Martins: Another second lieutenant who tried to come to Sanchez's rescue.

Remberto Lafuente: A lieutenant who led Bolivian soldiers into the jungle to rescue Sanchez and his men.

Juan Vacaflor: A lieutenant, he was briefly captured by the rebels during the raid on Samaipata.

Bernardino Huanca: A sergeant with Prado's B Company, he took out a guerrilla nest during a firefight near La Higuera, leading to Che's capture.

Sergeant Mario Teran: Another member of Prado's company, he was the soldier who volunteered to "take care" of Che in the schoolhouse.

CIVILIANS

Epifano Vargas: A civilian guide who was shot by guerrillas as he was helping an army patrol in March 1967.

Honorato Rojas: A farmer who betrayed Che's men at Yado del Yeso.

Dioniso Valderomas: A resident of La Esperanza, he lived near the sugar mill where U.S. Special Forces soldiers trained the Bolivian Rangers.

Dorys Roca: One of fourteen family members who lived in a three-room house in La Esperanza, she fell in love with American soldier Alvin Graham III.

Erwin Bravo: The mayor, he supported the presence of U.S. troops in La Esperanza.

Manosanta Humerundo: As the Holy Hand, he was a medicine man who treated sick villagers in La Esperanza.

Bolivia
South America

1967

N

3000 km

Peru

La Paz

Cochabamba

Brazil

Santa Cruz

Vallegrande

Nancahuazu

Chile

Camiri

Paraguay

Argentina

300 km

© 2013 Travis Rightmeyer

HUNTING
CHE

PART ONE

MANY VIETNAMS

3 November 1966

The passengers on the flight were buckled in and braced for landing, crossing themselves and breathing deeply.

Flying into La Paz was almost always a white-knuckle experience, and most of the passengers on the packed DC-6 were too busy praying to ponder the spectacular Andes views outside their windows. The pilots pointed the plane at the runway of El Alto International Airport, thirteen thousand feet up, the world's highest. They knew what to expect, but the blasts of wind off the mountaintops rocked the craft from side to side and wrung cries and shouts from the people in the seats. They'd come fifteen hundred miles from Sao Paulo, Brazil, to the Bolivian capital, three hours of bucking and pitching. The air in the cramped cabin was clammy with fear.

One man did not seem to notice the atmosphere of imminent death. He sat on the aisle seat near the front of the cabin, his white shirt and Windsor-knotted tie crisp and fresh. Adolfo Mena

Gonzalez maintained the comfortable calm of a man whose plans are carefully laid, a man accustomed to being obeyed. He was a pudgy, clean-shaven, middle-aged man with black horned-rimmed glasses and flecks of gray along the edge of his receding hairline. In his pocket was a Uruguayan passport.

On his mind was his mission.

He felt confident no one in Bolivia would recognize him. It was thirteen years since he'd been there last, and he looked nothing like the unwashed young medical-school graduate who'd passed through with a friend on a transcontinental motorcycle journey. They were scruffy kids then, carefree thrill-seekers. But that trip opened Gonzales's eyes to the ugly sides of South America, country after country where a few wealthy people controlled the riches and resources while the rest struggled through lives of horrifying poverty. At the end of the journey the idealistic young doctor changed his career path. He abandoned medicine to fight for social justice.

He was coming back to Bolivia to take on the biggest challenge of his life. After two years of meticulous planning, everything was now in place: the cars he would drive, the routes he would follow, the remote farmhouse where he would live. He wasn't sure how long he would stay in Bolivia. A few months? A year? Much depended on the people on the ground. All he had to do now was survive this landing, and make it through customs.

The plane's wheels bounced onto the runway, the engines screamed. Gonzalez felt adrenaline shoot through his body. He pushed his glasses up onto his nose and nodded to Antonio Garrido, the white-faced man in the next seat, his comrade.

When the cabin door opened, the men bounded off the plane into the glorious mid-afternoon sun. They breathed the thin air deeply and moved quickly from the tarmac to the terminal. A slim, sexy woman with long black hair approached them, her black beret tilted so rakishly down it covered her eyebrow. Heads turned toward her. Her high cheekbones and upturned nose singled her out as a European, and her clothing said she was a Bohemian intellectual, maybe a poet or a sculptor. She trained her brown eyes on Gonzalez and embraced him like an old friend.

Into his passport pocket she slipped a folded paper. The trio made for the security gates, and as the woman greeted Garrido, Gonzalez reached for his passport and opened the new document. It was invaluable, exactly what he had hoped for:

The Director of Information of the Presidency of the Republic has the pleasure of presenting:

Adolfo Mena Gonzalez

Special Envoy of the Organization of American States, who is undertaking a study and collecting information on the social and economic relations that prevail in the Bolivian country-side.

The undersigned, who has presented this credential, ask all national authorities and private persons and institutions to lend Senor Adolfo Mena all the cooperation that they can in order to facilitate his research effort.

Signed:
Gonzalo Lopez
Director of Information
Presidency of the Republic of Bolivia
La Paz,
November 3, 1966

With this document, Gonzalez and his friend could travel freely through Bolivia. It was his "get out of jail free" card—a rare treasure for any traveler. The woman was well connected to rich and powerful figures in Bolivia. Hard things were easy for her.

Having walked calmly to the customs table, Gonzalez handed his passport and the letter to the agent. The man in the khaki uniform inspected the documents and closely examined the suit-and-tie photo of Gonzalez. He glanced at Gonzalez to see if the faces matched, then stamped the passport and waved him through.

Gonzalez sighed and waited for Garrido to clear customs. The pair had memorized the airport layout months before, and they hurried out of the terminal to the curb where the woman was waiting in her Jeep. They kept silent on the ten-mile drive, passing roadside stands where vendors sold fruit, vegetables, and clothing. La Paz was built in a canyon with homes and apartment houses climbing the steep hills alongside. Low stucco shops and cafés stood along crowded, narrow streets. In the distance, through the haze of exhaust, Gonzalez glimpsed the majestic snowcapped peaks of the Illimani, the highest mountain range in the Andes. They traveled north into the city center, on to the fashionable tree-lined Prado district, and up to the Hotel Copacabana.

More friends greeted him there. He checked into a third-floor suite and they followed him upstairs. For hours they discussed their plans and marveled at how well he looked, until the exhausted Gonzalez excused himself to his private room.

He was in a fine hotel at the urban heart of Bolivia, but Gonzalez had no intention of staying. He would rest tonight and leave for the ranch first thing in the morning. The trip would take two days, following the edge of a mountainous jungle. Most of the roads were unpaved.

The noise in the next room died down. He was too tired to fall asleep. He thought about leaving straightaway. He paced the room for a few minutes to calm himself, then brushed back the thick white balcony curtains. The Illimani filled his view and marched away to the horizon, rank after rank of snow-covered glory. He lit a cigar and stared at the dusky vista, then took his trusty Minolta camera from its bag. Gonzalez carried his camera everywhere, snapping pictures like an enthusiastic tourist. He looked around the luxurious room, memorizing details. He was accustomed to the finest hotels and superb restaurants. This would likely be the last such indulgence, he told himself.

It was worth it. This mission was vital to his greater plan. Here he meant to start "two, three or many Vietnams" in Latin America, and ultimately bring the capitalist warlords of the United States to their knees.

Gonzalez sat in a chair by the window. On the wardrobe door directly in front of him hung a full-length mirror. He stared at his reflection, startled at his transformation into a middle-class business traveler. Maybe he wanted to document the start of his great journey. For whatever reason, Gonzalez poised his camera in his lap, scowled into the mirror, and snapped his portrait.

He changed out of his suit and back into himself. The time was right, he knew, for revolution in Bolivia.

CHAPTER 1

Ambush

Captain Augusto Silva Bogado felt a trickle of sweat run from his collar down his backbone. The morning sun was pushing the shade out of the steep valley, shining off the river and turning the jungle into a steam bath. His men walked along the banks below, while he and the higher ranks stayed among the trees on the hillside.

Silva and his men were part of the Bolivian Army Fourth Division, based in the oil town of Camiri. The men below, thirty-five conscripts under his command, were looking for suspicious foreigners, men with guns and money. They were following up a tip uncovered by Silva himself. It would probably turn out to be nothing, Silva thought. Troublemakers stayed up north near the tin and copper mines. There wasn't much to occupy a foreigner down here in the southeastern scrubland.

But no one could afford to ignore rumors repeated several times, in several places. He had to be prepared.

The men spread out across the valley. Slowly, carefully, the soldiers walked in a jagged line along the Rio Nancahuazu. They wrestled with thick vegetation that lined the valley floor, and they cradled their Mauser rifles as they walked, occasionally splashing into the water and swearing. Silva thought they looked more like reluctant hikers than soldiers. They'd been trained for war, but none of them had ever smelled gun smoke.

Most of his men were campesinos—poor and mostly illiterate Indians doing their required year of military service. It was their duty to serve, and they were resigned to it. Some even seemed to enjoy army life, and why not? There was no war. Food, shelter, and wages in the barracks usually far exceeded what they had at home, and they received technical training they could use after leaving the military. For the soldiers, this was a routine reconnaissance mission in Bolivia's remote badlands. The only real danger was a backwoods cocaine producer, or a poisonous snake or spider.

From his position near the front, Silva scanned the brush on the rocky slopes. So far, he saw nothing. It had been like that for days. He pushed forward.

He made a mental review of the report he'd turned in:

9 March, 1967. Dropped off by an army patrol near property owned by Segundino Parada near the village of Tatarenda.

Assignment: Determine whether there were enough ovens, water, and firewood on the land for turning local stone into calcinated lime, a possible explosive.

After examining the property, Silva was ready to return to Camiri. There were few army vehicles in the area, so the soldier hitched a ride back with a Bolivian State Oil Deposits truck. During the ride, oil workers told about the strange men with foreign accents roaming the area, "big, bearded men carrying backpacks and with plenty of money," "forty to fifty million pesos."

Silva still smiled at the memory.

That seemed highly unlikely. Few men in rural Bolivia carried that kind of cash. When Silva told his commander about the rumor, a pilot was sent up for an aerial reconnaissance. Four men were spotted along the Grande River, so Silva and his men were sent out here to gather more information. On the way they learned that in Tatarenda, two men dressed in olive-drab trousers and jackets had bought and cooked two pigs and taken canned food and cigarettes with them into the jungle. Police in the nearby village of Lagunillas arrested two "paramilitary types" for trying to sell weapons. Not a good sign.

Silva shook his head. Who were these men? What were they doing?

The army thought it important enough to send another unit to help Silva. After the two units joined forces, they marched on an isolated farmhouse with a tin roof. Inside they found food, blankets, and the key to a Jeep parked outside. A fire was still burning in the kitchen. If the men in the olive-drab trousers had been at home, they'd left in a hurry.

The dirt paths surrounding the house were worn—a sign that there had been plenty of organized activity.

Silva had to find these men. They were probably drug dealers, and the army would have to shut them down. First, though, Silva called for more reinforcements—just in case they needed to use deadly force.

The extra men arrived with Major Hernan Plata, a mixed blessing—Plata had little on-the-ground experience. Silva and Plata organized the morning patrol along the Nancahuazu, with Silva taking the first section and Plata's men following about forty-five yards back. A well-armed third section, led by Lieutenant Lucio Loayza, took up the rear with 60mm mortars and a .30-caliber machine gun.

The plan was to advance up along both sides of the Nanca-huazu. If they found the foreigners or ran into trouble, they would call for air support.

On March 23, they commenced at dawn. Silva had just brought his mental report up to date when one of his soldiers called him forward.

"Footprints," the man called to him. "They head up the path cut along the canyon."

Silva came up to where the soldier was standing on the bank. In the mud he could just make out the waffle-prints of boots leading down a path that went farther into the canyon.

"Good job," Silva said.

Signaling the point man, he gave the order to move forward.

The path meandered deeper into the V-shaped valley. Boulders and brush thickened as the walls grew steeper on each side. Silva and his men walked in the brush along the bank for a few minutes before the zigzagging riverbed straightened itself into a narrow arroyo. Boulders dotted the banks. A small stretch of woods stood where the river once again curved away out of sight. The valley was strangely silent.

Silva glanced upstream at his men. Lieutenant Ruben Amezaga and Epifano Vargas, a civilian guide, stood in the water, cooling themselves in the weak current.

Someone shouted. A man's voice in a foreign accent: "*Viva la liberacion nacional.*"

A gunshot cracked from the ridge high above. A second later the valley exploded into confusion. A barrage of gunfire made it impossible to hear anything. Rounds sliced through the brush, wood slivers and mud flew upward and perfumed the air. Silva's men shouted and screamed as the patrol scrambled for cover.

Lieutenant Amezaga charged forward from his exposed position in the river, firing his weapon toward the woods. Several rounds smashed into him, and the young officer fell headfirst into the water. Vargas turned away from the barrage, but he, too, crumpled into the brown river.

Silva knew he was in trouble. He and his men were between the hillsides with the enemy above them. They were trapped in the kill zone. They couldn't move forward—the fire was too intense. Behind them Plata's men were also pinned down. Bullets raked the path. They were trapped.

Silva tried to fire back, but it was impossible to get a clear shot at the shooters' concealed positions in the rocks. He could hear the wounded men screaming. Several lay along the bank, blood pooling around them. Glancing down the path he'd just traveled, Silva saw another of his men stagger to the earth.

Over the gunfire he could hear the foreign voice calling him to surrender. The accent was not Bolivian, he thought. Cuban, maybe? Silva's brother was studying in Cuba. He knew the accent.

With no response, more rounds from the guerrillas' guns cracked ahead and behind. There was no escaping the cross fire. Silva shouted to his men to cease firing. He glanced at his watch. Six minutes after the first shot, the gunfire stopped.

Looking behind him, Silva saw Plata's men drop their weapons. But the rear guard didn't surrender. Burdened by heavy weapons, the eight soldiers had stayed in place during the firefight. Now they retreated back along the river. Silva could hear the soldiers frantically tearing through the jungle. Maybe they would make it back to Fourth Division headquarters in Camiri. The commanders would send reinforcements, Silva hoped.

But for now, he had to survive. Atop the hill Silva saw guerrillas emerging from the thick brush. There were only a handful of them, dressed in olive-drab fatigues. Seven Bolivian soldiers lay dead. Four more were wounded. Fourteen more soldiers surrendered.

A small, bearded man was in charge, Silva saw. The guerrillas called him "Inti." He wore a green cap over his black hair, and he barked orders at Silva's men like a drill sergeant.

"Move the dead onto the riverbank," he shouted, and the new prisoners rushed to obey. The guerrillas moved down the valley, rounding up more soldiers as they went. Major Plata emerged from behind a bush, crying like a baby. The soldiers looked at the officer with disdain. When Lieutenant Loayza and his men arrived with their hands on their heads, Silva thought he might cry, too—there was no one left to run, or to radio for help.

The body of Vargas, the oil company guide, was the last pulled from the water. One of the guerrillas kicked it in the ribs. "That's the way informers die," he said.

Led at gunpoint, Silva and his men carried the wounded into the brush and up to the guerrilla camp. Plata followed close on Inti's heels, babbling about his plans to retire from the army in only a few months. He offered to show Inti his papers, details of the intelligence and battle plans, if the guerrillas would set him free.

"We are to signal our position soon," he said. "If they don't hear from us, the planes will come."

One of the attackers took Plata's papers and disappeared with them over the hillside.

Inti took Plata aside, but the soldiers could still hear him, weeping and chattering. He gave up the army's mission, its position and plans.

The guerrillas gathered Silva and his men into a circle and passed canteens of water among them. They hunched on the ground and swallowed the water in grateful gulps.

One of the conscripts handed back the bottle to its owner.

"Please kill that coward Plata. He's not one of us," he told the guerrilla. "He's a despot. He punishes us with no mercy if we break the smallest rule, but look at him now."

"He's a coward," another of Plata's men said, spitting on the ground.

Silva just shook his head and kept his eyes down. Plata embarrassed him, but he knew the commander was trying to save his own life. They couldn't fight their way out, and only God knew what these men had planned for them.

Silva listened while his commander "sang like a canary." He formed a plan of his own. If he pretended sympathy with the guerrillas' cause, maybe they wouldn't execute him or his men.

When Silva's turn came to talk with Inti, he hinted at Communist ties. "I joined the army on request of the party," Silva said. "My brother is studying in Cuba."

Silva told the stranger about life in the Bolivian Army, how hard it was to fight when resources were stretched so thin, the food was bad, and no one could be bothered to communicate. A little later, he passed along the names of two officers he thought might collaborate with a revolution.

Inti listened to Silva ramble, and ordered the guerrillas to treat the wounded. As they bandaged the wounds, the guerrillas talked about the cause, how theirs was a struggle for freedom and the people, how the Bolivian campesinos were being exploited by the government and the military. The Bolivian people deserved a better life, they said. They finished up by offering the Bolivian soldiers a place in their ranks.

The men listened quietly to the speeches.

"I don't know why I have been sent to fight," one of the wounded said.

"We have no choice. Our fathers had no choice. We do what we are told," another conscript told them.

They were in survival mode. No one wanted to die.

Night fell, but nobody slept. Silva didn't know what would happen. He considered his options, and prepared to die. When? He didn't know. He thought about his family, his wife and children. Silva had to find an escape. But there was no way out of the camp. They had too many men, too many guns. This wasn't some ragtag gang. They were well-trained, well-armed fighters.

At daybreak Inti addressed the prisoners. Silva's heart raced: Was this it? he thought. But Inti surprised them all.

"All the prisoners will go free," Inti told them. "We don't kill unarmed enemies. We treat them with dignity and respect. You have until noon March 27 to gather your dead."

One of the fighters brought two large satchels into the clearing and dumped out a ragged assortment of shirts, pants, and oddments of clothing. The soldiers were ordered to strip down to their underwear and exchange their camouflage for civilian clothes. Only Silva and Plata were allowed to keep their uniforms. Before they set off into the trees, one of the guerrillas turned to the prisoners and invited them to come with them, to join the movement to liberate the country.

But the men were moments from freedom. None of them stood to join the guerrillas.

The ragged men waited until all sounds of the guerrillas faded away before they rose to leave the camp. They were lucky to be alive, but the worst was yet to come, Silva thought. He and Plata had to tell their commanders they'd been ambushed, that more than thirty soldiers were captured, seven were dead and several more wounded. Their mortars and big .30 machine gun were gone, along with more than a dozen Mausers, three Uzi submachine guns, and thousands of rounds of ammunition. The soldiers had been stripped of their radios, boots, and the very clothes on their backs.

Later that afternoon the sorry group straggled into the Fourth Division headquarters in Camiri. By then Silva and Plata had agreed they couldn't tell their superiors that fewer than ten guerrillas had done so much shameful damage. Instead they reported an organized attack by dozens of paramilitaries, disciplined men, overwhelmingly armed. They told their commanders that the foreign-led guerillas had as many as five hundred soldiers in the Nancahuazu region.

CHAPTER 2

El Presidente

Bolivian President General René Barrientos Ortuno reread the last pages of the after-action report and slammed the folder onto the table. The report had shot up the ranks, traveling from desk to desk before it finally landed in front of Barrientos.

Somewhere along the line the story leaked to the public, and the newspapers and radio stations went crazy with conjecture.

At age forty-seven, Barrientos was already a wily old soldier and politico, an army general who'd achieved his country's top post via military coup. His government was fragile, and his country's economy and spirits were shaky from almost a century of bad leadership, military coups, and lost wars. Foreign guerrillas were the last thing he needed. The report said the rebels sounded Cuban. Was Cuban dictator Fidel Castro involved? If so, why would he involve himself in Bolivia? Che Guevara? But Che Guevara had disappeared two years before, was probably dead in a ditch somewhere, the president thought. He shook his head in disbelief. It just didn't make sense. Nothing about the skirmish made any sense.

In Bolivia, violence usually came after clear warnings, and attacks almost never came from outside Bolivian borders. Antigovernment demonstrations were not unusual—the students marched in the cities, and the powerful labor unions out in mining country.

This was something new.

The ambush occurred on the wrong side of the country, in the remote Rio Nancahuazu valley. There was simply nothing out there but cacti and a few old Indians, the president thought, illiterate campesinos scratching a living from the jungle-covered mountainsides. It was a trackless, mosquito-infested wasteland.

Barrientos knew his army was not prepared to fight off an uprising, especially if professional revolutionaries and foreign money and weapons were involved.

Bolivians were good soldiers, he told himself, but history proved they weren't much good at waging war. A hundred years before, a fight with Chile over mineral-rich deposits of bird and bat dung had cost Bolivia its entire coastline. Thirty years later, Bolivia and Paraguay had sacrificed a generation of their young men in "the Chaco War," a battle over access to the Paraguay River. It was the bloodiest war of a bloody century in South America. It devastated the Bolivian economy but opened the way to political change. "The Chaco generation," veterans galvanized by the war, returned home to a land where educated whites—only 5 percent of Bolivia's four-million population—held most of the power, and only men who could read and write could vote in elections. In 1941, the National Revolutionary Movement (MNR) was formed and attracted the miners, union members, and farmers who made up most of the population. On April 9, 1952, the MNR rose up and seized power. Party founder

Victor Paz Estenssoro's reforms included the universal right to vote, massive land reform, education for rural children, and nationalizing mines. Indians integrated into national society, with the articulate, half-Quechua General René Barrientos at the forefront.

The country settled in for a period of peaceful reform. Since Bolivia won independence from Spain in 1825, the country had suffered more than one hundred government coups. The people were worn out by war and instability, so the MNR decided to rein in the military by abolishing the army and closing down the military academy. Both were resurrected within six months, but once the soldiers went home it took years to put the forces back into fighting form. Paz Estenssoro had made powerful enemies.

Bolivia remained relatively quiet until early 1964, when someone allegedly tried to assassinate General Barrientos. Accounts of the attack are full of cloak-and-dagger secrecy, American CIA agents, and colorful tales. One newspaper said his life was saved when the assassin's bullet ricocheted off the U.S. Air Force silver eagle wings he wore on his uniform. The general was airlifted to a U.S. military hospital in Panama—two thousand miles distant—for treatment. Credible Bolivian witnesses to the attack could not be found. Still, this "Silver Bullet Affair" turned Barrientos into a dashing national hero. Within the year he used that machismo celebrity to build support and topple the MNR.

President Estenssoro handed Barrientos the reason he needed by tampering with the constitution to enable himself to run for another term. Estenssoro was reelected by 70 percent of the vote, but General Barrientos and what remained of the Bolivian high command were fed up with what they perceived as an antimilitary regime. They staged a "restorative revolution," another military coup. Paz Estenssoro fled Bolivia. Barrientos and another army commander ran the country for the next two years, and in 1966 Barrientos resigned from the military to run for president.

He was a reformer, too, he said, born in the provinces, fluent in indigenous Quechua as well as Spanish. He was a self-made man, a pilot, a born leader, married into the ruling class. Bolivia elected him president in a landslide vote.

Since then the general-turned-president had kept careful watch on the opposition, but even with all the security measures in place they'd still somehow missed this threat.

Today's news had been even more alarming.

The day after the ambush, police discovered important documents in a Jeep parked on a deserted street in Camiri—160 miles southeast of Santa Cruz. Camiri was an important town, a main stop between Santa Cruz and the borders of Argentina and Paraguay. Parked cars were not unusual, but this Jeep—with La Paz license plates—hadn't moved in weeks. When police searched the dust-coated vehicle, they found papers detailing guerrilla operations in a secret camp in the Nancahuazu. In four notebooks a woman called Tania listed an entire Bolivian network of urban contacts, friendly Communists outside Bolivia, and several bank accounts.

Barrientos planned to raid those addresses and arrest the criminals. "They will pay for their treasonous disloyalty," he promised.

The evidence pointed to Che Guevara. A week before the ambush, police had arrested two Bolivian men who were trying to sell rifles in Camiri. The men said they'd stayed in a rebel camp for a week or two, but were disillusioned with the harsh conditions and deserted. When introduced to interrogators at Fourth Division headquarters, they revealed even more information: The guerrillas had set up a camp at a farmhouse in Nancahuazu. Barrientos read transcripts of the interrogation:

Q: *Tell us who is in command of those guerrillas where you were.*

A: *The main leaders of this guerrilla war are Che Guevara at the top, whom I didn't have a chance to see because he had gone exploring at the head of twenty-five other men.*

The other man said the same thing.

The investigators, though, said they doubted Che was in Nancahuazu, but the prospect was disturbing. A few weeks earlier, a journalist had asked the president a routine question about Che and revolution. "I don't believe in ghosts," the president said then. "I am convinced that Che Guevara is in the world beyond, together with Camilo Cienfuegos and other martyrs of the Castro regime."

But the papers found in the Jeep were clear: Che was almost certainly alive, and possibly working in Bolivia. If he really was out there, he probably had hundreds of fighters. How many of those were Cubans? Che never traveled without his trusted Cuban bodyguards. The ambush survivors said their captors were Cuban, and a guerrilla leader had preached to them about the glory of revolution. That was vintage Che, Barrientos thought.

While the nation struggled to make sense of the ambush, Barrientos went on the offensive. He monopolized the airwaves, promising an anxious nation he would crush the rebels and their supporters. With newspapers and radio stations reporting what they could of the ambush, Barrientos issued a carefully worded government statement—a bit of creative writing that embellished the facts to save face and appealed to Bolivian national pride to unite the country. These foreign killers threatened the nation's very sovereignty, the president said.

This outrageous and cold blooded act . . . is even more serious because it has brought pain and mourning to the families of the soldiers, workers, and campesinos.

The timely report by the survivors permitted a quick reaction with troops of the Fourth Army Division, backed up by planes of the Air Force, which dispersed the attackers, causing casualties and taking prisoners. In their flight, they left suitcases containing clothing, pieces of equipment, pamphlets on guerrilla warfare and Castro communist propaganda of Cuban origin as well as a tape recorder, a portable high frequency radio and a Jeep.

The prisoners, local inhabitants and surviving soldiers, reported that a large group of persons of differing nationalities, among them Cubans, Peruvians, Chinese, Argentines, Europeans and also Bolivian communists are involved.

The statement ended with a warning: "The army has ordered the drastic and immediate eradication of these insurgents." Citizens were told to report any suspicious movements. The bluster bought Barrientos the time he needed to figure out his next move.

There was no mention of Che Guevara.

CHAPTER 3

The Dinner

Bolivian Army captain Gary Prado Salmon was a meticulous man.

He donned his crisp khaki pants and polished black belt, buttoned his white shirt, and tugged on his shoelaces to make sure they were just so. His olive skin was shaved smooth and his black mustache neatly trimmed. Everything was perfect. It had to be.

Prado was headed to his neighbor's house for dinner, and a special guest was expected to attend—President Barrientos.

Prado's family knew Bolivia's first family well—they were *parientes*, relations. Rosario, Captain Prado's wife, had grown up with the girl who later married General Barrientos, and the women were still like sisters. Rosario's mother was married to Barrientos's father-in-law. It was like that in Bolivia. The ruling class was very small—maybe two hundred families—and they all were connected somehow. The elite controlled it all: the military, government, mines, and media. They kept within their own social circle and made decisions for the masses.

Prado's neighbor, the evening's host, was Santa Cruz governor Colonel Felix Moreno Ortiz, a fellow who loved to throw dinner parties. When Ortiz learned the president was coming to Santa Cruz, he invited Barrientos to dinner. Nothing fancy. It was just an informal gathering with a few couples, including Prado and his wife. Ortiz said the president was looking forward to relaxing with a few old friends after a trying week.

Prado understood. It was a stressful time for everyone in the military.

Prado couldn't stop thinking about the ambush. He'd read the report and knew some of the soldiers involved. He had trained a few, including Lieutenant Amezaga, one of the first casualties. Prado was an instructor at the military academy—and a damn good one, according to his men. Now, he was part of the Eighth Division cavalry unit and had helped turn Amezaga and other raw recruits into military officers. Prado was soft-spoken and whip-thin, but he commanded respect. An expert on military tactics, he led by example, painstakingly showing soldiers how to shoot and maneuver, skills he had learned from his father, Julio Prado, an exceptional cavalry officer.

Prado did everything he could to make his father proud. The oldest of three sons, Prado was the only one to join the military. Prado's father had been an officer during the Chaco War, rising from second lieutenant to captain. Afterward, Julio Prado was among three dozen Bolivian officers selected to train in Europe. He went to Rome in 1938, and that's where his first son was born. When World War II began in September 1939, Julio Prado returned to Bolivia, where he went on to become the commander of two divisions: military attaché in England and Bolivian minister of defense. He retired as a major general, the military's highest rank.

As a child, Prado watched his father train cadets at the military academy. As a teenager, he joined the army and, like his father, was assigned to the cavalry. He intended to speak with Barrientos sometime in the evening, to offer his service as an officer in the field. If there was a rebel force in Bolivia, he didn't want to be stuck behind a desk. He wanted to avenge his student's death, he thought, and ultimately his country's honor.

He felt Rosario enter the room, felt her arms wrap around him from behind.

"You look so handsome," she said softly. Prado smiled uneasily. He didn't take praise well.

"*Te amo, querida,*" he said.

"*Te amo, mi alma,*" she whispered back.

Rosario was a petite, pretty woman with brown eyes and an engaging smile. She wore a colorful cotton dress that hugged her trim figure.

"We should get going," she told her husband.

He reached for her hand. It was a beautiful, starlit night, and the neighborhood was alive with music.

Santa Cruz was a working-class city, home mostly to factory workers and campesinos fresh from the mountains. The city's wealth traveled out to the edges, and the ruling class was insulated from the gritty city center by old trees and carved stone walls. This was one of the affluent streets, lined with brightly painted houses, elegant wooden balconies, red-tiled roofs, and wrought-iron garden gates.

The Prados passed through their neighbor's gate, and a servant opened the front door before the captain could knock. Laughter rolled toward them from inside the house, along with the mouthwatering aroma of roasted chicken. The tile floors shone almost as brightly as the living-room chandelier.

Prado spotted the president right away, chatting with Ortiz and several other guests. The couple approached to pay their respects.

Prado held his tongue. He wanted to talk about the ambush and ask Barrientos how he planned to counter the guerrilla movement. But this wasn't the time. Not yet.

Barrientos had a way of making everyone in a crowded room feel special. The general was a handsome man, tall, with a tan complexion, slicked-back black hair, and a strong handshake. He was a charismatic, skilled politician, but short-tempered and sometimes ruthless. The public rarely saw that side. To them he was a daredevil pilot, jumping into army helicopters and flying from village to village, giving passionate speeches about land reform, law and order, and the evils of Communism.

He wasn't all talk. He'd worked for months to fulfill his campaign promises. Now his full attention was focused on the guerrillas.

The hostess led her guests to the dining area. Ortiz's cook had prepared picante de pollo—chicken in a spicy sauce with rice and potatoes. As they passed the plates, one of the guests broached the topic everyone had been waiting to discuss: the ambush. Weary as he was with the topic, Barrientos had known it would come up eventually. It was the talk of Bolivia, all over the airwaves—every radio station interrupted its broadcast when news updates arrived. That morning a newspaper had reported that the president had personally flown an army helicopter into the mountains to see firsthand the government drive against the guerrillas. Barrientos told reporters his fighting units "had adequate resources" to deal with an estimated four to five hundred guerrillas who had been receiving "foreign aid for more than a year."

Barrientos put the best face on a dire situation. He wanted to quell fears that violence might break out in towns and cities. Then one of the guests shared the latest scoop: Che Guevara was part of the ambush plan, advising the guerrillas. He might even be hiding somewhere inside Bolivia. The guest had heard it on the radio, he said.

Che was both feared and adored in Bolivia, in equal measures. Che Guevara was a romantic hero, an Argentine doctor who'd abandoned his middle-class life and profession to help Fidel Castro overthrow Cuban dictator Fulgencio Batista. When Batista fled Cuba on January 1, 1959, many people in Bolivia and throughout Latin America expressed joy and solidarity with the guerrillas. Cuba reminded them of their own countries' struggles for independence, when campesinos all over the continent took up arms to overthrow Spanish rule.

The Cuban Revolution translated well into the region's modern struggles. Cuba was not the only country where a ruthless dictator had turned his country into a fiefdom, exploiting is people and the natural resources. If a small group of revolutionaries could topple an entrenched dictator in Cuba, thought people in other such places, why not in their own country?

Castro was the leader of the Cuban Revolution, but Che was its icon—and his message resonated with insurgents fighting injustice all over the world. With his long hair and scraggly beard, green fatigues and beret, he preached a simple message: The duty of a revolutionary was to make more revolution. And the ultimate goal of any armed struggle was to topple corrupt governments that exploited the people.

Behind the noble rhetoric, Che was as brutal as any Third World dictator. After Castro seized power in Cuba, Che was the man in charge of executing political prisoners. He worked efficiently and showed no mercy.

Che embraced his revolutionary image and exported it throughout the world along with ideological how-to books on armed struggle. If it worked in Cuba, it would work in other places. He called his theory *foco* ("focus"): A small group of dedicated guerrillas, based in a rural haven, could quickly overthrow an established government and liberate a nation.

Che had seen the value of rural support while fighting in Cuba. On November 25, 1956, he and eighty-one other guerrillas boarded a rickety old cabin cruiser called *Granma* and set sail on rough seas for Cuba. Within two weeks they'd landed, engaged the enemy, and lost almost all their men in a disastrous skirmish with Batista's soldiers. The survivors, including brothers Raul and Fidel Castro, fled to the Sierra Maestra Mountains, where they regrouped and recruited anti-Batista farmers to their cause. It took some time, but two years later, Castro and his guerrillas—known as the 26th of July Movement—overthrew the Batista government and seized power.

Che held several positions in the new government, but he continued to preach revolution in other developing nations, building himself into a "revolutionary statesman of world stature."

The revolutionary delivered his last blistering speech in Algeria on February 24, 1965, at an economic seminar on African-Asian solidarity. There he criticized not only the United States, but also the Soviet Union, saying both governments exploited the world for their own gain. Two weeks later, Che vanished.

Time passed. Cuba mourned. Fidel Castro went public with a letter Che Guevara had sent him some months earlier. Che affirmed his solidarity with the Cuban Revolution but declared his intention to leave Cuba to fight for the revolutionary cause abroad. He'd resigned from all his positions in the government and party and renounced his honorary Cuban citizenship.

But Che stayed in the news. He was blamed for uprisings in Africa, Latin America, and Asia. The U.S. State Department declared him "a dangerous enemy to democracies," and the CIA was charged with tracking him down. But Che had slipped away. He'd become a ghost, a boogeyman.

And now he might be here in Bolivia, in Barrientos's backyard.

The diners finished their entrées, and Barrientos exuded his usual confidence. He told the guests that he was continuing to push the United States for more military aid and was getting a positive response. And why wouldn't they help us? Barrientos asked. Look what happened in the skirmish. Bolivia needed arms to keep these Communist guerrillas at bay. With more weapons our army will crush the bastards, he boasted. It was just a matter of time.

The guests nodded their heads in grave agreement, but Prado was incensed, torn by indecision. He supported Barrientos, but he also knew it would take more than just weapons—and bullshit—to defeat the guerrillas, especially if Che was their commander. The Bolivian military was headed for disaster unless it adopted new tactics to fight the rebels. It would be disrespectful to publicly disagree with the president's optimistic assessment. This was a dinner party, not a debate, and his father had taught him to respect authority. But so much was at stake. Prado had spent six months of extensive training in counterinsurgency at a U.S. base in Panama. It had confirmed what he already knew: that his commanders were living in the past. They still embraced tactics used in World War II—where you had a front line and a rear area. That was fine in a conventional war, but his commanders didn't understand that in a guerrilla war you had to move quickly—and aggressively—to root out the enemy. He had to make Barrientos understand that the old military ways wouldn't work anymore. Prado thought about the soldiers killed in the ambush. If nothing was done, more would die.

"No, Mr. President, I don't think more weapons will solve the problem. We're doing things wrong," Prado declared, flattening his palms on either side of his plate.

A hush fell over the room. No one spoke to the president like that. Not even the son of one of Bolivia's most respected generals. But Barrientos admired his balls—his machismo—and let him continue.

"Why do you say that, Captain?" Barrientos asked.

Prado explained that conventional tactics wouldn't work on the guerrillas.

"We should isolate the area and train troops to hunt the insurgents. They are always hiding, always on the move. So you have to find them, fix them in place, and destroy them in close order," Prado said. He felt passion creeping into his voice. "What we're doing now is sending out untrained troops—we're sending them to be picked off by disciplined killers. Our officers, without training in this kind of combat, will suffer the same."

There was an uneasy silence. Barrientos stared into Prado's eyes. He could feel the young officer's determination. *We need more men like this one*, Barrientos thought.

"You make very good points, my friend. Very good points. Very soon we will see."

Barrientos turned his attention back to the other guests. Prado, meanwhile, began to wonder if he'd done the right thing. He slipped away from the party soon after. Was the president going to follow his advice, or had he just sunk his military career?

Two days later he got his answer, and his orders.

He was to report to a new Ranger battalion being formed to hunt and kill guerrillas. He would be part of the experiment.

CHAPTER 4

Pappy's Mission

Major Ralph "Pappy" Shelton picked up his old blue-and-tan Gibson guitar, strummed a few chords, and then leaned it against the barrack wall.

It was late afternoon at Fort Gulick, Panama, and Shelton was ready to go home. He had been in the army for twenty years and was getting ready to retire from active military service. *It's time*, he thought. He just had to sell himself on the idea.

His wife, Margaret, wanted him home. She was tired of being a single mom, shuffling five kids to Little League games and art class, doing the parent-teacher meetings. She did a two-person job, and he knew it. He was already a soldier when they'd got married, and she handled it pretty well for a long time. But as the years dragged on and the kids got bigger, it became more difficult. When orders came for a move to Panama, she and the family shipped out alongside him, as they always did. But Panama didn't agree with Margaret. She couldn't adjust to the island-like life on the base. After she'd given it her best try, the family packed up and went home to Tennessee. She waited for Shelton there, ready for a secure, settled civilian life.

Shelton promised her he'd leave the army when this rotation was over, and he always kept his word. But he was struggling. Despite all the bullshit—and there was always a lot of shit you had to put up with in the military—he loved army life. He had no qualms about living in the barracks. He enjoyed the camaraderie and was beloved by his men. His combat experience in Korea and Laos was well respected. He lived for the action, which he had been seeing more of since joining Special Forces in 1961. In fact, all the good things in his life could be traced to the military.

His was born in Corinth, Mississippi, and his father left before he was born. Shelton had enlisted in the army as soon as he was old enough. Back then, joining up was a smart move for a young man at loose ends, an opportunity to see the world and get some job skills. No matter what branch, it was honorable to be in the military. He worked his way up from private to major. He fought in Korea and served with the Green Berets in Laos and the Dominican Republic. Only dumb luck had kept him out of Vietnam—and maybe his ability to speak Spanish.

But what would he now find to do in civilian life? He was thirty-seven years old, with a big family to support. How would a lifelong professional soldier fit into a country that had lost its respect for him?

The Vietnam War had changed things. Over decades of Cold War maneuvering, America found it couldn't win anymore with sheer troop strength and military hardware—it was mired in a brutal war with guerrillas who used frustrating hit-and-run tactics. The enemy brazenly attacked U.S. troops and then disappeared into the triple-canopy jungles.

By April 1967, nearly 400,000 U.S. soldiers were stationed in

Vietnam. Casualties mounted: Close to 10,000 men had been killed—6,100 in 1966 alone. Still the generals in charge called for more troops and more weapons—it was the only way they knew to stop the Communists in the north from conquering South Vietnam. If that happened, other Southeastern Asian nations would fall like dominoes to the Communists—and that would threaten U.S security. At least that was the theory.

But the public was tired of the war and souring on the once-respected military institutions—and soldiers. They were questioning military and political leaders and losing patience and trust in the government. Antiwar protests were breaking out in cities and colleges, and things there were turning ugly—tear gas, arrests, draft protesters who refused to go and fight for freedom. Heading into the "Summer of Love" in 1967, rock musicians tapped into the discontent, some, like the Beatles, preaching: "All You Need Is Love."

For Shelton, the venom aimed at soldiers was disturbing. It was one thing to attack politicians. It was another to criticize fighting men. They didn't create policy. They were bravely fighting—and dying—for their country, to stop the spread of Communism. He wondered what he would do if, back home, hippies insulted his choice of a military life.

A soldier tapped on his door and poked his head inside.

"Major Shelton, Colonel Smith wants to see you."

Shelton was curious because he had only told a few people he was planning to leave the army. Maybe the colonel had found out and wanted to talk him out of it.

He headed over to Quarry Heights, headquarters for U.S. Southern Command (SOUTHCOM)—the office complex that oversaw U.S. military programs and actions in the Southern Hemisphere and the Panama Canal Zone.

The door was open to Colonel Magnus Smith's office, and the

big man told Shelton to close it behind him and take a chair. Smith was a straight shooter. He'd known Shelton for years, and he didn't waste any time detailing his next mission.

Smith was in charge of the Eighth Special Forces Group, and SOUTHCOM had told him to assemble a mobile training team (MTT) for a secret mission in Bolivia. The army there had formed a new, 650-man Second Ranger Battalion in response to an imminent threat. The Americans would have only nineteen weeks to train the Bolivian Rangers in the intricacies of counterinsurgency tactics. They didn't have much time. Communist guerrillas were already at work in the jungles there, threatening Bolivia's stability.

"We need a Ranger-qualified Special Forces captain or major," Smith said. "There are only two Ranger-qualified officers available, and one of them is in Vietnam. That leaves you, Shelton. I know you are ready to bug out of here, but we need you to take this."

Shelton simply nodded and sat back in his chair.

The colonel told Shelton that SOUTHCOM had planned a similar training school for Bolivia in the coming year, but the guerrilla attack on Bolivian troops in March had pulled the plan onto the front burner. Bolivian President Barrientos had asked Washington for immediate military help, and the Johnson administration had approved the request. The last thing Johnson needed was a Communist-led insurgency in Bolivia—or anywhere in Latin America. They didn't want another Cuba or (God forbid) another Vietnam. That's why Shelton's Special Forces team would only train Bolivian soldiers. They would not conduct any missions there. The U.S. ambassador to Bolivia, Douglas Henderson, was adamant about that: no American troops in the field. The Bolivians would have to take care of the mess themselves.

One more thing: Shelton could handpick his sixteen-man team, but they would have to deploy as quickly as possible. Smith's voice was urgent. Shelton knew this was serious. He stood up, ready to start organizing his team, with all thoughts of home banished from his mind.

"Oh, one more detail, Major," the commander said. "It's possible Che Guevara might be behind the trouble."

"Che?" Shelton asked. He felt his eyebrows reaching for his hairline.

"Yeah. Sit down another minute," Smith said.

There were so many unanswered questions about Che. U.S. intelligence had no idea whether he was alive or dead. If he was leading this guerrilla war, was it from a distance or actually in the field? Everyone agreed this operation had Che's fingerprints all over it. Guevara hated the United States, and what better way to cause headaches than to start a revolution in Bolivia? Che probably hoped he could drag the United States into the conflict and open another front in the war on Communism. That's why the mission was so vital, Smith said.

Indeed, it was the reason Ambassador Henderson had visited SOUTHCOM a few days earlier. Henderson had spent a morning briefing the high command about the deadly ambush and the guerrilla threat. Henderson was a no-nonsense career diplomat who had for years downplayed the Communist threat in Bolivia. He had been telling Washington that Communism presented little menace to Bolivian stability—even though that opinion ran counter to U.S intelligence reports.

In May 1965, the CIA's Office of Current Intelligence in Latin America released a study that placed Bolivia second in line, after the Dominican Republic, as being at risk of a Communist insurgency. It called the political situation in Bolivia "highly unstable" and warned of "Communists and leftist extremists [who] are armed and determined not to permit a prolongation of the Barrientos regime."

Even after the ambush, Henderson believed that the uprising had little chance of success in a country so thoroughly sick of war. But with Che Guevara figured in, the equation added up to something much more serious.

After meeting with Henderson, General Robert Porter Jr., chief of SOUTHCOM, sent U.S. Air Force brigadier general William Tope to Bolivia. SOUTHCOM needed an accurate military assessment of the Bolivian crisis, and Tope was an affable, trustworthy man who could speak fluent "military" with anyone, from the lowliest private to the top brass. Ambassador Henderson gave his blessing.

Shelton, meanwhile, had his work cut out for him. He would have to find a suitably remote location in Bolivia to train the Second Ranger Battalion and then teach them counterinsurgency theory and practice, all in the space of three months.

Shelton realized this would be his last mission. Once the training was over, so was his military career. He made himself a promise: When things got tough, he would stay strong and do things *his* way. This was his unit. His mission. All he had to do was pick the right team.

CHAPTER 5

The Meltdown

Shelton's driver carefully navigated the bumpy dirt road leading to the village of La Esperanza.

It was an obstacle course, filled with crater-sized potholes and cattle darting into the road. Animals owned this narrow stretch of dusty brown soil. The herds moved and grazed in clusters, escaping the flat white sunlight in the shade of palm-tree groves.

"This could be northeastern Mississippi, in July and August," Shelton told the driver. "Lose the palm trees, add some cotton patches." Nothing could be worse than toiling in the cotton patches, he thought. He first earned calluses on his hands during those long-ago days in the fields.

Shelton had worked all his life. It was all he knew. In early days he was a logger, a sawmill operator, an assembly line worker at an auto plant. When the Great Depression came to his hometown, it saw that there was already nothing left to devastate. Corinth, Mississippi, was an old railroad junction for the Mobile & Ohio, surrounded by endless cotton fields. Many farmers lost their land in the 1929 bank collapse, and just about everyone, black and white, seemed to struggle to put food on the table. Growing up rough had made him tough, Shelton said—and there was no substitute for plain hard work.

Shelton had taken a few of his trusted soldiers on this reconnaissance mission, and Bolivian Army officers accompanied them. The convoy of jeeps stopped in the village plaza, and they jumped out to stretch. It had been a long drive.

Shelton looked at the small groups of children running and playing in the front of shabby adobe homes with thatched roofs. Most of the huts sat back from the road, shaded by thick overgrowth. There were a few businesses—one-story wood and brick buildings with tin roofs. The general store doubled as the bus depot, where villagers could embark on the daylong, forty-mile trip south to Santa Cruz. The thatched-roof school was dilapidated. The village had no electricity, running water, or indoor plumbing. Chickens outnumbered villagers, and herds of cattle trotted by the jeeps, raising huge clouds of dust. To Shelton, it resembled the set from a spaghetti western. All they needed to see was Clint Eastwood riding down the main street in his poncho.

Then Shelton spotted a building that was out of place—an abandoned sugar mill. It stood five stories tall, about fifty feet high in front. It had been built a few years earlier with money from the U.S. Alliance for Progress—a program that helped finance economic development projects in Latin America. The factory created jobs and strengthened the local economy for a few years, and people from surrounding villages came to La Esperanza to work. But poor management finally shut down the enterprise. It was a blow to the area, but a stroke of luck for Shelton. The vacant, steel-framed building was the perfect place to train Bolivian soldiers. The structure could provide ample housing for the troops and a perfect site for rappelling and other exercises. It also had its own well and a storage cistern for water.

"What do you think?" asked Captain Edmond Fricke, who was Shelton's deputy.

Shelton grinned.

"It could work," he said.

That's what Fricke loved about Shelton—not only was he a professional soldier, but he was upbeat, with an engaging smile. Shelton was about five feet, eight inches tall and thin. He wasn't muscular, but you could tell he was tough from the way he carried himself. He stood straight and looked you in the eye. His skin was dark from years of working outdoors, and he spoke with a slight Southern twang. People just naturally gravitated to him.

Shelton walked through the village, ensuring there'd be enough room for maneuvers. He didn't want too many people living nearby, because night training might disturb them.

This was supposed to be a secret mission. They didn't need word leaking out about U.S. Special Forces training Bolivian soldiers. If newspapers found out, it could create a shit storm for Ambassador Henderson, who was fighting to keep U.S. troops well away from the action.

Shelton counted about twenty homes. Maybe 150 people lived here, and in the neighborhood.

La Esperanza was surrounded by a wide expanse of abandoned cane fields. They could easily create a rifle range. The village was isolated at the end of a bad road—it would be easy to set up a security perimeter. They had looked at other possible spots on this trip, but this site had no flaws. Shelton turned to Bolivian Eighth Division commander Colonel Joaquin Zenteno Anaya and asked if the place was available. Zenteno nodded his head yes. Shelton smiled. The search was over.

With the first part of his mission complete, Shelton and his men jumped back in the jeeps and headed to Cochabamba for a return flight to Panama. Two of his men—Sergeant Hector Rivera-Colon and Master Sergeant Roland Milliard—stayed behind to work out the logistics with the Bolivians.

Bumping along in the jeep, Shelton reflected about the mission. They would only have a short time to train the men. Could they do it? It was a challenge, but Shelton never shied away from one. His life had been filled with people who'd told him what he couldn't do.

He was only seventeen when he moved to Detroit and landed a job on an auto plant assembly line. It was 1947—two years after the end of World War II. America was still basking in the glow of defeating Japan and Germany. The Great Depression was in the past and America was looking to the future. That was Shelton's plan, too. When he heard about possible layoffs, he joined the army for the educational opportunities and job security. No more bouncing from job to job. With the military, there would be structure, stability, and a chance for a better life.

He was a tank crewman in Japan and was there when the Korean War broke out in 1950. Shelton was one of the first U.S. soldiers on the scene. Two weeks into combat, shrapnel injured him. He returned to battle three months later and was awarded a Silver Star—the army's third-highest award for combat valor—for destroying an enemy machine-gun nest. After four more months of combat he was wounded again—this time by a hand grenade—and was shipped back to the United States.

He married and soon had two children. When his enlistment ended in 1953, Shelton went back to Mississippi to try farming. His father had a little land, and Shelton poured most of his savings into cotton and corn seed. He didn't take long to change his mind. Drought withered his crops as soon as they pushed up from the ground. Shelton realized he missed the army.

Soldiers who left the service could return to the same rank if they did so within ninety days. Shelton reenlisted on Day 87. During the next five years, he served on bases in Georgia, Germany, and South Carolina. Always looking to advance his career, Shelton went to school for noncommissioned officers, graduating first in his class. Then he applied to Officer Candidate School. At first his wife was skeptical—she was already pushing for him to leave the military. But Shelton was admitted just before his twenty-eighth birthday, the cutoff age. He seemed to be an old man to his younger classmates, and they gave him an affectionate nickname: "Pappy."

He graduated as a second lieutenant in 1958 and then went through strenuous Ranger training, returned to Korea, and then joined Special Forces in late 1961. It was a time when a young president and war hero, John F. Kennedy, turned to the Green Berets to help stop the spread of Communism. A hard-liner, Kennedy was elected in 1960 in part because of his Cold War stance. He was a student of military affairs and had developed an interest in counterinsurgency—the art and method of defeating guerrilla movements. Special Forces were the ideal anti-guerrilla weapons, and Kennedy began sending his Green Berets to troubled areas to train foreign troops.

With that, Shelton soon deployed to hot spots. In 1962, he went to Laos with a training team. He returned to a failing marriage. Three more babies did not solve their problems.

Meanwhile, Shelton told military career planning that he wanted to attend an intensive Spanish-language training class. If he was going to spend time in Latin America, he wanted to speak the language—he didn't want anything lost in translation. Soon, Shelton was fluent in Spanish, a real plus when he traveled in 1965 with another training team to the Dominican Republic. The team was part of twenty-three thousand U.S. troops sent to the island to help protect U.S. interests during an insurrection.

Fearing another Cuba, President Johnson ordered the troops there to restore order during a coup. Shelton stayed in the Dominican Republic for eight months and then was posted to Fort Gulick, Panama. Now it was Bolivia.

After that, the screen was blank.

He didn't have time to worry about his future. His team had to train these troops quickly, and his commanders were pushing him to get started. He had his location and his team in place. The heat was on.

Like Harry S. Truman once said: If you can't stand the heat, get out of the kitchen.

Shelton was ready to jump into the fire.

The Bolivian Army had been chasing ghosts for weeks in the Nancahuazu wilderness and had nothing to show for it but cuts, fevers, and insect bites.

Every step the three companies took was sown with thorns, vines, spiders, and scrub, and much of that on steep hillsides. There were few paths in these twisting valleys, as there was nothing here to attract human or even animal visitors. The tops of the hills were largely barren, the valleys choked with dense vegetation that demanded strong arms and machetes to pass through.

A Company commander Major Ruben Sanchez was charged with finding guerrilla encampments in this morass. He and his men had been hiking the valleys for days looking for clues, but they'd found nothing. It was as if the guerrillas had simply disappeared.

Worse, many of the conscripts in his unit were out of shape. They had to stop often to catch their breath in the rugged terrain, and several had fallen ill. *Maybe it's better if we don't engage the guerrillas*, Sanchez thought. The outcome was far from certain.

Their plan was simple.

Sanchez's team, along with the other companies, would set up three bases, and each one would carry out reconnaissance in a different direction. They would spread out across the Rio Nancahuazu valley, find insurgents, and destroy them. They had more than a hundred soldiers on the hunt, but Sanchez wasn't sure they could accomplish the mission with even a thousand. With dusk settling over the valley, the companies set up camp. Sanchez stayed awake that night. Something felt wrong.

At dawn on April 10, A Company sent three patrols up the Rio Nancahuazu. Second Lieutenant Luis Saavedra Arambel's team of fifteen men was to follow the course of the river northward. About noon the men reached the confluence of the Iripiti River, a tributary stream. Suddenly, someone started shooting at them.

The soldiers panicked and ran. Saavedra fell dead, and two more soldiers fell alongside him. Another was seriously injured. Seven were captured, and the remaining four managed to escape along the riverbed. They frantically retraced their steps back to the patrol base. Sticky with sweat, dirt, and blood, the soldiers recounted the ambush. Sanchez listened, then quickly organized his sixty men and marched toward the ambush site. Jorge Ayala and Carlos Martins, both second lieutenants, were among the soldiers.

It was another shameful ambush, but they'd found the guerrillas at last. Sanchez prayed he could get there in time. Expecting normal guerrilla hit-and-run tactics, he advanced without taking many precautions. He thought that the guerrillas would be long gone. But as he and his men approached the ambush site, a burst of gunfire echoed in the valley.

They drew closer and heard the crack of a few rounds, followed by the steady beat of machine-gun fire. Sanchez's squad was under attack. The guerrillas had been waiting for them, hiding in the brush and trees.

Sanchez yelled for his men to take cover and return fire. But the bursts seemed to come from every direction, kicking up dirt and shredding leaves. Ayala barked orders but was suddenly silenced by a shot in the head.

Sanchez was stuck.

The terrain allowed no escape. Probably dozens—if not hundreds—of enemy soldiers surrounded them. Sanchez quickly did the battlefield calculus: They could keep fighting and die, or surrender and perhaps be spared.

He ordered his men to give up.

Martins's soldiers, meanwhile, had been trailing Sanchez's unit. When the firing began, they retreated. At the same time, a patrol led by Lieutenant Remberto Lafuente heard the firefight and immediately headed along the riverbed in the direction of the fighting. His patrol was unaware of the ambushes. They had no radio.

As Lafuente's men approached the ambush site, they found terrified soldiers falling back in disorder. Lafuente spotted Martins, and they decided to regroup. Dusk was falling, and soon it would be too dark to see. The officers didn't want to walk into another trap. They stumbled back to the patrol base and spent a tense night worrying about their comrades and fearing for their own lives. How close were the guerrillas? What would happen if they were captured? Would they ever see their families again?

As the sun burned away the morning mist, Lafuente's men were ready to begin tracking the guerrillas. But as they rose to leave, they were surprised by the sounds of limbs cracking along the pathway to the riverbank, footfalls, a sneeze. It was men, walking in their direction. The soldiers took up position and waited. Lafuente looked for the first sign of the guerrillas. His men raised their rifles around him, but stopped when Sanchez and the other Bolivian soldiers suddenly appeared in a clearing with their hands folded behind their heads. Just behind the prisoners walked ten guerrillas, leading the Bolivian soldiers along the riverbed.

When the guerrillas realized they were surrounded, they pointed their guns at Sanchez and told him to order the soldiers to fall back. If he didn't, the guerrillas would shoot him and all their prisoners.

It was a standoff. For a moment, no one moved a muscle.

The Bolivians aimed their rifles at the guerrillas, and the guerrillas' guns pointed at the Bolivian prisoners. The prisoners sweated and sobbed. Sanchez blinked, tried to stay in control. He knew that one wrong move and he would be dead.

Sanchez shouted to Lafuente: "Go back. They are setting us free."

He said it twice before his men truly understood the message. Reluctantly, his soldiers lowered their weapons and drew back. When they were out of sight, the guerrillas melted away into the brush.

Humiliated, Sanchez and his soldiers regrouped with the others. They were safe, but everyone was shaken. It was one thing to fire a weapon in training; another to stay composed enough in combat.

At nightfall, a team headed out gingerly to recover the dead. It was a gruesome task. Their bodies were torn, their uniforms stiff with blood. Some were missing chunks of skull where rounds had hit, and wild animals and birds had begun their work. In all, eight soldiers had been killed in the two ambushes, including two officers. Eight others were wounded. Twenty-eight soldiers were captured and released, and the enemy ended up with a fine cache of weapons: twenty-one M1 Garand rifles, twelve M1 carbines, nine Mausers, four M3 submachine guns, and one Browning automatic rifle.

Sanchez brooded all the way through the march back to a base near Camiri. The guerrillas had given him a letter for release to the media, but he was too upset to read it. His men were ill prepared for battle. They were campesinos, not soldiers. Look at how they behaved under fire, he thought. Some fought, but most ran like cowards. He shook his head in disgust.

"My God. What's next?" he mumbled.

The April 10 attacks triggered widespread panic. News of the ambushes spread quickly through the streets of Bolivian cities as people received the grisly details from newspapers and radio. Even conservative pro-Barrientos media reported that the military was in tatters, unprepared to fight. The nation was helpless against foreign invaders. It was just a matter of time, the reporters thought, before La Paz came under siege.

The government found itself with a new problem: spin control. The authorities usually could deal with Bolivian media. A few well-placed phone calls to publishers or threats of violence usually worked to silence anti-Barrientos publications, but those tactics were useless with foreign journalists who operated under a different set of rules. Reporters had been snooping around the country for weeks, trying to find "fixers" to take them into the jungles to look for Che and his guerrilla fighters. Though Che might cringe at the thought, he had become an international media star. Articulate, handsome, mysterious, Che was hip. Students at privileged college campuses in the United States read insurgent doctrine to one another from his 1960 book *Guerrilla Warfare*: "The guerrilla struggle is a mass struggle, it is the struggle of the people," they intoned. Che was the symbol of rebellion, willing to challenge authority and fight for his vision of social justice. He was a romantic revolutionary—ready to sacrifice his life for a noble cause: "In the arduous profession of the revolutionary, death is a frequent occurrence," he said.

That he had not been seen for years only added to his mystique. And so journalists from posts all over the world were tripping over one another in Bolivia. An interview with a live, cigar-chomping Che in the Bolivian jungle would be the scoop of a lifetime.

For Barrientos and his government, the guerrilla attacks were more than just embarrassing: They threatened the nation's stability. In less than a month, dozens of Bolivian soldiers had been killed or wounded—or humiliatingly captured and released by the guerrillas. It had to stop. Barrientos had warned the United States about the Communist threat. His country, their ally, faced an organized and experienced enemy with deep ties to Cuba, the Soviet Union, and possibly China. He asked for more weapons, but every time he broached the issue with Ambassador Henderson, he was told no. The threat wasn't serious enough. The ambassador believed that Bolivia's military could handle the crisis on its own.

The American didn't understand Bolivia, Barrientos thought. It wasn't just the guerrillas. Miners in the northern part of the nation were protesting for better working and living conditions. Many of the students and the educated class in La Paz still despised Barrientos for his mixed blood and for the 1964 coup. They thought the overthrow had undermined all the Democratic principles and reforms born out of the bloody 1952 Bolivian revolution. If the guerrillas tapped into that discontent, Barrientos's hold on power would be seriously threatened. He had worked too long and hard to let that go easily.

Barrientos recalled the words that young Captain Prado had blurted out at that dinner party: The army needed new tactics to fight an elusive enemy. Yes, the United States was going to train the Second Ranger Battalion, but it would take time to get them in the field. Barrientos was a military man; he had rebuilt his country's military from scratch since seizing power in 1964, and it still wasn't much. There was a dearth of experienced leadership. His standing army comprised 6,200 conscripts—raw recruits—supplemented by 1,500 soldiers who had served more than two years. And what troops he had were badly demoralized.

The soldiers who survived the skirmishes passed along astonishing tales of guerrilla prowess to new units arriving to replace them. They described large groups of guerrillas and how their fellow soldiers had panicked under fire. The new units knew what to expect: long days in the hot tropical climate, searching for an enemy that blended into the rugged terrain. There were no roads, few supplies, and obsolete weapons. The president felt desperate. He explored every option as it occurred to him, and turned to his high command for answers. General Alfredo Ovando Candía, commander in chief of the armed forces, was in Europe when the guerrillas first struck in March. He had returned to Bolivia and had helped calm the president.

One of his first steps was organizing an anti-guerrilla operations command in Camiri and establishing a military zone. Ovando wanted to confine the guerrillas to one area, to make it easier for the army to track them down. He contacted the intelligence services of other countries, including the United States, Brazil, and Argentina, to determine if Che Guevara was alive and behind the trouble in Bolivia.

Ovando didn't stop there. He courted military cooperation from neighboring countries. If Che was indeed in Bolivia, he was a threat to its neighbors, too. Argentina sent arms and ammunition to replace Bolivia's Chaco War–vintage Mauser rifles. Brazil promised a major shipment of combat rations, which would help solve the troops' supply problems in the operations area. Intelligence agencies agreed to increase surveillance on the common borders to detect and track guerrilla movements.

And to stop the incessant rumors, Ovando decreed that only the military high command could make statements about the insurgency. All news would come through official communiqués. No other information was to be released.

Barrientos made another bold move: He declared military law. He outlawed the Communist Party of Bolivia and the Revolutionary Workers' Party and arrested forty-one of their leaders. Barrientos wasn't going to allow them to support the guerrillas. He also took the opportunity to crack down on labor unions. He kept track of the information flowing from the notebooks found in the parked Jeep—police had rounded up anyone whose name was listed there, and the interrogation transcripts were delivered to the president's office every day. Bolivia suddenly seemed to teem with Communists.

The president next considered forming a military "hit squad"—a group of forty or fifty young officers charged with sneaking into the jungles on a top-secret mission to kill guerrilla fighters. But U.S. officials in La Paz feared the group might morph into a palace guard, a private army dedicated to keeping Barrientos in power. They rejected the plan, saying the Second Ranger Battalion was being trained for that very reason: to destroy the guerrillas.

Then Barrientos seized on another solution: napalm. Inquiries went to Argentina, saying the Bolivian government might buy enough of the incendiary bombs to defoliate the forest along the Rio

Nancahuazu. An appalled Henderson quashed that plan and told Barrientos it was "unacceptable." As another American diplomat told the *London Times*: "We are certainly not going to supply means for Bolivian hotheads to start bombing and napalming villages or even suspected guerrilla hideaways. Civilians would inevitably be killed, and we have a long experience that this inevitably produces a stream of recruits for the guerrillas."

Barrientos was embarrassed and angry with Henderson, and called him to a meeting at the presidential palace in La Paz. Henderson stood his ground. He believed in speaking his mind—even if it meant offending high-ranking officials of host nations or members of the U.S. diplomatic corps.

Henderson was tall and thin with a square jaw, silver hair, and high cheekbones. In his tailored Brooks Brothers suits he looked like a powerful business executive. He was born in Weston, Massachusetts, his father a hardworking carpenter and military man who served in the Philippines insurrection (1899–1902), the Mexican border campaign of 1916, and later World War I. He infused his son with stories of war and travel in foreign lands. Henderson's uncle spent years as a mining engineer in Latin America, and filled the boy's head with similar tales of adventure.

Like Shelton, Henderson attended public schools and worked odds jobs to get by. When one of his high school teachers saw him working at a gas station, he helped the bright young man get a scholarship to Boston University. That was the beginning of Henderson's career. After graduating, he attended the Fletcher School of Law and Diplomacy at Tufts University. He was twenty-seven when he took the Foreign Service examination in 1941. He learned he had passed on the day before the Japanese attacked Pearl Harbor.

The State Department interceded with Henderson's draft board to have him excused from military service, then sent him to a series of consular jobs in small cities in Latin American countries, including Mexico, Chile, and Bolivia. He gained a reputation as a no-nonsense, tireless worker. In the late 1940s he was assigned to Washington because of his expertise in Latin American economic issues. He helped President Truman craft a point in his 1948 inaugural address, about the importance of offering technical assistance to foreign nations. In the fullness of time, President Kennedy appointed him as ambassador to Bolivia.

Henderson had been dealing with Barrientos for years. He knew the president could be charming at times, but prone to whining, too. The big meeting at the presidential palace began with a wheedling ramble about how the United States had to send more aid, how Bolivia's national security was threatened. Nothing new.

The ambassador told Barrientos that he would discuss the issues with Tope, the Air Force general then in Bolivia on a fact-finding mission for SOUTHCOM. Barrientos nodded. It was a good move. The president liked Tope. They both were air force officers, and Barrientos could talk candidly to him—military man to military man. Tope would *understand*, Barrientos thought. Over the last week, Barrientos had met twice with Tope and other Bolivian commanders to discuss military strategy. This next time, though, the two men would chat alone.

When Tope arrived, Barrientos told him his army needed high-powered, up-to-date military equipment. He claimed that the better weapons would boost troop morale. He warned Tope that if the guerrillas gained a foothold in Bolivia, the revolution would spread like a cancer to neighboring countries, and the United States would face another Vietnam-like dilemma. He asked Tope: Could the United States stand by and watch as Communist-backed insurgencies toppled the stability of Latin America nations?

Tope sat for a moment and collected his thoughts. He had been interviewing Bolivian military officials for weeks. He had visited outposts and watched as the men trained. In a detailed report on the Bolivian crisis that he was preparing for SOUTHCOM, Tope concluded that the Bolivian military was a mess. The command structure was appointed on the basis of "personal loyalty and political patronage," and "military training at higher levels is generally archaic, impulsive and self-aggrandizing." In addition, there was no field intelligence or communications equipment. The entire military needed an overhaul, but there wasn't time for that. Tope termed the situation "highly volatile." Threats in urban areas and the mines remained very real, he said, and their "immediate impact on both the economy and the government could be much more disastrous than the present guerrilla activity."

Sitting there with the hopeful president, Tope knew that new rocket launchers were not the answer. His answer was blunt. Barrientos had to make systemic change in the Bolivian military.

"An untrained conscript will drop a modern weapon just as quickly as a Mauser," he told the president. He pointed out that the Viet Cong guerrillas supplied themselves largely by picking up U.S. equipment dropped by South Vietnamese soldiers. Tope brought the conversation back to the present crisis. How many guerrillas were out there? he asked.

Barrientos didn't know for sure. But he firmly believed there were several hundred of them, hard-core, professional Cuban-trained paramilitaries, spread out in different locations in the Rio Nancahuazu valley. For some reason, Ambassador Henderson was deliberately underestimating the rebel band's strength.

Tope was on Henderson's side, but he didn't have facts to counter Barrientos. He didn't know the size of the force, and nobody else knew, either. Even after years of work and millions of dollars of aid in the region, the United States still did not have a reliable intelligence network in Bolivia. Information gathering was just as skimpy in other Latin American countries. Hell, they didn't even know for sure if Che was dead or alive.

It was inexcusable.

Tope knew that had to change. U.S. troops were banned from the combat area in Bolivia. But that didn't mean the CIA couldn't help. They needed proper intelligence, and they needed it right now.

CHAPTER 6

The Intellectual Revolutionary

Roosters crowed up the sun at Muyapampa, a farming pueblo in the Andes foothills. Macaws and parrots fluttered overhead. About two thousand campesinos and shopkeepers lived in the dusty town, but no one but a soldier would be up so early.

The soldier was on checkpoint duty, part of the regional security alert. His platoon had only arrived the night before, and he had drawn the short straw. When he saw three men walking down the dirt road into town, he couldn't be sure the sunlight wasn't playing tricks on his tired eyes. Dressed in dirty civilian clothes, they were taller than the usual Bolivian peasant. They didn't belong there. As they drew closer, the soldier saw that one of them had a camera draped over his shoulder.

"*Alto o disparo*," the soldier shouted.

The men stopped and lifted their hands over their heads.

The soldier had no idea if the three were guerrillas. He only knew they looked suspicious. Who the hell would be walking down the road at 5 A.M.?

"Don't shoot. We are international journalists," the cameraman said. He spoke with a foreign accent. The soldier called for backup.

"They say they're journalists," he told his sleepy companions. The strangers put out their hands to shake, as if they'd been introduced. The soldiers answered with their fists until an officer finally arrived and ordered his men to stop.

The sun was up before Captain Julio Pacheco sat down with the men and started asking questions.

George Andrew Roth, the man with the camera, said he was British. A photographer chasing a story, he said he had worked on stories with the Bolivian Army, too.

The second man said he was Ciro Roberto Bustos, an Argentine painter and a salesman. The third man was thin and sunburned, with sandy hair and a beard. Jules Regis Debray, a twenty-six-year-old French philosophy professor, said he was on assignment, writing about the guerrillas for a magazine in Mexico. Pacheco transferred them to the Fourth Division headquarters in Camiri for additional questioning.

The Frenchman knew it was only a matter of time until the Bolivians figured out who he was. Debray, a well-known Marxist, had close ties to Fidel Castro. He literally wrote the book on the very guerrilla strategy being used in Bolivia, the widely read *Revolution in the Revolution*. He'd got himself into this mess. He was smuggled into Bolivia the previous September by Tania, the East German sleeper agent who'd set up the ratline from La Paz to the guerrillas' camp near Camiri. Finally, after years of theory and rhetoric, Debray made his way to the jungle hideout to live the life of a revolutionary.

It was nothing like he'd expected. It was horrible, in fact—

months of filth, insects, and uneducated men playing macho games in a steaming, stinking jungle camp. Bustos had been out there even longer and was just as fed up.

When Roth showed up at the camp, Debray saw him as his ticket back to civilization. Roth was the only one of the three with journalism credentials. He'd arrived in Bolivia a few weeks before from Chile, hell-bent on interviewing real guerrillas for a story. He'd weaseled his way into a Bolivian Army unit and persuaded the officers to let him read a diary seized from the guerrilla hideout in the Rio Nancahuazu valley. He gleaned enough clues there to help him track down the rebel group. Roth had a childlike disregard for his own safety, and one afternoon he simply showed up unannounced in the guerrilla camp.

The reporter received a cool reception. The interview he'd risked his life to get consisted of terse yes-and-no answers to his many questions.

As soon as the interview ended, Debray approached the rebel leader with his plan. Everyone knew he and Bustos wanted out. Roth, with his camera and notebooks, could help them past the army patrols. They all could pretend to be journalists, and their foreign accents would uphold the story, and the leader wasn't sad to see them go.

Debray and Bustos offered to share their stories of life in the camp in exchange for Roth's help. Roth didn't have a lot of options, so he agreed. The trio walked out of the rebel camp the evening of April 19. They were in government custody within hours.

The Frenchman could feel his luck running out.

A line of campesino faces watched silently as he was led down the street and through the gates of the police station. Standing off to one side of the patio was a local photographer who'd been tipped off that some captured guerrillas were on their way. He stepped forward, raised his camera, and snapped several frames as the soldiers shoved the three men into the station. Debray decided he was going to die within the next few hours. He did not have to tell any secrets beforehand. And so the following hours were a hail of fists, kicks, and elbows, then a sudden shift to the cabin of an airplane. As the plane climbed over the jungle canopy, a Bolivian officer slid the cabin door open and dragged Debray to the edge.

"Talk to me, or out you go," he shouted.

Debray simply closed his eyes and tried to enjoy the cold wind on his face. His bluff called, the officer pulled him back from the brink.

The following day, the Bolivian government released a report claiming "three foreign mercenaries" were killed in a battle with guerrillas. But when photographs of the trio emerged, the report was amended—the three men were in prison in Camiri, it said.

The local photographer had saved their lives, providing evidence they were alive and in custody.

Roth was released in July, three months after his arrest. He was never charged with a crime, which led to rumors that he was a CIA informant. A former Peace Corps language teacher, Roth said he took up journalism to make more money.

For the first few days, Debray and Bustos were shuffled between their cell and long interrogation sessions. Debray kept silent until the Bolivians used a hammer to pry the information out of him. Once, a Bolivian officer emptied the magazine of his .45 pistol into the dirt floor between Debray's knees.

At first, the Frenchman stuck to his story, saying he was at a nearby guerrilla camp for a story. After a few days, a Cuban-American CIA operative named Gabriel Garcia showed up. He didn't hit Debray or threaten to throw him from a plane. Instead, he sat down, took out his pen and pad, and started asking questions about why

Debray was really in Bolivia. He wanted to know about the guerrillas and the camps.

Sitting across from the CIA man, Debray was beaten. Worn out from his ordeal, his ears ringing from the point-blank barrage, the Frenchman was ready to trade information for survival. Maybe the CIA could save him.

Garcia just asked questions and took notes. It took a long time, but finally the subject of Che Guevara was raised.

Che was the reason Debray had come to Bolivia, the Frenchman admitted. He'd always wanted to meet and interview him, and he'd learned Che was helping start a revolution in the Bolivian jungle.

Garcia soon put away his notebook and excused himself. Within the hour, his report shot back to La Paz and Washington—a captured guerrilla with clear ties to Castro had confirmed that Che Guevara was working in Bolivia.

He might be lying. They would need more proof.

The Bolivian government, meanwhile, decided to make an example of Debray. Charged with murder, arson, armed insurrection, conspiracy against the state, and illegal entry into Bolivia, Debray was paraded before press cameras in the striped uniform of convicted criminals. Propaganda posters labeled him an assassin. "He who kills with steel will die by steel," one poster declared.

For Debray, the revolution was over. He languished in a dirty cell, wondering if he would ever get out of Bolivia alive.

The arrest of Debray added to the presidential frenzy.

First the ambushes, then the Bolivian high command proclaiming that hundreds of Cuban-trained fighters were flourishing in the scrubland, and now Debray, a foreign Marxist, was wandering the same neighborhood, with two accomplices.

In public President Barrientos exuded cool confidence. Privately he screamed for blood. Here was more proof that outsiders were plotting his overthrow.

At the end of April, Ovando finally publicly admitted that Debray, Bustos, and Roth were alive and in custody, that the military was investigating suspected links with the guerrilla movement. That was all. There was no more news about the men for the time being.

Stony silence may have suited the government, but the world outside was not satisfied with so little. Debray's friends and family were campaigning for him in the international media. French president Charles de Gaulle called Debray a "young and brilliant university student" and demanded his release.

Barrientos was incensed.

Debray and his followers were involved in a war that was spreading death in Bolivia, he told reporters. They deserved to pay the maximum price, he said. He intended to petition the Bolivian Congress to reinstate the death penalty. Groups formed to support Barrientos's position, including one comprised of families of the soldiers slain in the ambushes. Their statement to the press reads thus:

> *Mrs. Debray wants her son back. We say to her that she lost him long ago, even before he arrived in Bolivia. She lost him when he distanced himself from God and his mother to join the pack of criminals without God, without homes, without a flag. She lost him when he was the instigator of cowardly assassination, when he became the theorist of cowardly slaughters in Venezuela, Peru and Bolivia.*
>
> *Now the mother of the idealistic guerrilla should resign herself, and realize that her son no longer belongs to her. He will be put before a court that will judge his exploits as a mass murderer.*

They wanted Debray dead.

So did Barrientos, who was tired of stories that painted him and Bolivia in a bad light. He wanted to show journalists that the military was in control. He brought them along to inspect military posts in the war zone. At several stops he gathered locals to hear him denounce the guerrillas' actions and promise to destroy the uprising. But he knew there was a long way to go. The uncertainty was driving him mad.

CHAPTER 7

Welcome to Bolivia

The two C-130 cargo planes raced down the runway at Howard Air Force Base in Panama and lifted off one at a time. As they climbed into the clear night sky, Shelton stretched his legs out and tried to sleep.

But his mind kept going over the mission. They had nineteen weeks to turn a bunch of conscripts into an elite Ranger battalion. It wouldn't be an easy job, even if his commanders gave him twice as much time. But Shelton felt good about his team—sixteen Special Forces officers and sergeants. This was a textbook Special Forces mission. He knew his men were up to the task.

Small mobile training teams were the heart of Special Forces. Shelton was the officer in command, with a warrant officer as his assistant and a senior noncommissioned officer to handle details. The team had the requisite sergeants in charge of weapons, communications, medical needs, engineering, and intelligence. Designed to spend months deep inside hostile territory, the unit could survive without extensive resupply from the outside. The men were cross-trained in one another's specialties, and most spoke at least one foreign language.

It was a long road to the Green Berets, and each man had had to prove his worth to be admitted. It began with an extensive training course at Fort Bragg, a series of tests to determine which soldiers had the physical and mental toughness necessary. If they made it through, they might move on to full Special Forces training.

Training "host nations" soldiers was a big part of the Green Beret mission, taking the best men from a foreign force and turning them into elite fighting units. The strategy was simple: Train their armies, and they would defend their own borders. Thus, Communism could be checked without risking the lives of U.S. soldiers.

Shelton knew his team could slip into the jungle and take down Che themselves, but they were barred by diplomacy from going near "the red zone"—the Bolivian operations area. They would have to watch from the sidelines. That was fine with Shelton because he'd already seen men blown to pieces on the battlefield. There was no glory in war, only carnage and confusion. He had seen war up close, and he wasn't looking for more of that ugly shit.

The team was fully briefed on Bolivia, well aware of how sensitive their mission was. The communications sergeants held the highest security clearances. They were simply the two best radiomen on the Panama base: Sergeant Alvin Graham, a handsome man whose thick mustache and dark sunglasses gave him a "Hollywood" look, and Staff Sergeant Wendell Thompson, a clean-cut African-American from upstate New York.

With Special Forces teams deployed throughout Latin America, the Eighth Special Forces Group Operations Center (OPCEN) maintained a twenty-four-hour communications watch. The team would be in constant contact with headquarters. Graham and Thompson assured Shelton they'd prepared for anything; they'd laid in extra batteries, spare antennas, tubes, and screws. He made them double-check before they left Panama. No one knew how well the radios would work so deep in the jungle, so they packed civilian radios, too, just in case. The plane was crammed with equipment, ammunition, and food.

"We're a small team," Shelton said. "This is the tip of the spear. If something happens, we need to be in touch with the OPCEN. I want twenty-four-hour contact."

It was a long flight down to Santa Cruz. Shelton tried to relax, but the C-130 was made for hauling cargo, not people. He had to get some sleep. He hunkered in, pulled his cap over his eyes, and took a deep breath. Consciousness only returned when the cargo plane roared onto the dirt runway in Santa Cruz.

A shaft of sunlight cut through the dark cargo hold. Shelton rubbed his eyes. He looked out the window so he could see Bolivia. A cluster of trucks idled near the rickety control tower. As the plane rolled to a stop, Master Sergeants Milliard and Rivera-Colon stood near the cargo door, their berets on their heads.

"Shit," Shelton said under his breath. "So much for a low profile."

He decided to make the best of it.

"We're going to make a grand entrance," he said to the soldiers waiting in the cargo bay. "Put 'em on."

Graham, Thompson, and the rest of the team fished their berets out of the cargo pockets of their fatigues and pulled them on over their crew cuts. The engines muttered into silence, the propellers chopped the window light into shadow-light-shadow. After some shouts, bangs, and hydraulic groans, the air force crew got the great back ramp open. Hot air rolled up into the plane's vast belly.

The team trudged down the ramp, shaking the blood back into

their stiff legs. Milliard and Rivera-Colon stepped up to greet them. Milliard, a grizzled Massachusetts Yankee, had spent the last couple of weeks clearing brush and building a firing range, lining up deliveries of food and supplies to La Esperanza. It took a lot of doing, but Milliard, with his thick Boston accent, was the perfect soldier for the job. His career mirrored Shelton's—they had both served in Korea and spent time in Vietnam. Milliard was one of Shelton's go-to guys.

The Special Forces team and Bolivian soldiers unloaded the two cargo planes and packed a convoy of trucks. By noon, the convoy was bouncing along the rutted road to La Esperanza, the team's new home.

The soldiers were surprised when they arrived. They thought they would have to start from scratch, but the abandoned sugar mill gave the training a head start. The building had a roof. The original power lines were still there, so they could hook up generators and have lights in their little huts in the village. When they drove through the village the people seemed genuinely friendly, smiling and waving at the convoy.

Once the trucks were unloaded, Milliard and Rivera-Colon briefed everyone on the latest guerrilla activity south of Santa Cruz.

The ambushes of March 23 and April 10 were old news, but there'd been a few brief skirmishes since then, and the discovery of Bustos, Debray, and Roth. In fact, Debray was being held in La Esperanza, if only temporarily.

Milliard and Rivera-Colon told them the country was full of fear, but that no one was more scared than Barrientos and his high command. No one knew how many guerrillas were out there, and the phantom of Che Guevara seemed to hang over every conversation.

The briefing heightened the Americans' feeling of urgency. If

Che was there, they'd have to work quickly to train the Bolivians, who would be arriving in the next few days. For now only a small Bolivian security force was assigned to La Esperanza. Shelton reviewed their mission: teaching the Bolivian Ranger battalion "basic individual, advanced individual, basic unit, and advanced unit training." All would learn counterinsurgency tactics, and officers and noncommissioned officers would be briefed on command and control techniques.

After the briefing, Milliard and Rivera-Colon gave the team a tour of the village. Two armed guards stood outside the nondescript shack where Debray was jailed, waiting for his trial. One of the guards brought the captive outside for air. He wore a white jumpsuit with black vertical stripes, like a cartoon convict. He looked tired, the men thought.

The men toured the sugar mill site. Most of them were preoccupied with mundane things—latrines, sleeping quarters, fly screens. The men were accustomed to tropical Panama, with its deadly snakes and insects, but there at least the men had their own barracks. This place was almost primitive. Yes, they might jerry-rig some electricity to the shacks. But there was no air-conditioning. No indoor plumbing, either. Mosquitoes and flies descended as the sun went down.

When they reached the edge of a field, Rivera-Colon pointed to the marksmanship ranges. The sugar mill would be the focal point, with classroom instruction in the workshops, garages, and storage areas of the huge structure. A foursquare brick warehouse near the mill was chosen for the communications and storage depot. Shelton knew he'd be spending a lot of time there. He walked inside and looked around. There were few doors and windows, a red tile roof. Weeds grew up from cracks in the floor tiles, and birds nested in the ceiling timbers. It was hot and miserable inside, but he felt at home.

He'd been in a lot of godforsaken places. He'd done a similar mission in Laos, training men to fight the Pathet Lao guerrillas, in even more primitive conditions. Talk about dense jungles, he thought—in Laos, there were places where the foliage blocked out the sun for square miles, where you could sometimes run into tigers, or even an elephant. This was quaint by comparison, charming.

Shelton had seen enough. He bounded outside and told his men to unpack. Everyone was road-weary. The team needed time to unwind. No one could say when they'd get that chance again.

Dioniso Valderomas watched the military trucks roar into his village, scattering the cocks and hens that usually ruled the streets. Even the tiny chicks ran out of the way.

The villagers were just as worried, but they had no place to run.

Strange soldiers in green uniforms jumped off the trucks. Some stretched to loosen up. Others headed straight to a squat white-brick building that had been abandoned a few years before, along with the sugar mill. Dioniso watched them from his front yard.

These were not local police officers or Bolivian Army soldiers. They were tall and clean-shaven and wore yellow stripes on their sleeves. They carried complicated rifles and unloaded dozens of crates with words stenciled on the lids in black paint.

His neighbors peeked from behind the trees, wondering what the soldiers were doing. There had been a lot of strange activity in La Esperanza in the past few weeks, and nobody bothered telling the locals what they were up to. Trucks and heavy equipment arrived, and men from out of town cleared abandoned fields. No one had seen this kind of activity since the sugar mill was open.

Valderomas had lived through the sugar mill era, and he recalled those days with satisfaction. He raised meat and vegetables and sold them to the men who worked at the mill. He'd saved enough money to build a four-bedroom house with a fine tin roof. It was right in the middle of town, but set back enough that the palm trees shaded it from the sun. He'd married the beautiful Helena, and the two of them were raising four babies. Dioniso was thirty-five, but he looked ten years older, with strong hands and dark brown eyes. The sun had turned his skin leathery, and he'd lost a few teeth over the years. But his was a good life. Every morning he and his wife rose to the music of crowing roosters. It was a good, peaceful life, and he did not want anyone to come and change it for him.

The men lounged on the porch of Kiosko Hugo store and discussed every truck that rolled by, every rumor, every report they heard over their transistor radios. No one knew how it all fit together, and no one cared too much. They'd heard about the Frenchman in the old house, and they'd heard about Che Guevara, the elusive Communist who might be behind the killings up in Nancahuazu. Maybe he was the reason these foreign soldiers were here?

Valderomas listened as the literate told what they'd seen in the newspapers and the men with radios relayed the morning's news reports. The old schoolteacher said the guerrillas were trying to overthrow the government. They wanted better living and working conditions for the campesinos and miners. Che was a person who cared for the poor, he said—the guerrillas were right.

For Valderomas, that didn't make sense. Life wasn't so bad in La Esperanza. The government mostly left them alone. They were free to come and go as they pleased. If they had money, they could buy land and make a living. Politics were for people living in Santa Cruz and La Paz, unhappy people.

Valderomas could think of only one way he would change the local scene: the school. He and his generation pushed their children to go to school. La Esperanza had a small schoolhouse, but it was so poorly kept that class was canceled every time it rained. On really hot days the classes moved outdoors. Dioniso knew his children might not be happy with the simple rural life he'd chosen, and that education was the only way to increase their options.

He felt protective of his family, and warned Helena and the *niños* to stay inside the house when the strange soldiers were around. He didn't want his family anywhere near them.

"This is no good. These foreigners should not be here," he told his wife.

But as time went on, the soldiers seemed to settle in for a long stay. The children couldn't live indoors forever. Dioniso couldn't help but feel that their quiet life, like the bustling sugar mill era, was soon to be a memory.

CHAPTER 8

The Men in Bolivia

CIA officer Larry Sternfield flipped some papers on his pad and looked across the table at Félix Rodríguez.

Cuban, descended from Basque stock—Spaniards who didn't consider themselves Spanish—Rodríguez was clean-cut and thickset, with wavy black hair and the mind of a chess player. He could store away facts and think several steps ahead—something extremely helpful during interrogations. He was easygoing, with a disarming smile that built rapport. He could coax needed facts from even reluctant sources. He was fearless, with a deep sense of duty and a character strong enough to withstand repeated disappointments. Rodríguez had dedicated most of his life to fighting Communists. It was that dedication, coupled with his aptitude for intelligence work, that kept him high on the CIA payroll.

For the last couple of days Sternfield had been ensconced in a Homestead, Florida, house interviewing Cubans for a secret mission to Bolivia. Humidity hung in the air, and both men could hear the air conditioner dripping and laboring in the kitchen window.

Sternfield liked what he saw.

Born on the island in 1941, Rodríguez was the only child of an upper-middle-class family with social ties to Cuban dictator Fulgencio Batista. His uncle, José Antonio Mendigutia Silvera, had been minister of public works. Rodríguez came to the United States in 1954 to attend school in Pennsylvania. In 1958 he headed to Cuba for a visit, stopping on the way in Mexico to spend New Year's Eve with his parents.

While the world sang "Auld Lang Syne," the Rodríguez family learned that Batista had fled and that guerrillas led by Castro's 26th of July Movement had taken power in Cuba.

Rodríguez's parents, along with thousands of middle-class Cuban refugees, poured from their Caribbean island into Miami, where they set up a byzantine society in exile designed to last for generations.

Young Félix never returned to Cuba. He dropped out of school to join the Caribbean Anti-Communist Legion, created by Dominican Republic president Rafael Trujillo. The Legion aimed to overthrow Fidel Castro, but its invasion was an embarrassing failure. Rodríguez finally graduated in June 1960 and went to live with his parents in Miami.

Thoughts of freeing his homeland consumed his life. In September he joined a group of CIA-funded Cuban exiles in Guatemala for military training. They were called Brigade 2506, and they were supposed to infiltrate Cuba a few weeks before America made its own guerrilla attack on the island.

The Eisenhower administration conceived the plan in February of 1960. Rodríguez's unit was groomed to slip into the country and work with the resistance in the Escambray Mountains, training recruits with an eye toward creating a guerrilla force big enough to hold territory. Once the rebel state was created, the rest of the brigade would land with a ready-made provisional government. The United States would immediately recognize the new government.

But President Kennedy scrapped the plan soon after his 1960 election. He preferred a full-on invasion, starting with the city of Trinidad and expanding afterward to the Escambray Mountains. But invasions are too obvious, and America wanted the world to think Cubans themselves were orchestrating the takeover on their own. The Trinidad plan was scrapped, too, and the planners turned their eyes toward a swampy backwater called the Bay of Pigs.

From there the exiles could control the air, secure the area, and bring in the provisional government. But when Adlai Stevenson, the American ambassador to the United Nations, learned that U.S. pilots would be responsible for the air strike—not defecting Cubans—he told the administration to either stop the air strike or he would resign. Air support was critical to the plan, but the people in charge decided to forge ahead without any.

That decision was fatal.

Rodríguez was already in Cuba two months before the planned invasion. On April 17, 1961, he listened to radio news reports as the invasion died on the beach. He immediately sought sanctuary at the Venezuelan embassy in Havana. After five and a half months in hiding, he finally made it back to Miami. Rodríguez had worked closely with anti-Castro forces and the CIA ever since. His wife, Rosa, fully supported his activities.

On the eve of the Cuban Missile Crisis in 1962, Rodríguez was kept on alert for days, ready to parachute into rural Cuba with a radio beacon for U.S. air-strike guidance. While her husband waited for a go-ahead in a Miami hotel room, Rosa Rodríguez waited at home by the television, wondering what part of the unfolding crisis involved her husband. Days passed, and the standoff was settled. Rodríguez's call never came. So when the CIA called again, the expatriate wasn't so excited.

Sternfield knew Rodríguez was qualified for the Bolivia mission, but what he wanted to know was if Rodríguez was willing to risk another disappointment.

"You might be in South America for some length of time," Sternfield said. "You ready for that?"

Rodríguez nodded. He knew Rosa was willing to wait, and this wouldn't be the first time he'd been called to catch an overseas flight with little notice.

Sternfield asked Rodríguez about his time in the Dominican Republic and his familiarity with radio equipment. The interview was pretty standard. Sternfield didn't reveal any mission details until he'd almost finished.

"There's a good possibility that Che Guevara is engaged in guerrilla activities in Bolivia," Sternfield said. He saw Rodríguez snap to attention. "Your assignment would be to help the Bolivians track him down and capture him. If I choose you, when would you be able to travel?"

Rodríguez's pulse jumped when he heard the revolutionary's name. If Che was in Bolivia, he wanted to be there. He took a deep breath and tried to play cool. He didn't want to get too excited about a mission that could be shut down at a moment's notice.

"Well, if I have time I will go to my house say good-bye to my wife. I will pick up my luggage and we leave right now," he said. "If we don't have time for that, then I'll call her and tell her I have to go."

Sternfield smiled. Rodríguez continued.

"If you tell me we've only got a couple of hours, I will call her from the airport to say I'll be away for a couple of months. And if you say 'right now,' then let's get in the car. I will give you my phone number on the way to the airport, and you can call Rosa for me."

Sternfield smiled. Rodríguez's sense of urgency impressed him. The CIA man knew he had one member of the two-man team needed for the job. But Sternfield wasn't going to tip his hand too soon, either.

"We'll call you in a few days," he told Rodríguez.

As Rodríguez drove home, he had no idea if he'd impressed Sternfield or if he'd got the job, but he packed his bag as soon as he arrived. When the call came two days later, he kissed Rosa and told her he would see her soon.

Bill, Rodríguez's usual CIA contact, was waiting at the CIA-rented apartment in downtown Washington, D.C. He didn't wait for Rodríguez to sit down.

"Do you know Gustavo Villoldo?" Bill asked. "Do you mind working with him?"

"I met him at Fort Benning, at the Army School of the Americas. We were second lieutenants together," Rodríguez said. "I have no objection to him at all."

"Fine," the case officer said. "Take a walk for a while. Come back in a couple of hours."

Rodríguez put his luggage away and left the safe house.

Villoldo arrived only minutes later. He, too, was excited at the prospect of hunting Che in Bolivia, but he, too, had been disappointed in the past. Two years earlier, Villoldo had traveled to the Congo to track down the wily Argentine. After three months of listening to Che's radio messages, he was closing in on his position. Che suddenly fell ill and fled into Tanzania. Villoldo was sent home.

When rumors began circulating that Che had resurfaced in Bolivia, his CIA contact urged Villoldo to "volunteer" for the new mission.

Meantime, Rodríguez walked the Lincoln and Jefferson memorials, pausing to gaze at the U.S. Capitol at the far end of the Mall. Rodríguez loved his adopted country more than most Americans because he had felt the pain of losing his own homeland. Castro was still in power in Cuba, and here Rodríguez was, living comfortably in the United States. The soaring monuments only made the pain worse.

The CIA gave him chances to pay Castro back. While waiting in Havana for the Bay of Pigs invasion, Rodríguez had three times volunteered to assassinate Castro with a sniper rifle. If he couldn't take out Castro, Che would be as big a prize. Che commanded the revolutionaries who'd rolled over the Las Villas Province, where Rodríguez was born, where his house and land would be if the Marxists hadn't seized it all. Che held a special place in the hearts of romantic leftists around the world, and a different spot in the hearts of Cuban exiles. Che was a thug, a killer, and "the butcher of La Cabaña."

La Cabaña was a gray stone prison. In January 1959, Che's men captured it and used it as a revolutionary headquarters. During his five-month tenure there, Guevara oversaw the kangaroo courts and summary executions of hundreds of what he termed war criminals, traitors, informants, and former members of Batista's secret police. It was a bloodbath, a purge of anyone who might have opposed the Cuban Revolution.

For Rodríguez, this mission would be his best chance for payback.

Rodríguez returned to the apartment. The planning began, and continued over the next several weeks. They had to work around several obstacles set up by the United States itself. Ambassador Henderson had banned Americans from operating in guerrilla areas, so the Green Berets were already in Bolivia training the Bolivian

Ranger Battalion, but they could not accompany the Rangers into the combat zone. But Villoldo and Rodríguez were Cubans, not Americans. They could get around the directive. They would travel under cover as Cuban nationals—U.S. residents looking at business opportunities in Bolivia.

"You'll fly into La Paz," Bill briefed them. "The Bolivians know who you are, but this cover should throw off the press and Cuban agents."

Once on the ground, Villoldo and Rodríguez would split up.

"Gustavo will lead a training course on intelligence-gathering for ten Bolivian soldiers. You, Félix, will work in Santa Cruz at the Bolivian headquarters. You know the radios; you can keep everyone connected and informed," Bill said.

The CIA man handed Rodríguez dossiers on his Bolivian counterparts: Colonel Joaquin Zenteno Anaya and Major Arnaldo Saucedo.

"Get to know these guys," Bill said.

Rodríguez knew that brutality was common in Bolivia. The officers treated their own troops harshly and prisoners worse. High on Rodríguez's list was convincing Zenteno and Saucedo that treating prisoners well worked better than beating and threatening them.

He also looked forward to getting a look at the documents captured at the abandoned guerrilla camps in the Rio Nancahuazu valley. He knew the papers often were the most valuable. Guerrillas were pack rats, and Rodríguez knew they had books, papers, diaries, and codebooks with them.

For two weeks, Rodríguez and Villoldo studied Bolivia. The briefings, held in the rented apartment, covered the current military and political situation. They were brought up to date on the backgrounds and attitudes of all the key players. Rodríguez created a signal plan and a tapping code for the radios. Transmissions would be relayed through a station in La Paz, to overcome the high mountain obstacles.

The pair took particular pains with the dossier of Debray, the captured French Marxist.

They combed over Debray's interrogation transcripts, hoping to find some scrap of useful information.

Debray had fallen victim to Bolivian police tactics, which translated to being slowly beaten to death. CIA operative Gabriel Garcia had stepped in and saved Debray's life. Garcia interrogated Debray for days after his arrest, and the Frenchman gave up everything he knew about the guerrilla's operations.

Rodríguez took particular note of a rebel named Castillo Chavez, known as Paco. Debray said the young Bolivian complained frequently about being lied to by the Communist Party. Paco was a thirty-year-old upholsterer who was recruited with promises of an education in Havana and Moscow. Instead, the Communists sent him to a guerrilla camp, where he was issued a gun and a heavy backpack and forced to march over the mountains. Rodríguez knew that if they could get to Paco, he'd be a valuable resource.

Paco was his target.

After weeks of study and discussion, Rodríguez was eager to leave for Bolivia and get to work. There was no doubt in Rodríguez's mind that if Che was in Bolivia, they would find him. But before they left Washington, they had to sort out what to do when they caught Che.

Bring him back alive, Bill told them.

"If by any chance Che is captured alive, which is very doubtful, try to keep him alive," Bill said. "Try and keep him alive at all costs, and we will make arrangements to fly him to Panama. Planes and choppers will be standing by if the situation presents itself."

PART TWO

PREPARATION

CHAPTER 9

The Trainers

The Rangers-to-be straggled into La Esperanza in early May in jeeps and troop trucks. Drawn from cities and villages throughout Bolivia, they were almost all illiterate and undernourished. Dirty beige fatigues hung off their bony frames.

Shelton watched them unload and fought back an attack of despair. He had only four and a half months to make Rangers of them.

The first six weeks would be hardest: basic individual training—boot camp. The Bolivians would learn to handle and fire weapons and endure tough physical training. Shoot, move, and communicate—the basic soldier skills. They had only one way to go: up. They had to improve.

While Shelton spoke Spanish, he needed a liaison with the Bolivian men, an officer he could trust, someone with some experience. Shelton turned to Captain Margarito Cruz. "Let's go talk to the Bolivian officers," he said.

Cruz followed Shelton from their operations center over to the sugar mill, where the Bolivians were gathering. Among the sad-sack soldiers stood a tall Bolivian officer in a crisp, freshly pressed uniform. Other officers gravitated around the man. He seemed well liked.

"*Hablas inglés?*" Shelton asked the officer.

"Yes, sir," the man responded.

Shelton shook his hand. "I'm Major Pappy Shelton, U.S. Special Forces."

"I'm Captain Gary Prado Salmon, Braun Eighth Cavalry Group, sir."

Shelton smiled. "Cavalry, huh?"

They spoke in English for the next half hour, discussing tactics and counterinsurgency. Shelton said he was the commander of the Green Beret team. Prado told him about his training in Panama, and that his father was a Bolivian general. The more they talked, the more Shelton liked Prado.

"Look around you," Shelton said. "I have nineteen weeks to train this battalion. We don't have time to dwell on any one skill. I need to know how the men are picking up the lessons. I need a Bolivian officer to report on their progress. Can you do that, Captain?"

"With pleasure, sir," Prado said. He felt himself blush red with excitement.

They would meet every day in late afternoon, Shelton said. And he wanted an honest assessment. No bullshit.

Prado smiled. "I will always speak my mind."

"Now, let's see what we can cut from this training. I'm not going to waste time on things they're not going to use. We don't need marching or parade drills. It's unnecessary. We have to train them to fight."

Shelton and Prado were to meet with the Bolivian commanders that night to look over the planned program and assign weekly goals. The entire Second Ranger Battalion—all 650 men—would be in La Esperanza by May 8, when training would begin in earnest. Prado would serve as Shelton's advisor, to help tailor the regimen to the Bolivians' needs and abilities.

"You are going to be an important part of this training, Captain," Shelton told the young officer.

Prado was proud. He had just arrived and had just earned the trust of this important figure. "I liked him from the beginning," Prado recalled later. "The other officers were more reserved, but Shelton was more open."

The commander's next order of business was the villagers. Local rapport was vital to Special Forces missions because the neighbors saw and heard things that a foreigner might miss. The village "grapevine" was an intelligence network in itself, an early warning system. If the villagers knew anything, and they trusted the Americans, they might volunteer information about the guerrillas. They had to wonder what the hell the Americans were doing there. They deserved some answers, Shelton thought.

So while the rest of the team was setting up communication wires and digging latrines, Shelton decided to do some public relations. He went back to his room, opened his guitar case, and pulled out his pawnshop Gibson. He asked Milliard to walk him into town.

"You know the key players already," Shelton said. "Let's meet them."

They grabbed Captains Fricke and Cruz, and the men went door to door, meeting some of the shopkeepers and village elders. They talked to the mayor—Erwin Bravo—and other shopkeepers. They introduced themselves to Jorge, a teacher at the dilapidated schoolhouse.

Shelton told them why the soldiers were there, how long they would stay, and the kind of training they would be conducting. The Rangers would stay until the end of September, and when that was done, they'd conduct more exercises with other Bolivian units. The trainers wanted to be home by Christmas, Shelton said. The village could return to normal with the New Year.

Meantime, they intended to benefit La Esperanza however they could. Special Forces medics would provide free health care to villagers. If anyone had questions or problems, they could be brought directly to Shelton, who was in charge of the entire operation.

Furthermore, the soldiers would need to hire locals to cook, do laundry, and run errands. The Americans had money. They would spend it there, in the village.

The mayor told Shelton they'd been leery of the strangers and put off by the lack of information. Now that he had some facts, he would spread the word. The mayor then conducted a village tour, ending it up at the three-room schoolhouse on the edge of town. About 280 children from La Esperanza and surrounding villages came to classes there, but the building was falling apart. There were no public funds for maintaining the building, the mayor said with a shrug of his shoulders.

Shelton shook his head in disbelief. He didn't want to make any promises, but he felt compelled to do something. He would give the problem some thought, he said.

The tour ended at Kiosko Hugo. The store was the village center, where everyone stopped for a cold drink and a chat. Shelton stepped onto the porch and began tuning his guitar. He was a self-taught guitarist. He wasn't much good, but he wasn't shy about playing in public. He loved all types of music: blues, rock and roll, country. Once he learned to play, he was never short of entertainment.

So standing there outside the Bolivian general store, Shelton strummed the chords to one of his favorite songs: "Mr. Shorty," a Marty Robbins country song about life and death in an old West bar.

The Bolivian men smiled and gathered closer. They tapped their toes and hummed along. Shelton couldn't sing a lick, but it didn't matter. A couple of the villagers hurried home and returned with their own guitars, and after Shelton finished, they started in playing Bolivian folk tunes. Shelton tried to follow along. He missed a few chords here and there, but he kept going, bobbing his head and flashing his smile as he played. Shelton had a blast. With just a few chords, he'd started winning them over.

Sergeant Mario Salazar leapt from the back of the troop truck and dropped his duffel bag in the dirt. This was it. He had made it to La Esperanza. A warehouse by the sugar mill would be the barracks, and if he hurried he could grab a good bunk. But Salazar stood in place. He needed time to think.

He'd been waiting for this moment since joining the army. When he heard about the ambushes, Salazar took his patriotic fury to the army recruiting office. When he heard about the new Ranger unit, he asked to join that, too. If he was going to risk his life, he wanted to be with the best. Now here he was, ready to take the first steps on that journey.

I can do this, he thought.

Salazar was a short, stout twenty-one-year-old with muscular arms. He wore his black hair short and parted to the side. His thick hands had deep scars from working in the fields. Salazar was a farmer, like his father had been before him. He never knew his father—he died before Salazar was born—but his mother, Angelina, filled him with stories of the old man's hardworking honesty.

Salazar was the man of the house. His mother had two more children after his father died, but it was Mario who raised fields of watermelon, peppers, corn, and beans to support them all.

Salazar had actually thought about enlisting the year before, when a friend joined up, but there still were crops in the field. After the attacks, he couldn't wait any longer.

The day arrived for him to leave, and his mother cried. Salazar made her a cup of coffee and sat down with her at the kitchen table. He promised to be careful, promised to send her at least ten of the twenty-five bolivianos he'd be paid each month. Every young man in Bolivia was eventually drafted, he said. It was their duty to serve for a year.

Yes, she responded between tears, but they didn't face real combat. They just trained and marched and played soldier. They didn't have to fight Che Guevara.

People in the countryside were sure Che was out there. Some were spreading tales of robbery, kidnapping, murder of innocent civilians. The radio waves and newspapers were filled with so much talk about guerrillas that Salazar didn't know what to believe. But he knew he couldn't stay at home.

He was going to be a Ranger—an elite soldier in a country with a poor military tradition. Salazar was proud to be part of a unit that could turn around Bolivia's troubled army. That's why he was here—to get ready for action. Like so many Bolivians, he wanted to avenge the deaths of his countrymen, to purge these Communist foreigners from the countryside.

Salazar looked at the sugar mill in the waning light and whispered a prayer: "Jesus of great power, have mercy on me and make me strong." It was a prayer he said in the fields at home when the sun drained away his energy, when he felt he couldn't work anymore. He added a line of his own. He promised Jesus he would train hard—no matter what. That he would keep moving forward, no matter how tired.

Salazar made the sign of the cross, picked up his kit, and headed into the barracks.

CHAPTER 10

179 Days

General Ovando, commander of the Bolivian armed forces, decided it was time for decisive action. Ovando and Barrientos were long-time friends, close in age, but Ovando took a decidedly parental role. Where Barrientos had flamboyant charisma, Ovando had quiet gravitas—and the unwavering support of the Bolivian elite.

Ovando commanded respect. He looked like a general, tall and thin with a receding hairline and a pencil-thin mustache. He was always impeccably dressed—his uniforms tailored and shirts freshly pressed.

He was forty-nine years old, and his military career dated back to the Chaco War. When the guerrilla attacks sent the country and the president into a frenzy of fear, it was Ovando who urged calm, and kept foreign nations updated on the insurgency. While Barrientos boasted that he would crush the guerrillas, Ovando convinced Bolivia's neighbors and friends that it was in their own interest to send them weapons. If Bolivia fell, they might, too.

Ovando encouraged Barrientos to keep the United States in the loop. Barrientos called on Bolivia's ambassador to Washington, Julio Sanjines-Goytia, a West Point graduate with Pentagon ties. Wealthy and charming, Sanjines-Goytia was friends with many senators and key U.S. military men who attended his fabulous Washington parties. Now it was time to call in some favors.

Sanjines-Goytia appealed to U.S. secretary of state Dean Rusk, asking the United States do nothing about the insurgency for now but increase Bolivia's financial aid. Barrientos wanted $6 million—including $4 million in direct military cash.

Rusk liked the idea. There was little support for U.S. military intervention while the Vietnam War continued to escalate. Rusk brought up the plan during an April 9 meeting with the Joint Chiefs of Staff about the Che Guevara crisis.

CIA director Richard Helms shot down the idea, saying the Bolivians could not be trusted with the money. He came prepared with bar graphs and charts. Helms showed how U.S. funds sent to keep civil service payrolls up to date had disappeared. Bolivian government employees, he said, hadn't been paid for months.

Bolivians had also squandered a fund to buy cross-country vehicles essential for counterinsurgency operations. Instead of buying rugged 4x4s, the Bolivians had invested in a fleet of Mini Mokes—light jeep-style military vehicles. The Mokes' small wheels and low ground clearance made them impractical for off-road use. There was no way a Mini Moke could hope to get within shooting distance of Che's hideout.

Army chief of staff General Harold Johnson made another point: "One of the most important lessons we have learned in Vietnam is that guerrilla flare-ups must be smothered immediately, without a moment's delay." Johnson said the army was already planning to send some advisors, and maybe troops.

Rusk interrupted Johnson, reminding him of the president's position: No U.S. fighting units in South America. No U.S. soldiers on the ground. It was a policy being pushed by Ambassador Henderson, who had State Department support.

"We urge that this hands-off policy be maintained," Rusk told the generals sitting at the table. "I know that something must be done about this problem," he said, but sending American troops into Bolivia, even as advisors "would mean the fat's in the fire."

The Green Berets were the only American troops going to Bolivia, and only as trainers.

When Barrientos heard about the push-back from Washington, he was incensed. He wanted military supplies and money—not Green Berets training campesinos. What good would that do?

Ovando told Barrientos that he would ask other nations for military aid. He assured Barrientos that the Bolivian military would prevail. And when the guerrillas were wiped out and stability returned, the Bolivian Army would have new weapons and equipment.

Ovando knew that was easier said than done. They still had no idea how many guerrillas they were facing. He was sure the Communists were using the unrest to recruit new soldiers.

After the last ambush, Major Sanchez had brought out of the jungle a note from the guerrillas, meant for release to the press. The major instead turned it over to military officials in Cochabamba for analysis. But someone leaked the letter to a local newspaper, which published it on May 1.

The Bolivian Liberation Army said it wanted to reveal the truth behind the first ambush—that the guerrillas had dealt a crushing blow to government troops.

We regret the innocent blood shed by fallen soldiers, but peaceful roads are not made with mortars and machine guns, as the puppets with decorated uniforms assert. There has not been nor will there be a single campesino who can complain about the way we have treated him or about our way of obtaining supplies, except for those who, betraying their class, volunteer to serve as guides or informers.

Hostilities are under way. In future communiqués we will expound our revolutionary position clearly; today we issue a call to workers, campesinos, intellectuals, all those who feel that the time has come to meet violence with violence and to rescue a country sold piecemeal to Yankee monopolies and to raise the standard of living of our people who grow hungrier every day.

Barrientos ordered the editor arrested, but it was too late. The damage was done.

Ovando knew the letter would appeal to the miners and trade unions. The mines in the northwest part of the country were the lifeblood of the Bolivian economy. They provided good incomes for workers, but the miners had always made trouble for the Bolivian government, even after the 1952 revolution. The mining unions were powerful and lobbied hard to improve working and living conditions for miners. Tension increased enormously after the military coup in 1964. In May 1965, the government jailed and exiled many leftist union chiefs and killed at least one. Troops occupied the mines, unleashing a bloody confrontation that raged for several days at the mines and on the outskirts of La Paz. By the time a truce was reached, 48 miners were dead, and 284 were wounded.

Ovando and Barrientos were worried that fighting could flare up again, and that the guerrillas would capitalize on the discontent. It didn't help that international news organizations were writing negative articles about them. A *Washington Post* headline blared: ISOLATED GUERRILLAS POST GROWING PERIL TO BOLIVIA. The story warned that the guerrillas threatened Bolivia's stability: "The significance of the guerrilla force lies in the potential as a catalyst amid the highly volatile elements of the Bolivian political structure. By simply remaining at large, the guerrillas could touch off explosive reaction in a country unrivaled in South America for the bloodiness and instability of its political history."

The harshest comments were reserved for the military: "Underscoring the possibility has been the armed forces reaction to the threat as though they were following the script for a Keystone Kops two-reeler. Lurching from tight-lipped news blackouts to statements that are contradictory and preposterous, the military has managed to confuse just about everyone regarding the threat and the campaign against it."

The article concluded by calling the armed forces "small, ill-equipped and, for the most part, poorly trained."

Ovando knew there was some truth to that. He had been trying for years to rebuild the military, which had been stripped of power after the 1952 revolution. The anti-military government was why he and Barrientos risked all in their 1964 coup. That's why American Green Berets were in Bolivia, training his soldiers.

Now, nearly two months after the first ambush, Ovando wanted to know when those soldiers would be ready—not only to hunt guerrillas, but to put down an uprising in the mines. It was time to visit La Esperanza.

By the middle of May, the streets and fields in La Esperanza were teeming with uniformed men. But with all the commotion, there was no confusion over who was in charge.

Major Shelton was everywhere, bounding from one meeting to the next with his clipboard in hand. He was in the fields, keeping tabs on construction as Special Forces soldiers used hand tools to build a full-scale Ranger training camp. They erected an obstacle course, confidence course, quick-reaction course—where jungle footpaths were rigged with pop-up cutouts of enemy figures—a river course, a target range.

He inspected the work. He even helped with the construction, working alongside his men and the Bolivian soldiers in the tropical heat.

Shelton enjoyed every minute of it. Wherever he walked, he flashed that wide, friendly smile as he chatted with soldiers, officers, and villagers. He listened and offered solutions. Shelton was often exhausted at the day's end, but so what? He took great pride in solving problems and getting the most out of his men. His cool demeanor rubbed off. They worked hard and relaxed afterward at Kiosko Hugo.

One of the first things Shelton did was set up a "pipeline" to bring much-needed supplies to La Esperanza. Usually Special Forces teams went into the field with footlockers, and they would be resupplied once or twice a month by a C-46 long-range commando transport plane. But with this mission, they had a C-130 at their disposal. Shelton used it.

Days after arriving, he had a refrigerator brought in on the cargo plane, a special request from a local bush pilot assigned to the team. When the icebox arrived, the pilot hauled it away. After that, there was nothing the pilot wouldn't do for the team. He flew all over the region, picking up men and supplies.

Once Shelton had primed the pipeline, he used it for critical supplies. Early on, he noticed the Rangers seemed hesitant to pull the trigger during live fire exercises, and they didn't seem to carry many bullets. He questioned Bolivian captain Julio Cruz.

"How many rounds per rifleman for the course?" he asked Cruz. "How many live rounds does your army issue for each man's training?"

"Ten bullets are authorized for each recruit."

"Ten rounds?" Shelton was shocked. "How can you teach them anything?"

Captain Cruz explained the Bolivian method of training soldiers: "First we tell them. Then we kick them."

Shelton had heard enough. If these farm-boys ever were going to learn to shoot, they had to practice. He requested enough ammunition to allocate each rifleman five thousand live rounds.

Shelton noticed that the Bolivian soldiers had only one uniform each, and no canteens, ponchos, or packaged field rations. That had to change. And their rations were shit: coffee and some bread for breakfast and lunch. Dinner was no better. Bolivian army cooks—throwbacks to the Chaco War—started dinner preparations by filling fifty-five-gallon drums with water. They dumped in rice, potatoes, and a few scraps of meat—sometimes a chopped anaconda, when they could catch one. They lit a fire under the drums and an hour or so later ladled the soupy concoction into bowls. It was classic slop.

The men weren't getting enough calories to keep up with the rigorous training. They didn't have stamina or upper body strength enough to complete some of the exercises, especially rope climbing.

Shelton stared at the to-do list on his clipboard. Getting additional funds to buy quality food was high on the docket.

He found himself opening up more to Prado, who came into his office at the end of each day. They reviewed training and schedules, the feedback that Prado would hear from the soldiers.

"You're my eyes and ears out there, Gary," Shelton told him

after one meeting. "If this mission is going to be successful, I'm going to need your help. You're as important as any man on this mission."

Prado beamed. Decades later, he still remembered those words of praise.

Shelton convinced Harry Singh, an American with the U.S. Agency for International Development, that helping the Green Berets build a training area and a school would improve relations with the villagers. So Singh, who was assigned to an AID-funded road-building project near La Esperanza, used his bulldozers to carve out a road to connect the camp to the larger road Singh was already building. Suddenly La Esperanza had direct access to the Santa Cruz highway.

Shelton told Singh that civic projects like his were part of the American counterinsurgency strategy. Singh agreed to help Shelton and his Green Berets rebuild the school in La Esperanza by the end of the year. The Americans were scheduled to leave in December, and the school would be their legacy to the village.

Shelton's populist streak served him well. He had a sense of social justice—a belief that Americans were obligated to improve the lives of others. And knowing this was his last mission was liberating. He didn't have to be cautious about tapping other agencies for help. He no longer had to worry about pleasing superior officers who could hold up a promotion.

Shelton was finished playing bullshit games. He was doing the right thing, his mission was high-priority, so the bureaucrats in upper echelons pretty much left him alone. It helped that he had the respect of SOUTHCOM's high command. They knew his work. He had their trust, and every day he used one of the team's powerful radios to update them on his progress. The musical evenings continued at Kiosko Hugo. Villagers joined in with their instruments most nights. Local cowboys loved it and often stopped to drink beer and bullshit with the men. They told Shelton the gossip flowing around La Esperanza and the region.

When Captain Harvey Wallender arrived from Panama to take over the team's intelligence section in the fall, he found that his work in La Esperanza was already done. Shelton's men had built up a friendly rapport between the village and the Rangers. Wallender marveled at how the Bolivians followed Shelton around, laughing at his jokes. It looked like they worshiped him, he said.

And that helped when Shelton ran up against a sanitation problem.

The Bolivians knew nothing about field sanitation. There were no indoor toilets at the training camp, and many of the men had never seen toilet paper. In La Esperanza, when they felt the urge, they pissed and shat just outside their warehouse barracks. The stink was eye-watering, and the filth posed a health hazard. So Shelton's team taught the Bolivians how to dig—and use—a slit trench latrine, the simplest type of pit toilet. Still, the Bolivians were reluctant to use it. Sergeant Dan Chapa finally broke it down for them—shit and piss do not belong anywhere within twenty yards of inhabited buildings, and hands should be washed with soap and water afterward. Those found doing otherwise would personally dig the next trench.

It was basic, but Shelton could see progress.

Ovando swept into the camp unannounced on May 10. Shelton was glad things were in good order. Once inside Shelton's office, Ovando questioned him closely about his progress.

Shelton was honest. It was only May 10, they had really just started training, but everything was going well. They'd spent the last two weeks getting settled in and building the training facilities. Ovando furrowed his brow. He'd hoped for much more.

"Show me the place," he said. As they walked to the training field, Shelton described the four-phase program, how they had just started the first: six weeks of basic training.

One group of soldiers was learning to assemble, disassemble, and clean their M-1 Garands. It wasn't unusual to see the soldiers struggle at first with basic exercises. After all, the average Ranger recruit had a fifth-grade education. The general tapped his feet and appeared tense. "I must return to La Paz," he said, turning toward his motorcade. "How much longer?"

"Sir, our training calls for 179 days. That's how long it will take. But when they're finished, they'll be ready to tackle any mission," Shelton said.

The general's shoulders sagged. "That long?"

Shelton was firm: "Yes, sir." He struggled to keep his composure. He looked Ovando in the eyes. "We can do this right or we can do this wrong. When I do something, I do it right."

"Bolivia needs those men in the field now," the commander said. "There's no time to lose."

"Sir," Shelton said. "They just started training. They're not ready."

Ovando could tell Shelton was giving him an honest assessment. He agreed: It was too risky, sending more untrained men into the jungle.

"Very good, Major," Ovando said. "Keep up the good work."

Shelton watched as the convoy headed back to Santa Cruz. He said nothing.

Valderomas stood under a dark sky lit up with stars, feeling good. He'd spent the evening at Kiosko Hugo, drinking beer and singing with his friends and the happy, guitar-playing American. The soldiers seemed to bring an excitement with them, and the villagers' initial trepidation had faded. A man at the camp had paid him well above the average price for a barrow-load of fruit and had asked him to bring some onions next time—it was much like the sugar mill workers used to do. A military crew was seen over at the derelict school, measuring the walls and windows—the mayor said they would fix up the place.

Valderomas was happy about that. But still, he didn't entirely like it. Too many people had converged here at once, too many strangers. Something bad was bound to happen.

Valderomas still forbade his family any contact with the soldiers—especially the Americans. He minded his own business.

Not all families felt that way. Cooks and maids, local girls, were over there every day, serving the American soldiers. He could see the way some of the soldiers looked at the women. The Roca family, a respectable tribe, was a bit concerned about their daughter Dorys. She obviously had a flirtation going with that tall American with the mustache. Valderomas wasn't blind. She was young and pretty. Heading for trouble, that one.

And there was too much noise. Gunfire, bulldozers, trucks, shouting—nonstop, night and day. Good as they might be for everyone else, Valderomas hoped the soldiers would leave soon, so he could sleep again.

CHAPTER 11

"We're not sure."

By early June, Ranger training was becoming grueling for Mario Salazar. He had thought he was in good condition when he arrived at La Esperanza, but field work hadn't prepared him for the long days of full-speed running, climbing, and diving. At the end of the day every muscle ached and throbbed. Now they were starting night maneuvers, so there was less time to heal between onslaughts.

He stood outside the makeshift barracks at dawn and watched the men heading to the training fields. Some stuffed folded-up bits of bread into their pockets, energy for later. Salazar stared at the sky, a riot of pastels—red, orange, and yellow. He was headed into another hot day on the obstacle course. Rope climbing.

He struggled with rope climbing. Hell, most of them struggled with it. It was new to them, they couldn't see the point of it, and many simply didn't have the strength to pull themselves up.

The rope dangled from a steel beam twenty-five feet above the sugar mill floor. Some were afraid of the height, but for Salazar, the burns on his hands were the problem.

He'd finally got the concept on his last trip up the rope. He wrapped the bottom part of the rope around his right calf and pressed it with his left foot to hold him in place. But as he was climbing up, he slipped. He slid back down the rope, holding on for his life. He made it to the ground without breaking any bones, but the friction left deep burns on the palms of both his hands. He was too proud to go to a medic. He washed the burns carefully, but during the night the mosquitoes and biting bugs attacked the wounds. Now his hands were swollen. Pus oozed from the edges of the black scabs. Salazar closed his fists on the pain and headed to the field.

Prado noticed and told him to get the wounds treated.

"End of the day, sir," he replied. "Don't want to lose my rhythm."

Nothing was going to sidetrack him. He wanted to earn the officers' respect. If he left for treatment, he might be sidelined for days.

He found his spot in formation, and one of the Americans began chanting: "*Lo mas duro! Lo mejor!*" "The toughest! The best!" The soldiers joined in. It was the Special Forces way of boosting morale, building confidence. If they shouted it long enough, they would actually believe it. It was like a pep talk before the big football game, and it was beginning to work.

A few weeks before, the soldiers had hung their heads. They were hesitant to fire their weapons or even look the officers in the eye. Not anymore. Salazar realized he had just refused an order from an officer. He was gaining confidence.

As they lined up, Salazar spotted Bolivian Army colonel Jose Gallardo, commander of the entire new regiment in La Esperanza. He was heading this way. Salazar felt even more pressure.

The soldier in front of Salazar grabbed onto the rope and began pulling himself up, while the American instructor shouted words of encouragement. When the soldier reached the top, the American clapped his hands in approval. The man came down the rope like a monkey and handed the end to Salazar. His turn. He would show them he could do it, too. He wrapped the rope between his legs. He gripped the rope so tight his palms went numb, and from there he inched up. When he tired, he clamped his feet together to hold his place. The pain in his hands was excruciating—like a swarm of fire ants. He blocked out the pain. Somehow he summoned the strength until, out of breath, his skin raw, he made it to the top. When he looked around, he could see the entire training area—the firing ranges, the "slide for life" where soldiers would hang on to a pulley and glide into a pond. With the American clapping, he inched down slowly and made it to the bottom. The other soldiers slapped him on the back. Prado pulled him aside, said "well done," and ordered him to the first-aid station. The medic there washed and salved his hands and bound them in gauze and tape. The relief was spectacular. By the time the medic had finished, Salazar's unit had moved from the rope-climb to another obstacle—one even more daunting.

The soldiers climbed to the top of a huge storage tank—about ten feet off the ground—and jumped off. After some of the Bolivians twisted their ankles, the Special Forces soldiers put mattresses at the bottom. It was another exercise to build confidence and toughness. Salazar watched his friends climbing and leaping, rolling and standing up again. His medical condition meant he was excused for the rest of the day, but climbing up the tank and jumping? He didn't need his hands so much for that. He ran to the back of the line.

When he'd wriggled onto the top of the storage tank, Salazar jumped without hesitation. The first time, his legs buckled after hitting the ground. The second time, though, he landed perfectly. He smiled and ran back to do it again. As with all the training exercises, repetition was the key. They trained over and over until it became second nature.

That night, Salazar gripped a pencil in his bandaged hand and wrote a letter to his mother. "I am working hard, but I am getting used to it," he wrote. "After many tries I was finally able to climb a rope, and in another exercise I jumped from a high ledge and landed on my feet. After weeks, we all are getting the hang of it. We are coming together. I have faith that it will all work out. We feel like we are doing something great."

Salazar told her not to worry. He was doing something noble. He ended the letter by telling his mother he missed her and was thinking about everybody back home. Then he closed his eyes and fell asleep.

Medics James Hapka and Jerald Peterson were doing everything possible to keep the Bolivians healthy. For weeks, they had been conducting exams on the soldiers. They didn't like what they found.

A doctor had never treated some of the men. While the Special Forces medics were not medical doctors, they had more than enough training to prevent diseases, treat wounds, and keep soldiers alive in the field. Now was the moment for prevention, when there was time enough to isolate and treat conditions that might cripple the mission later on. Hapka and Peterson had their work cut out for them.

Before embarking on the mission, the two of them had studied up on local diseases, parasites, scorpions, spiders, and snakes. They learned that southwest Bolivia was a hot spot for hepatitis B and yellow fever. They were expected to treat illnesses and injuries at the training camp, set up a clinic for the villagers, and train several Bolivian soldiers to be medics for their companies. As time went on, the American medics found long-term health issues eroding troop strength. Dental hygiene was unheard of among the conscripts. Their mouths ached constantly from gum disease and rotting teeth. Some soldiers had to be ordered to bathe or wash their clothes, and then had to be shown how. The hygiene problem was only made worse when they were injured during training.

In the early weeks, dozens of men were scratched and cut while working and training alongside fields of thorns and thistles. *Venchugas*, a kind of boring insect, attacked the wounds and sparked infections. Flies deposited eggs inside the cuts, which created painful boils that had to be lanced and cleaned.

The Special Forces soldiers weren't immune. Shelton's men encountered venomous scorpions, as well as snakes and spiders, especially in wooded areas. They tried to protect themselves at night by using mosquito nets, but they were little help. The men were always covered in itchy welts and hives.

The medics knew that with all the guns and ammunition around, they would have to be prepared for more than bug bites. They kept their medical bags stocked with bandages, tourniquets, IV fluids, splints, and painkillers. At some point, they knew all of them would be needed.

Back in La Paz, it was one crisis after another—and Barrientos blamed it all on Che and the damn guerrillas. They were stirring up trouble in the cities. They had to be, he thought. Everything seemed to be going to hell at once, so someone had to be behind it all. A teachers' strike had paralyzed schools, and the miners' unions were making more demands by the day.

Fed up, Barrientos took strong steps in early June to exert total control. First, he placed the entire nation under a state of siege. All personal rights—and there weren't many to begin with—were suspended. Anyone who protested against the government was thrown in jail. No one dared call the president a dictator, but Barrientos's word was law.

In a move to undercut striking teachers, he declared an "early winter vacation." Children were sent home and schools closed, so it didn't matter if teachers were on strike.

A few days later, Barrientos lost patience with the miners.

They could not have been more provocative. At a June 6 assembly, the Huanuni miners held an open demonstration and declared solidarity with the guerrillas. Protests in other areas pointed out dangerous working conditions and unfair practices. The president sent in the army. The troops occupied the Catavi and Siglo Veinte districts—key tin mining centers. But nothing prepared the country for Barrientos's next move.

On the night of June 23—the eve of the Feast of Saint John and a major holiday in Bolivia—miners at the Siglo XX mine gathered with leftist political and union leaders. They rallied, calling for a restoration of wages and a reinstatement of miners who had been fired. Early the next morning, while the miners and their families slept, troops rolled into the mining camp. When the miners resisted, soldiers opened fire.

The government said sixteen people were killed and seventy-one wounded. But the miners put the number at nearly ninety dead, many of them women and children. They called it the Saint John's Day Massacre. Barrientos was unapologetic. He believed he had the authority not only to send in troops, but to use deadly force. The miners, he claimed, provoked his soldiers. They were the ones to blame.

And U.S. officials praised his action. Ambassador Henderson said it was justified. In Washington, Walt Rostow, a special assistant to the president for national security affairs, sent a soothing three-page report to President Johnson saying the crisis precipitated by the miners apparently had "run its course."

He painted a rosy picture of Bolivia: Student demonstrations were waning, and the miners seemed to have capitulated since Barrientos took a strong-arm approach. A successful threat from any other quarter had been prevented because the government and the armed forces remained unified. Rostow said that life in Bolivia was returning to normal and that the remaining problems were a "fall in government revenues" and "the guerrillas."

The report never explained that government revenues were falling, in part, because the Barrientos regime was riddled with corruption. Or that Che Guevara was leading the guerrillas.

The United States had been trying to keep track of Che for years, chasing his ghost across Africa, Latin America, and Southeast Asia. Intelligence analysts had put together an extensive profile. The bearded icon took the international stage when Castro rose to power in Cuba. Che and Castro were as close as brothers and shared a missionary zeal for Cuban-supported revolution. Che was a Communist evangelist, and his disdain for the United States and its economic hegemony was part of his appeal in an era of youthful rebellion and Cold War paranoia.

Che was a teenage rebel, too, back in his comfortable middle-class school days in Argentina. His friends called him "Chancho" or "Pig," because he always wore messy and dirty clothes. It was all a show. Che wanted to present himself as an outlaw.

He loved playing the loner, the rebel. He got the nickname Che—which means "hey" in Spanish—because he used it so much. It was the equivalent of saying "yo."

The Americans knew everything about Che except where he was. The CIA maintained he was dead, his body lying in an unmarked grave in the Dominican Republic. Ambassador Henderson held firm to his belief that Che was not in Bolivia.

But Bolivia had more information. A few days after the Saint John's Day Massacre, Ovando called national and international media to a press conference. He revealed comments Debray had made to authorities about Che Guevara's activities in Bolivia.

Debray "apparently has spoken more than is necessary, although we cannot know the implications of this, nor the circumstances in which he said what he has said," the general told them.

In other words, Debray had confessed that Che was actively involved with the guerrillas. Debray, the Marxist intellectual, had turned on his hero.

Ovando didn't say anything else. He didn't have to. His comments were enough to attract even more international attention to Bolivia.

The CIA dismissed Ovando's comments. Henderson pooh-poohed it all. Still, he asked the U.S. embassy to prepare a study called *Is Che Guevara in Bolivia?* to allay American fears.

The conclusion the study reached: "We're not sure."

But Barrientos was sure Che was alive and in Bolivia, creating this disaster just for him. It wasn't a matter of "if" Che would strike again—but "when."

CHAPTER 12

State of Siege

The bearded men in green fatigues jumped from the pickup truck and pointed their rifles in Lieutenant Juan Vacaflor's face.

The stunned Bolivian officer didn't have time to react. One minute he and some of his soldiers and villagers were standing at a snack stand, the next minute a half-dozen guerrillas were screaming "hands up" and waving guns.

They had no choice. They raised their hands and surrendered. The gunmen told them to sit in a line on the ground and keep their hands in sight.

These weren't drug runners, Vacaflor thought. A couple of them had Cuban accents. These were the foreign mercenaries his unit had been hunting in the forest. And here they were in broad daylight, on the outskirts of Samaipata.

Samaipata, a Quechua village, lay about seventy-five miles southwest of Santa Cruz, in the Andes foothills. Its cool, high-altitude climate made it a popular resort for city dwellers. It was also a strategic point, high up on the main road from Cochabamba to Santa Cruz.

If the guerrillas took control of Samaipata, they could cut off the main artery between the cities.

Vacaflor watched carefully as more guerrillas emerged from the truck, spread out, and corralled the villagers near the snack stand. For weeks now, he'd heard they were in the area. They always seemed to be one step ahead of the army, despite the campesinos telling his men their every move.

He had to warn his men in town.

The Bolivian Army was spread out in small units along the road. Vacaflor didn't have a radio. His only communication was the state telegraph system, which often didn't function. He was isolated, with no way to warn his men or the other units nearby.

Vacaflor listened as the guerrillas talked of food and medical supplies. This wasn't a full-scale attack, but a resupply mission, a shopping trip.

Still, Vacaflor knew he was in danger. He was acquainted with some of the men killed in the springtime ambushes, and everybody knew these were cold-blooded killers. There were six guerrillas in the truck: Ricardo, Chino, and Pacho were foreigners. The others were Bolivian.

A Gulf Oil Company pickup truck was parked near the snack stand. Pacho, a Cuban, sat down inside the cab of the truck. Villagers and two Gulf Oil men were standing nearby watching. No one moved. Like the soldiers, they were shocked to see the guerrillas in person.

One of the guerrillas went to the snack stand and bought drinks for everyone. As he walked, his arms full of bottles, he smiled like a host at a party. He stopped at Vacaflor and handed him a drink.

Before Vacaflor could finish, four of the guerrillas pointed their guns at him and told him to get up.

Vacaflor scrambled to his feet and the guerrillas escorted him and his sergeant to their pickup truck. Two guerrillas stayed on the road and guarded the highway.

"Take us to your barracks," a guerrilla ordered Vacaflor.

There was nothing he could do but take them. The truck drove down the rutted path toward the center of town. Vacaflor could see the colonial buildings and feel the cobbled streets under the tires. The truck stopped in front of the door of the school, which Vacaflor's unit used as a barracks. He watched in stunned silence as the guerrillas grabbed his sergeant and shoved him toward the gate to the courtyard.

"What is the password?" a guerrilla whispered. "Say the code. Tell them to open the gate."

Vacaflor couldn't hear what was being said, but he watched as the sergeant stopped at the door and leaned in close like he was talking to someone behind it.

The gate slowly opened, and the four guerrillas rushed in waving their weapons, yelling for the men inside to surrender. A burst from a Mauser cut through the yelling like a chainsaw. Vacaflor heard the guerrillas fire back. The firefight lasted several seconds before he saw a number of his men being led out of the school, their hands on their heads.

Moving to the gate, Vacaflor ran to the guardhouse inside the courtyard. Private José Verezain's body splayed on the floor. A bloodstain on his tunic grew bigger as Verezain's heart beat a few final times before stopping. Vacaflor made the sign of the cross over the man, then turned away and joined the other soldiers outside the school.

Two of the guerrillas brushed by him with an armload of Mauser rifles and a Bruno light machine gun. The Bolivian soldiers kept their heads down. If Vacaflor thought the guerrillas might execute him at the snack stand, he was sure they would do it now. He couldn't shake the image of Verezain's body, his empty eyes. At least the private had had the chance, and the courage, to fight back.

After loading the weapons into the truck, three of the guerrillas came over to Vacaflor.

"Come with us," one of them said.

This was the end, Vacaflor thought. The guerrillas left two men to guard his nine soldiers. The other two took him down to the grocery and the pharmacy. They bought canned goods and candy, and paid in cash for their purchases. At the pharmacy they picked up some bandages, alcohol, and aspirin. They demanded that the druggist get them asthma medicine, but the pharmacy carried only common remedies, no asthma drugs. The men paid and headed back to the pickup truck.

Vacaflor heard one of the guerrillas urge his comrades to hurry up, an army patrol might arrive and they didn't want to get caught in town. Vacaflor knew there were no patrols in the area, but he wasn't about to tell the guerrillas.

The men threw the supplies into the truck and then ordered Vacaflor into the cab. They collected their comrades at the school and snack stand, and gathered up Vacaflor's men as well. The heavily laden truck wallowed down the dirt road. Vacaflor had no idea where they were taking him. He silently prayed they would spare him and his men—the guerrillas had let prisoners go in the past.

After a half-mile ride, the guerrillas stopped along the road and ordered the soldiers out.

They lined them up and ordered them to strip. The guerrillas picked up the soldiers' clothes, documents, and money, climbed back into the truck, and drove away.

Vacaflor watched as the red taillights disappeared. He took a deep breath. He'd survived. The soldiers walked back to town. They were grateful to be alive but fearing what was to come. Vacaflor began framing the shameful report he would have to make to his commanders. Six guerrillas had taken his town, killed one of his men, forced him to give up uniforms and weapons, and disappeared. There was no way he could pursue them. It was a miserable defeat.

The lieutenant made one addition to his report. Instead of just six anonymous guerrillas, Che Guevara himself had come to raid Samaipata. The revolutionary had led the way into the schoolhouse, killed his soldier, and taken all of Vacaflor's equipment.

The raid made international news.

Press accounts suddenly portrayed bloodthirsty guerrillas overrunning the southeastern part of the nation. Residents of Samaipata claimed that between forty and seventy guerrillas had attacked—led by a fiery-eyed Che in a black beret. Some reports claimed the guerrillas had cut the highway between Cochabamba and Santa Cruz—a vital trade route for sugar, rice, corn, wood, alcohol, and tourists.

Barrientos and the Bolivian high command were in shock. More than three months after the first shots were fired, the guerrillas were getting stronger and more brazen. The high command counted its blessings: What would have happened if a passenger train had been going through Samaipata when the guerrillas struck? What if they'd stopped the train and robbed the passengers? Barrientos was trying desperately to keep things from spinning out of control. There already was panic. Families in the countryside were fleeing to the city, while city-dwellers pondered moving northward, away from the trouble spots.

International media covered the chaos. The *New York Times* said the Bolivian government was in "serious trouble," facing open rebellion from the guerrillas, rival politicians, unhappy businessmen, rampaging university students, and miners. "How the Barrientos government manages to survive while Bolivia is being ripped apart by such violence and disunity is the key question right now," the editorial intoned.

The U.S policy was to keep Barrientos in power as long as it could, the theory being that the "handsome former air force general" was the "best of a mediocre lot." But Washington's patience was running out.

By simply standing by, the government was allowing the guerrillas to win militarily. U.S. experts were appalled by the "poor quality and poorer motivation of the Bolivian foot soldiers."

"It is hard to imagine what a coup d'etat against President Barrientos would accomplish in the way of solving any of the nation's violent problems," a newspaper wrote. "Yet a coup does not seem far off. But after that, Bolivia's future is totally unpredictable."

Frustrated, Barrientos renewed his call for more U.S. equipment. Ovando pressed neighboring countries for more supplies. Barrientos turned his eye to the Rangers-in-training. He needed them now, not later. The country was facing an unprecedented peril.

He ordered them activated for immediate duty.

But what Barrientos didn't count on was strong push-back from Shelton. The Rangers weren't Rangers yet, he told SOUTHCOM. If they went into the field now, they would be in deep shit. They needed more training. The brass in Panama told the president no. The Rangers would stay in La Esperanza.

Barrientos didn't like it, but there was little he could do. The United States was providing most of the money to keep his country afloat. He just hoped that by the time the Rangers were ready for action, he'd still have a country.

CHAPTER 13

Shaping Up

After two months of intense training in the sticky heat, the Bolivian conscripts were grasping the finer points of soldiering. Many of them had never handled a rifle before they arrived, and now they could take apart and reassemble several weapons within moments. They could climb ropes and move quickly through a maze of obstacles without missing a step. The Rangers started their mornings with war chants, followed by thirty minutes of calisthenics. Then they sprinted to the range and back before tackling new assignments.

The Green Berets showed them how to secure jungle paths with warning devices made from coffee cans and string. They learned how to read maps and use compasses, and how to counterattack in an ambush. They were tired at the end of the day, but there was little rest—at night they went on maneuvers. It was coming together.

Training was getting more complicated. They moved into the advanced stages of individual training, which included rappelling off the side of the five-story sugar mill building. Everything was on schedule. Soon they'd move to unit training, learning to work as a team. Then, after two weeks of field exercises, they'd ship out to the jungles for the real thing.

One night in early July, Prado stopped at Shelton's office for their end-of-day review. Prado had become invaluable to Shelton. He told him if soldiers in a particular unit were having problems with a concept or tactic, and the pair would devise a schedule to give the struggling soldiers some extra tutoring, or time on the firing range. (The range was always a tricky issue, because villagers and their cattle sometimes ambled unexpectedly across, on their way to their pastures.) Prado sat in his usual chair. Shelton poured the both of them drinks and asked his colleague how things were going.

"Everything is going well today," Prado said, taking his glass.

"Are you telling me what I want to hear?" Shelton asked.

"No. I can see the difference. When they got here, they were not soldiers. They had no training. Now look at them."

Shelton smiled and downed his whiskey shot. "What do you think we need to do next?"

Prado took a deep breath.

"Well, one thing we still need to put into the heads of our soldiers is that this is not just a training exercise. They are not going home after this, we are going out to fight, to kill people. I think we still have to put that into their heads. They have to be mentally tough to go into the jungle."

"And how do you suggest we do that?"

"We need to keep telling them what's at stake. That this is more than just training. They are becoming Bolivia's elite force."

He paused for a moment to collect his thoughts.

"You asked me how things were going."

Shelton nodded yes.

"By the time the training is over, the men will be soldiers," Prado said. "I am not worried about that. My worry is whether I will be able to lead them. These men trust me with their lives. Am I ready for that? Can I lead them as they should be led?"

Shelton flashed that wide grin.

"Gary, I know that you will be more than ready. I've watched you with your men. They respect you. I respect you."

Prado was stunned. None of his army superiors ever said such things. To hear those words from Shelton filled him with pride. But he was uncomfortable with praise.

"I've never been in battle. I don't know how I will react."

Shelton didn't flinch. "Gary, I've been in battle. And I have a sixth sense about soldiers and officers. I can predict who will run and who will stand and fight. And I can tell you that when the time comes, you will fight. You're a good officer."

Shelton looked in Prado's eyes. "I think we're going to do this. We're going to deliver this battalion."

Prado nodded in agreement. "Yes. I think so."

Officers were so important to success, commanders even more so. And every one of them, in any military unit, had an ego the size of Texas. Shelton was sure the United States could win the war in Vietnam, but the commanders had to let the soldiers fight. The United States had the best soldiers in the world, but commanders, under political pressure, were holding them back. It was no wonder public opinion was turning against the war. And that just made it harder on the soldiers. They would fight like hell for a hill or a village, then they would give it up the next day. Vietnam was a classic guerrilla war, and for the most part, the United States was still fighting it like a conventional one.

That's not how you win, Shelton thought. You do it like Special Forces. You go in. Train troops. Live with the people. Build trust.

What they were doing in Bolivia was an example of what they should be doing in Vietnam. Hell, he did it in Laos, too. He built trust with the villagers. He was doing it again in Bolivia.

Prado cleared his throat and set down his empty glass.

"We're going to get Che," Shelton assured him. "I know things look rough now. The guerrillas have been playing hit-and-run. I know some Bolivians are worried."

"You mean the president?"

"Yeah. Barrientos. Ovando. All of them. But Che doesn't have a chance. And after this is over, you can go back to your wife and kids and tell them what you did. Tell them that you helped train a battalion that took care of Che Guevara. Hell, tell them you led a battalion that got the bastard."

"And when it's over, what will you do, Pappy?"

"Me?" Shelton grinned. "I'm going home for good. This is it for me. I'm riding off into the sunset." The smile faded from his face. "I don't really know what I'm going to do. I might go to college," he said softly.

College? Shit. This was his calling. But he'd promised Margaret he would leave. If he said he was going to do something, he did it. Besides, he missed his kids. While he was out here being Pappy for the goddam army, his kids were growing up without their dad.

"Before we leave, I want to make sure that school is built," he said. "That's something that can really help these people."

Construction materials for the school had started arriving in La Esperanza. U.S. AID was providing most of the money, and Bartos Construction, Singh's company, was donating equipment and expertise. The people of La Esperanza promised to help build it. On June 25, the village had kicked off the project with a fiesta, where the local priest blessed the site. Shelton hoped they would finish before the money ran out.

Shelton had heard that Ambassador Henderson was holding up some of the funding. He had no idea why. But if the situation didn't get better, Shelton promised himself he would confront the son of a bitch. It didn't matter that Henderson was technically his boss. Like Sidney Poitier in *Lilies of the Field*, Shelton was going to find a way to build the damn thing.

For medic Peterson, the long hours of training were tiring, but Hapka's presence made it easier. The American medics met a few weeks before the mission. But as they prepared for the assignment, they quickly became friends.

Peterson and Hapka were from two different worlds; Hapka grew up in Milwaukee, Wisconsin—a city with 740,000 people in 1960. At the time, it was the nation's eleventh largest city. Peterson spent his childhood in Bradford, Pennsylvania, a rural town in the Allegheny Mountains, where there were less than a dozen students in Peterson's graduating class.

But they had some things in common. They were only a year apart in age: Peterson was twenty-five, while Hapka was twenty-six. And they loved to hunt.

On most days, the medics taught first-aid classes on how to treat gunshot wounds and other potentially life-saving skills to Bolivian soldiers. They also treated sick soldiers and villagers. Sometimes they would ride horses to neighboring villages to provide basic health care. But on weekends, they'd sneak in the surrounding thick brush looking for birds, mostly quail and dove. They would spend hours, away from the others. Sure they'd talk about the usual soldier bullshit. But they'd also discuss their families and their lives.

The outgoing Hapka, who sported a moustache, graduated from West Milwaukee High School in 1959. The city was booming with factories. And there were sports teams—the Milwaukee Braves had been in the World Series in 1957 and 1958. And in nearby Green Bay, Wisconsin, there were the Packers, who, under legendary Coach Vince Lombardi, was becoming a National Football League powerhouse. After high school, Hapka enlisted in the army and joined Special Forces in 1962.

Peterson took a different path. He enrolled in a state college, but dropped out when he ran out of money. He enlisted in the army in 1961 and joined Special Forces a year later.

Both joined the army because of their sense of patriotism, and because the army offered them economic opportunities.

For Peterson, it also was a continuation of a family tradition. His father had joined the navy in 1942—the same year Peterson was born. He had siblings who also served.

Peterson was training as a medic in San Antonio, Texas, when he met a woman at a night club who would later become his wife. It was a hectic time in his life. In 1965, he was deployed to Venezuela for two months to train soldiers in that South American nation. Now he was in Bolivia.

The men didn't know Shelton before the mission. But the medics liked the major. Shelton was easygoing and didn't micromanage, Peterson recalled. He trusted his men.

Shelton would stop by the dispensary where Peterson and Hapka spent part of their day. He'd say: "You're responsible for doing this." Then he would ask them how they were doing and if they needed anything.

Usually, they'd respond: "No, sir. Everything is going fine."

Then Shelton would smile and leave.

Despite the harsh climate, Peterson and Hapka tried to make the most of the deployment. At night, they would hang out at Kiosko Hugo drinking and bullshitting with the other soldiers, and listening to Shelton play his guitar. When they got drunk, they'd sing along. There wasn't much else to do. They were isolated.

That's why those hunting trips with Hapka were so special. It gave them a much-needed escape. On one trip, Peterson found a farmer who was selling a musket from 1842. He bought it and planned to take it home. But Peterson tried not to think that far ahead. Not when he knew training was far from over. Not when the guerrillas were still on the loose. Not after Samaipata.

Prado ran up to the edge of the circle of men. Inside the ring was weapons sergeant Chapa, dug into a foxhole with a Browning .30 light machine-gun setup. Out in the distance a newspaper flapped from a tree branch—the target.

The American told a Bolivian sergeant to step inside. It was his turn.

For the last hour Chapa had been teaching the noncommissioned officers how to fire the weapon. Training NCOs was a critical part of Special Forces instruction. Once they were trained, they passed along their knowledge to soldiers who needed additional help.

Prado knew how to use the M-1919A6 machine gun, a military workhorse. It was a fixture during World War II, the Korean War, and Vietnam. It weighed thirty-two pounds without its tripod and could fire several hundred rounds a minute.

The Bolivian sergeant peered through the iron sight mounted on the boxy body of the gun and charged the first round. He adjusted his aim and squeezed the trigger. The gun let out a throaty burst as the rounds raced out of the barrel. The fire had a rhythmic pace as tracers arced toward the target. The newspaper exploded into shreds.

The sergeant raised a fist in celebration. Prado was impressed. The men were becoming deadly proficient, and the NCOs carried that confidence with them when they worked with the conscripts.

For Prado, this was the beginning of the rebirth of the Bolivian military. Over the last few years—under Barrientos's guidance and with Ovando's blessing—the military had been rebuilt. But there was a long road ahead. The most critical, most needed change was in the very culture of the military, Prado thought. There were too many dinosaurs in powerful posts, men who had served in the aftermath of the Chaco War. They had lost every battle they'd ever engaged in, and their pessimism permeated the fighting units. Even the Special Forces soldiers ran into the Bolivian past.

Weapons training was a good example. Sergeant Chapa was constantly squeezing the Bolivian supply officer for ammunition. The cantankerous bastard was reluctant to part with "his" ammunition.

"He always gave me half of what I requested each time," Chapa recalled. "It was a constant fight to get what was needed to train the soldiers properly."

The best riflemen were recruited to become snipers. Chapa took them under his wing. He taught them how to set up a shot and find the best vantage point. Wind, distance, shadow, and light—all can make a great deal of difference to the accuracy of the shot.

At the end of each session, Chapa stayed around for anyone who needed more help.

The Special Forces team also trained soldiers for the mortar squads. Mortars gave the light infantry real firepower in a portable form. Probably the most important defensive weapon in the battalion's arsenal, a good mortar team could beat back an attack with a steady barrage of high-explosive rounds.

Besides weapons, the Green Berets were training a platoon of intelligence officers. They learned to disappear into their civilian clothes and mix in with the locals. They would have to fan out across the operation zone to gather critical information, determine its worth, and get it to the right person with utmost efficiency.

Prado knew nothing could change Bolivia's awful military past, and real transformation would only come with a new generation. But there beside the machine gun in the training field he saw the plan coming together. Soon the army would have a battalion of three highly proficient and mobile companies. And with them they could take down the guerrillas.

Kiosko Hugo was filling up. Special Forces soldiers gathered around the outdoor tables, drinking and talking. Shelton's guitar was there against the table, ready to be picked up and picked at. The men sang along if they knew the words—especially to "Mr. Shorty," which had become the team song. Everybody laughed and drank a little more.

Work hard, play hard. There wasn't much else to do.

Graham was on the porch, talking to Dorys Roca, a village girl from a big local family—fourteen of them lived in a three-room shanty. Dorys was a tiny thing, probably still a teenager, with long black hair and big brown eyes.

Roca hadn't been there when the soldiers came to La Esperanza. She was working out of town, caring for a sick relation. When she came back and saw the camp taking shape at the sugar mill, she saw an opportunity to help her family. Roca took a job cleaning the quarters and doing the laundry for the Special Forces soldiers.

That's how she met Graham—the tall, handsome radio operator from Phoenix, Arizona, who always greeted her with a smile. Like most of the Green Berets, he wore dark, flashy sunglasses. He was only twenty-three years old. This was his first mission as a Green Beret.

The couple gave the village gossips something to talk about. The pair took moonlight walks, chattering and laughing in the dark. Dorys was easy to talk to. Graham told her about his life back home and said one day he hoped she would see it for herself. Dorys wished she could go—Arizona sounded so different and exciting. For now, though, Graham had this mission. They had to train the Rangers, then go back to Panama in December. But they had until then. And he would come back to La Esperanza to see her after that, he promised. The onlookers were skeptical. He was a soldier, a foreigner, an American—there was no way he would marry a simple girl from a backwater town in Bolivia. Poor Dorys was going to get her heart broken, but nobody thought to warn her. They didn't want to shatter her dreams.

Valderomas stood by his window and stared into the darkness. It was late July and he couldn't sleep. He couldn't remember the last time he had slept through the night. He'd lost track of the days.

It was the damn soldiers on their damned night maneuvers. It was one thing to shoot and march and make noise in the daytime, but no decent person stayed up all night, shouting and shooting guns and exploding things. And that's what was happening in La Esperanza. It seemed that the soldiers trained around the clock. The noise carried from the fields into his house. His wife and children didn't seem to notice, but it unnerved Valderomas. He tossed and turned all night. Some of the other villagers also felt like he did. They liked the money the soldiers spent, but they worried. What if there was an accident? What if they set the village on fire? What if the guerrillas won, and La Esperanza was punished for hosting the foreigners and the trainees?

Valderomas talked to the mayor about it, but his concerns were shrugged off. The mayor looked at him and said: "What do you want me to do? Tell them to leave?"

"Yes," he replied.

That wasn't going to happen.

The Bolivian soldiers were training for something big. Why else would they have called in the Americans?

CHAPTER 14

"He will not leave Bolivia alive."

The lemon-yellow Braniff DC-8 crested the mountains and started its approach to the airport in the bowl below. The plane seemed to fluoresce against Bolivia's brown-and-tan landscape. Rebelling against the sobriety of traditional airline images, Braniff had dressed its fleet in glad-rag colors like turquoise, lemon, and baby blue. It was an ostentatious arrival for two Cuban operatives on a secret CIA mission, but it was one of the only direct flights to the small South American republic.

Rodríguez was more than ready get off the plane. They'd started in Miami, flying first to Panama City and Lima, Peru, before arriving in La Paz. Rodríguez's new passport listed him as "Félix Ramos Medina." Villoldo, in a nearby seat, was now "Eduardo Gonzalez."

They hit the ground running. Bill, their CIA contact from the United States, and a Bolivian immigration officer met them at the gate. "He'll take your papers and luggage and get everything stamped," Bill said. "You can pick up your suitcases at the hotel. We've got a meeting right away at the president's house."

On the highway into the city, Rodríguez and Villoldo met John Tilton, head of the CIA station in La Paz. Rodríguez noticed an electric blanket folded neatly on the seat beside Tilton.

Rodríguez was curious.

"What do you need an electric blanket for?" Rodríguez asked.

"You'll see soon," Tilton said.

The president's house stood in a splendid plaza in downtown La Paz. The colonial home had rows of windows and columns in front of the main doors.

Rodríguez and Villoldo were escorted inside. The cold hit Rodríguez like a shot. The house, like most of La Paz, was freezing cold inside—it was the altitude and the thick walls, Tilton told them. They were ushered into a small office and introduced to Barrientos. Tilton handed the electric blanket to the president, who smiled and accepted it graciously. It was for his wife, he explained. Her feet were always cold.

The men sat down around a table. Coffee was delivered on a tray.

Like a good CIA operative, Rodríguez had learned everything he could about the Bolivian government. He knew Barrientos had only been president for a year and was extremely close with Ovando, the leader of the Bolivian armed forces.

Despite the current crisis, Barrientos touted Bolivia's economic turnaround. He said Comibol, the state-run tin mining company, had turned a profit in 1966. His regime was encouraging foreign investment, and Gulf Oil Company was signing on for rights to export petroleum and natural gas from Bolivia.

But Rodríguez knew Barrientos's government was in trouble. The miners hated him. The unions despised him. He faced a relentless guerrilla movement—one so strong that Cuban-trained fighters went shopping in Samaipata. It was a huge psychological blow. If that wasn't enough, Barrientos was under increasing pressure to release Debray. He would never attract foreign investment under such unstable circumstances. If he didn't gain control soon, Barrientos would be gone.

The president had also done his homework. He'd seen dossiers on the two CIA operatives: Rodríguez and Villoldo were veterans of the 2506 Brigade, the exile invasion force at the Bay of Pigs and other Cuba missions. These men could hunt down the Communist agitator. But first, he wanted to know about their other battles with Castro and Che. Barrientos, like most old soldiers, loved a good war story.

Rodríguez went first. Sitting back in his chair, he let himself unwind. It was February 1961 and he was part of the second seven-man advance team sent to Cuba from Florida to prepare the invasion.

They set off in a twenty-five-foot-long boat loaded with weapons and explosives. Crossing from Key West to Cuba in heavy seas, the four-hour journey punished the men. Rodríguez felt better as soon as he saw his homeland on the horizon. He saw fishermen on the pier and couples and families picnicking on the sand.

The two-man crew motored parallel to shore, waiting for the signal—three flashes of light—for the team to start toward the beach. Rodríguez shepherded the team's equipment. Once they were on land, a dozen farmers and workers from a local sugar mill helped them unload the weapons on the isolated, rocky beach.

Anti-Castro groups were running up and down the Matanzas-Havana Highway at fifteen-minute intervals waiting for Rodríguez and his team to arrive. Soon the first of several cars pulled up. The men were shocked to see Rodríguez wearing fatigues, but he quickly changed. The CIA had told the team to hide in the jungle and wait for the invasion, but they soon learned that the anti-Castro resistance had safe houses and a network of messengers set up already. Theirs was a civilized country.

Rodríguez made contact with the resistance. The invasion plan was to open up two fronts, force Castro to split his troops, and divide the island.

But on April 17, 1961, Rodríguez woke to aircraft overhead and news of the invasion on the radio. Cuba's radio network was broadcasting emergency messages, ordering soldiers to report to their bases. Rodríguez called other resistance fighters, but none of them answered. Castro's security forces had already arrested most of them.

Villoldo then told what he did that day—the luckiest day of his life, and the most heartbreaking. A pilot from boyhood, Villoldo flew a B-26 bomber over the beach at the Bay of Pigs, but the napalm bomb on his wing refused to drop. For several minutes he and his copilot tried to wiggle the aircraft's wings to dislodge it. No luck. On the ground the invasion was falling to pieces. Up above, the pilots had to figure out what to do next. They could sacrifice the plane and parachute to the ground, or make a risky landing with the bomb on the wing. They chose the latter and headed back to "Happy Valley," the unit's Nicaraguan base.

Like Rodríguez, Villoldo had escaped to Miami a few months after the revolution and was recruited by anti-Castro Cuban exiles. The CIA soon offered him a job flying bombing missions to support the invasion.

Villoldo circled the dirt runway, preparing to land. The wheels hit the ground first, and then the bomb, which skidded down the runway with sparks flying from underneath. Villoldo braced for the explosion. The airplane rolled to a halt. Villoldo scrambled from the plane, staggered to the edge of the runway, and cried.

The bomb never exploded, but Villoldo was distraught. He believed he had failed his mission, and his family that was still in Cuba.

Meanwhile, Rodríguez laid low for three days in his safe house. From the window he glimpsed trucks full of soldiers, and on the television he watched his comrades, the men he'd trained with, driven away to prison. They looked beaten.

When Castro's forces started house-to-house searches, Rodríguez scurried to the Spanish embassy seeking asylum. All over Havana, diplomats from Spain and Latin America were offering asylum for infiltrators and resistance fighters. After some coordination, Rodríguez was finally able to earn asylum from the Venezuelans, but only if he could make it to their embassy. Alejandro Vergara, a Spanish diplomat, set it all up.

"We'll take the ambassador's car," he said. "The chauffeur will take us right up to the Venezuelan embassy. You'll be sitting in the back with me. Don't look left or right. Don't pay any attention to the Cuban soldiers out front. Just act like a diplomat."

Rodríguez wasn't convinced the plan would work. He hadn't shaved in days, and his hair was long and wild. He didn't look anything like a diplomat.

"You won't be safe until you are actually inside the embassy building itself," Vergara explained. "We will drive through the Cuban guardhouse, up the driveway, and along the side of the embassy, right next to the kitchen door. I'll get out and go inside. You'll wait for me in the car. As long as you stay in the car you're under the protection of the Spanish embassy, so don't move, even if the Cuban militia starts pounding on the doors or breaks the windows. Then, when I open the kitchen door and signal, you run like hell to me."

Sitting in the bright-green vintage Mercedes flying a Spanish flag, Rodríguez couldn't reconcile in his mind how he'd slipped into Cuba at dusk on a boat and now was leaving Cuba by car, in broad daylight, right in front of Cuban soldiers.

The ride took a few minutes. The whole time, Rodríguez plotted different escape scenarios. Could he jump in the front and rush off in the car? Maybe he could grab a soldier's rifle. Rodríguez's mind was in survival mode. Vergara shook him out of his plotting, his hand on the door handle. They were there. "Just wait, Félix," he said. "Don't run anywhere but the door. And not until I signal."

Félix sweated. Time stood still. Cuban soldiers were standing nearby, watching the car.

And then he heard the shout: "Félix! Run!"

Rodríguez dashed from the car and into the kitchen, almost smashing into Manuel Urrutia Lléo, the former president of Cuba, who'd been installed and then ousted by Castro.

"Good morning, Mr. President," Rodríguez said, catching his breath.

Five months later, the paperwork was done, and Félix returned to Miami. Villoldo spent two weeks in Happy Valley before going back. They met a few months later at Fort Benning, where they became army second lieutenants at the same time. Once back in Miami, Rodríguez and Villoldo started working the CIA's Cuba infiltration plan. Villoldo volunteered to hunt for Che in the Congo. Now they were here in Bolivia, looking for some payback.

After the meeting, Barrientos presented Rodríguez and Villoldo with personally signed cards addressed to all military and civilian personnel. The message was clear: Bolivians must cooperate with Rodríguez and Villoldo.

A formal meeting with Ovando followed soon after, where the agents were given the rank of captain and issued official military identification. For a day or two they rested and adjusted to the altitude, then they headed for their deployments.

Villoldo headed to "the red zone," the guerrilla-controlled area surrounded by Bolivian troops. Rodríguez stayed in Santa Cruz, to work with Major Arnaldo Saucedo, the Bolivian officer in charge of intelligence, and several other Bolivian commanders. At first they kept to the rules issued from Washington, meeting secretly and only wearing civilian clothes. But between meetings in Santa Cruz, Rodríguez commuted to La Esperanza in military vehicles. His civilian clothes made him stand out there. So soon, when in the company of soldiers, both Rodríguez and Villoldo donned Bolivian Army fatigues with no rank or insignia attached.

One of Rodríguez's first suggestions to Saucedo, a thin man with a neat mustache, was to consolidate and share the scraps of intelligence they gleaned in the field. The guerrillas' camp was on the south side of the Rio Grande, in the Fourth Division's area of operations. But so far the insurgent attacks had taken place on the other side of the river, on Eighth Division turf. Che knew how commanders compete, jealously guarding tips and intelligence lest the wrong man take credit. Guerrilla movements worldwide used this against them. American commanders were seeing the same thing in Vietnam.

When Rodríguez asked the Fourth Division commander about guerrilla activities in his area, the response was what he expected. "We don't have a guerrilla problem here," the man said.

Right, pal, thought Rodríguez.

He had to convince the Bolivians to work together.

Rodríguez left at seven each morning for the division headquarters, where he spent hours combing through every scrap of paper captured from the guerrillas. He read intelligence reports and interrogation transcripts. He started a file for each of the known guerrillas, with name, nicknames, rank, age, and citizenship. The files detailed the traits that gave Rodríguez insight into each man. He knew which ones smoked, what kind of weapons they carried, what they wore, how they spoke.

Rodríguez wanted to know the cliques, the quirks. He needed to find the seams in the guerrilla band. Who liked whom? Did they like Che? If he ever got his hands on any of the men, he needed to know as much as he could to plot every move. The one he wanted most was Paco, the young Bolivian fighter tricked into joining Che's group with the promises of a university education.

When Rodríguez wasn't studying guerrillas, he worked on radios. His goal was to network the Bolivian soldiers so they could simply coordinate their operations. A critical piece of the puzzle was the spotter-plane pilots—they had no way to tell the men on the ground what they saw from above. Rodríguez improvised an antenna that allowed the pilots to use a PRC-10 radio to talk with ground troops. He also set up a radio network for the CIA station in La Paz.

For weeks, both CIA men slowly built networks of informants and listened up for any scrap of intelligence. Occasionally they were summoned to La Paz, where the president often asked them to tell more tales of their dashing adventures. Late one evening over dinner, Villoldo told the tale of his father's death.

The Villoldo family was part of Havana's high society. By the time Villoldo was born in 1936, his family owned a General Motors plant and a thirty-thousand-acre farm in northwest Cuba.

When Villoldo was eleven, his father taught him how to fly an airplane, and like Rodríguez, the boy was sent to school in the United States. Villoldo thrived there but returned to Havana in 1952. He started working at the family's GM dealerships and took business classes at the University of Havana.

After the revolution in 1959, Castro's forces started confiscating property and shaking down wealthy landowners. Villoldo's father was on the list. Bearded guerrillas surrounded the family home one afternoon and took Villoldo Junior into custody.

After three days of trying to get the young man to call his father a traitor, the guerrillas let him go. But that didn't stop the harassment. For weeks, guerrillas came to interrogate Villoldo's father. Che came twice to the house. The second visit was in February 1959. Villoldo Junior was at the family's business headquarters in downtown Havana when Che met with his father.

That night, father and son took a walk together to discuss the meeting with Che. The old man was shaken. During the meeting, Che had given him a choice: Either Villoldo Senior would conveniently die and leave the family's assets to the state, or his two sons would go before a firing squad.

The next morning, Villoldo found his father dead in a spare bedroom. Next to him was an empty bottle of sleeping pills. Villoldo promised to avenge his father. Che would die. Castro would pay.

Silence fell on the room. "I am sorry for your family," Barrientos said.

Villoldo turned to the president.

"If you tell me that you are planning to return Che to Cuba after you capture him, I am boarding the next plane back to Miami," he said.

Barrientos was quiet for a moment and then answered. "You have my word, as the president of Bolivia, that if we capture Guevara, he will not leave Bolivia alive."

CHAPTER 15

Holy Hand

Shelton sat inside the operations center, feeling keyed up. A rickety fan shoved the hot air around but did little to relieve the sticky heat of August. For weeks, he'd been hearing about the two CIA operatives collecting intelligence on Che, and now he was going to meet them.

He did not envy them their job.

U.S. Intelligence had been tracking Che Guevara for years, and if the man was here leading the Bolivian guerrillas, their decades of work had been proved a total failure. In the Cold War days of *spy vs. spy*, how could the spooks not know where their man was, or if he was even alive? How could Che have slipped so cleanly away for so long? It didn't make sense.

Newspapers seemed to have more of a grasp on Che than the CIA. Reporters were sneaking into the fields, talking to campesinos, and printing their wild stories about the guerrillas. The U.S. newspapers speculated more and more about Che's possible presence in Bolivia. In a July 23 article, Jack Anderson and Drew Pearson wrote:

> *When President Rene Barrientos of Bolivia announced that the mystery man of Cuba, Che Guevara, was directing guerrilla forces in the Bolivian mountains, the story was discounted. However, United States military intelligence has now reported that Fidel Castro's right-hand man is in the Bolivian mountains leading about 100 well-equipped, highly trained troops.*
>
> *The significance of this operation has not been lost on various Latin American presidents. Bolivia is the most mountainous country in the Western Hemisphere and the easiest in which to hide out. Equally important, it is surrounded by the poorest sections of Brazil, Peru, Paraguay, Argentina and Chile.*
>
> *If a successful revolt can be organized in Bolivia, it could spread to poor sections of these neighboring countries, possibly on to their capitals. Presumably, this is Castro's strategy.*

By now, Shelton had no doubts that Che was leading the rebel band. But he knew the intelligence community still wasn't as convinced—even after the daring raid in Samaipata. His thoughts were interrupted when two men dressed in Bolivian Army uniforms walked into the room. He jumped up from his chair.

"Pappy Shelton?" one of the men asked.

"That's me. Who are you?"

"Félix Rodríguez."

Villoldo introduced himself and they sat down to chat. At first, they made small talk. Shelton asked them about their journey and their meeting with Barrientos. Then they talked about their pasts. Shelton told him about his long career, including his time in Korea and Laos. Rodríguez and Villoldo filled in their backstories. The three of them hit it off. The Cubans respected Shelton because he had fought Communists in Korea, Laos, and the Dominican Republic. He was a soldier's soldier. And in Shelton's eyes, Rodríguez and Villoldo were patriots, doing their part to overthrow Castro and his repressive regime.

The CIA men told Shelton their plans. Villoldo would stay at La Esperanza to help train the Rangers intelligence unit. Once trained, the unit would dress in civilian clothes and work the villages, searching out information on guerrilla locations. They would be the Rangers' eyes and ears. Rodríguez, meanwhile, would work in Santa Cruz with the Eighth Division.

To Shelton, the CIA mission made sense. Intelligence was critical. Without it you were open to ambush like those poor Bolivians. They had had no clue guerrillas were even in their country until the shooting started.

Shelton told Rodríguez and Villoldo that the Ranger training was going as planned but that he wished things were different. His team could easily sneak into the jungles and take out Che in no time. Rodríguez agreed. The United States was handcuffed by rules. In guerrilla wars, you had to use your own tactics. Yes, counterinsurgency worked. But there were times you just had to go in after the bad guys and kill them.

By the end of the meeting, Shelton knew he would work well with the CIA men.

A month after the Samaipata fiasco, Barrientos was still taking heat. Army troops continued hunting the guerrillas in the operations area, drawing fire now and then. The country was still reeling from the Saint John's Day Massacre. There were calls to lift martial law and let life return to normal. Reporters continued to flood his country, and they were asking how long Barrientos would stay in power. Many of the stories contained quotes from unnamed U.S. diplomats.

Barrientos knew who those sources were: Henderson. To his face, the ambassador was condescending. Henderson was always admonishing Barrientos as if the president were a petulant child: No, you can't have more aid. Your troops can handle the guerrillas. Behind the scenes, Henderson regularly criticized Barrientos for failing to eliminate the guerrilla threat.

Barrientos had friends in the U.S. military command. They wanted to send arms and even troops to Bolivia. But Washington was cautious. If they didn't want the guerrilla war to spread into a regional conflict, they'd better take off the handcuffs, Barrientos argued. He was particularly annoyed when U.S. pressure stopped Argentina from sending in backup troops. It was unusual in Latin America for one nation to ask another to send troops into its territory. Memories of disputed boundaries and land grabs reached back generations, but Barrientos was growing increasingly worried about the guerrilla threat. He reached out to Argentine president Juan Carlos Ongania, who was just as paranoid about Che as Barrientos was.

Barrientos lost his temper when a *New York Times* story trumpeted the request around the world. The newspaper said the Bolivian appeal "appears to demonstrate the increasing concern of the government of President Rene Barrientos . . . over the effectiveness of the guerrillas both in combat and in creating a nationwide feeling of alarm." The story added that the guerrillas in southeastern Bolivia are "well organized, armed with modern weapons, and led by Cuba-trained Communists."

The president blamed Henderson for leaking the story. His talks with Argentina were supposed to be secret. No one was privileged to know about those conversations except the Americans, and it was

Bolivian vice president Adolfo Siles hands a diploma to one of the Green Berets who helped train the Bolivians. Each team member received a certificate to honor their service. The ceremony took place in Santa Cruz, Bolivia in 1967. JERALD PETERSON

Major Ralph "Pappy" Shelton's men stand in formation at a ceremony in Santa Cruz, Bolivia, in 1967. The men were being honored by Bolivian officials for training the Bolivian ranger companies. JERALD PETERSON

Above: Shelton's men sit in chairs during the same ceremony in Santa Cruz in September 1967.   JERALD PETERSON

Right: The patch created and worn by members of the Second Ranger Battalion who were trained by American Green Berets led by Major Ralph "Pappy" Shelton.
JERALD PETERSON

Felix Rodriguez stands to the right of Che outside the La Higuera schoolhouse where the revolutionary was being held prisoner.   FELIX RODRIGUEZ

The body of Ernesto "Che" Guevara after he had been killed. After his death, Che's body was cleaned and displayed in a laundry room at a Vallegrande hospital.
JERALD PETERSON

Left: Major Ralph "Pappy" Shelton as he appeared in 1967. He was the leader of the Green Beret team that trained the Second Ranger Battalion in La Esperanza.
U.S. ARMY SPECIAL OPERATIONS COMMAND PUBLIC AFFAIRS PHOTO ARCHIVES

Right: Captain Gary Prado in the Bolivian Mountains in 1967.

Left: A copy of the passport photo Che used to enter Bolivia. In the passport, Che identified himself as a Uruguayan businessman Adolfo Mena Gonzalez.

Right: Sitting in a La Paz hotel room in November 1966, Che snaps a self-portrait of himself before he heads to his base camp in the Bolivian jungle.

The remnants of the guerrilla band crossing the Rio Grande in mid-September 1967.

The tin-roof house; this was Che's first guerrilla base camp.

A photo of Tamara Bunke Bide, who was called Tania. She helped Che set up an urban support network in Bolivia.

Left: Regis Debray, a French Marxist intellectual, who joined Che in Bolivia and was arrested trying to leave the guerrilla camp.

Right: Ciro Roberto Bustos, an Argentinian painter and salesman, was with Che and arrested with Debray.

President Rene Barrientos Ortuno visiting troops in the field.

Bolivian soldiers transport three dead guerrillas on mules into the village of Pucara on September 26, 1967.

A group of Green Berets in La Esperanza, Bolivia in 1967.

Members of the Bolivian Rangers' B Company in La Higuera.

Captain Gary Prado's men capture Camba, one of Che's guerrillas.

A photo of Che after his capture in La Higuera.

A Bolivian ranger guards the schoolhouse in La Higuera where Che was held and later executed.

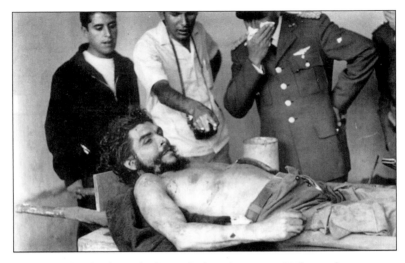

Che's body on display in the laundry room in Vallegrande.

Above: President Barrientos visits the Rangers troops after Che's capture.

Right: General Alfredo Ovando Candia visits Vallegrande after Che's death.

the United States that had again thwarted his plans. Argentina had already sent weapons, food, and equipment, and soldiers were just the logical next step. Argentina was worried that the guerrillas could spill across the border. They knew that Che—if he was indeed alive—would love the chance to lead a revolution in the country where he was born.

As one Argentine military official put it: "We just don't have enough troops to send to Bolivia right now. The people in the military are frustrated as hell because they all think that there is another Sierra Maestra getting started in Bolivia, and we can't really do anything about it under the circumstances." (Castro and Che had prepared their drive to power in Cuba's Sierra Maestra Mountains.)

In public, Barrientos tried to be diplomatic about the leaks. None of the stories he referred to quoted Henderson. Still, it was clear where the negative information had originated. Like most diplomats, Henderson spoke to the U.S. media on background matters, under cover of anonymity. It wasn't unusual for journalists to visit and interview Henderson at the embassy. The *New York Times* was probably the most influential newspaper in the world. It was the first newspaper politicians and bureaucrats in Washington grabbed in the morning. When Bolivian reporters asked Barrientos about the *Times* stories, he kept his cool but quickly assigned blame, using only suave diplomatic double-talk:

"Just as Mr. Henderson has his opinions based upon some information, so I can assure each Bolivian citizen absolutely that the guerrillas are not going to succeed in this country. Everything Mr. Henderson says, if it is as reported, is completely false. But I doubt that he would have said such things . . . because I do not believe Mr. Henderson talks such nonsense."

Henderson patched up his relationship with the president, assuring him he did not know who had made the comments or leaked the documents. Barrientos wasn't an idiot. He understood the way the game was played. He accepted Henderson's apology and sent a cable to the State Department saying, "I want to make clear that Henderson is my good friend and I do not believe he would have said those things which I call nonsense."

The telegram calmed the storm, but Barrientos knew he couldn't trust Henderson. He came to the nub of the matter: He could not expect much help from outside powers. No one could solve Bolivia's problems but Bolivians. Yes, they would accept U.S. aid and training. But in this conflict, they were clearly on their own.

In early August, Bolivian troops spread out and searched the area around the guerrillas' original base camp in Nancahuazu. They combed every surface for things they might have missed in earlier searches. But unlike on previous expeditions, they had a map—thanks to Ciro Roberto Bustos.

He had been in jail since his arrest with Debray and Roth in April. If the Argentine Communist thought life was tough in a guerrilla camp, his Bolivian captors showed him how much worse things could get. After a near-execution in the field by Bolivian conscripts, he'd spent the following months in a filthy prison cell, awaiting trial or perhaps official execution. Bustos had been a dilettante revolutionary, happy to bullshit for hours about Marx and Stalin, using his rebel warrior rap to pick up women at parties. But that was a long time ago. It was another world out on the front lines, carrying guns, marching over mountains, living in the jungle. He wasn't cut out for the real thing.

Psychologists say every person has a unique way of dealing with fear. Some can suck it up and perform well, while others crumble under the pressure. It all has to do with background and upbringing.

If your child is taught to hunt and fish at a young age, he becomes comfortable around guns and animal carcasses—things that more fastidious people might find disturbing. If the child is sheltered from harsh experiences, he tends to shun confrontation and violence. That's why in battle, some people run toward a firefight while others retreat. Bustos realized that he just hadn't been raised for the regimen of rebellion. He had no stomach for *real* revolution, even though he never saw combat during his months in the rebel band. Being a revolutionary was uncomfortable, dirty, and brutal. Sitting in his cell, wondering if he would die that day, Bustos caved in. He told the Bolivians everything he knew.

Bustos said the guerrillas had abandoned the original base camp, but that they returned from time to time. They had storage areas there, filled with critical supplies. He drew a set of detailed maps of the camp, showing everything the Bolivians needed. Once he started talking, he couldn't shut up.

At first, the Bolivian military moved cautiously into the area, afraid of booby traps or guards. But on August 6, the troops hit the jackpot: several caches of weapons, including submachine guns, grenades, and a mortar. They found medical supplies, passports and travel itineraries, a list of contacts in Bolivia, deciphered radio messages from Havana, and codebooks. And there were snapshots, dozens of candid photos of the guerrillas. There was even a cigar butt.

It was an amazing find. Barrientos was ecstatic. Here was even more proof that Cuba—and more specifically Che—was behind the nation's troubles.

For Barrientos, the most damning evidence was the photos. One woman in the snapshots was Loyola Guzman, a twenty-five-year-old member of the Bolivian Communist Youth. She was arrested immediately and taken to the Ministry of Interior building in La Paz. During interrogation she provided information on eleven members of the guerrillas' support network in the capital city. When the guards left her alone for a moment, Guzman threw herself out the third-floor window. A cornice of the building broke her fall, and she was only slightly injured.

Police took her to a hospital, where she told the press she would rather kill herself than betray her comrades.

"I am fully conscious of my situation. I am in this situation because of my conviction," she told the media. "Despite the error that I have committed, since many documents have gotten out that can be used by the authorities to arrest many people, I hold to my ideas. Although this is a blow to us, the struggle will go on, even if many more people will die."

The police had already started rounding up the suspected guerrilla contacts in La Paz. Guzman knew what would happen to them. They would be tortured and killed. Barrientos had no patience for disloyalty.

Barrientos was not the only one intrigued by the recovered paperwork and documents. Annoyed at American resistance to his demands for help, the president balked at releasing the materials to the United States—he and other cabinet members feared they would never be returned. After wrangling with Henderson and State Department officials, Barrientos agreed to hand over some of the items, but only after the Bolivians meticulously catalogued every scrap.

U.S. military officials particularly wanted the passports. The one of a clean-shaven, middle-aged man with glasses and a receding hairline was particularly interesting. They suspected they knew who he was, but wanted to make sure.

Word of the discovery reached President Johnson. Rostow, the president's assistant for national security affairs, included a brief note with the memo, explaining why the Bolivians wanted the materials returned quickly: They planned to use them to prosecute Debray.

Like everything else in the U.S.-Bolivian relationship, custody of the materials became contentious. Barrientos pressed for their return, but the United States kept asking for more time. Finally, the documents were sent back—but one key item was missing: the cigar butt. The Bolivians asked the State Department where it was, but officials there said they didn't know. They asked the CIA. Their answer was simple: "Consumed in analysis."

As the sun set over the fields, the Green Berets slipped off their gear and settled into the chairs at Kiosko Hugo. It seemed the entire unit was there, with Rodríguez and Villoldo as well.

Since arriving at La Esperanza, the CIA men had tried to blend in with the other soldiers. Few of the others knew who they were, or why they were there.

Villoldo spent most of his time with Special Forces' Captain Cruz, training the Rangers' intelligence unit. Rodríguez lived in Santa Cruz, working with Major Saucedo, Eighth Division chief of intelligence, piecing together news as it arrived from the countryside. Rodríguez tracked down leads and fattened his files on the individual guerrillas. He and the major were an important team. As the mission continued, Rodríguez made frequent trips to La Esperanza, just to clear his head and refresh his spirits.

Shelton and Rodríguez sipped beers at the makeshift bar. Rodríguez enjoyed Shelton's company. One Sunday morning, Rodríguez was awakened by music and clapping. When he walked outside, he spotted a guitar-playing Shelton flanked by a soldier twanging a washtub bass, another playing the washboard, and a Green Beret clacking a pair of spoons. The Bolivians loved it.

There was always a lot of talk about Vietnam around the bar. Everyone, even the Bolivians, wanted to know what it was like over there, how things were going. Was the United States winning? Shelton didn't mind talking about it. But like a good soldier, he didn't dwell on why they were fighting. Once the war started, that didn't really matter.

Rodríguez looked at it differently.

Vietnam was another front in the bitter fight against Communism. He had made a promise, after Castro and Che took his country, to strive for freedom for his "brothers and sisters living in slavery under Communist oppression."

But more importantly, he promised to stand firm to his last breath and defend the values of the United States, his adopted country. His homeland had been taken away from him, and his family was cast off to find their own way. But Rodríguez wasn't rudderless. Instead, he had found purpose in the struggle to right the wrongs brought on by Communism. And that meant taking the fight to guys like Che in Bolivia, even to Asia, if need be.

That night, Rodríguez told Shelton about his role in the Bay of Pigs disaster. He told Shelton how the original plan would have freed two thousand political prisoners, how it was changed after Kennedy was elected president. The president changed the location of the landing from Trinidad City to the Bay of Pigs—it had an airfield and was farther away from large groups of civilians. The brigade of Cuban exiles landed on a beach called Playa Girón.

The invasion in April 1961 was a disaster—everything went wrong. Castro captured more than eleven hundred soldiers from the U.S.-backed exile force Brigade 2506. Rodríguez later found out why it all went so wrong. Before the invasion, Cuban exiles in Miami had been shooting off their mouths. Soviet agents picked up on the chatter and warned their Cuban allies about the planned attack. So when the exiles stepped onto Playa Girón, Castro's army was waiting for them.

Rodríguez wasn't there. He was in Havana, he said, where he'd spent several months setting up a resistance network and smuggling weapons. "I was lucky to make it to the Venezuelan embassy in Havana," Rodríguez said. He spent five and a half months in the embassy before escaping.

In the aftermath of the Bay of Pigs fiasco, anyone in Cuba even suspected of taking part in the conspiracy was slaughtered. So many people around the world had bought into the image of Che as a romantic revolutionary. But to Rodríguez and the Cuban exiles, Che was responsible for the murders; he was nothing more than a thug.

Worse was Che's arrogance. In August 1961, during an economic conference of the Organization of American States, in Uruguay, Che sent a note to President Kennedy via one of the president's advisors, Richard Goodwin. It said: "Thanks for Playa Girón. Before the invasion, the revolution was weak. Now it's stronger than ever."

Shelton just shook his head. Rodríguez had gone through hell, he thought. Maybe it was the beer, or the balmy night air, but at that moment, all Shelton could think of was that Rodríguez was "one of us." He wanted to show him how much he appreciated his service. Shelton took out his pocketknife and made a tiny cut in his finger, just enough to bring a bead of blood. He squeezed the drop into his glass of beer. He looked into Rodríguez's eyes: "Blood brothers?"

Rodríguez smiled, charmed at the gesture.

"Yes, blood brothers."

He followed Shelton's lead. He cut his finger with the knife and let his blood drip into his beer. Then Shelton and Rodríguez exchanged glasses.

Shelton raised his and shouted: "*Salud.*"

"*Salud* to you," Rodríguez replied.

They downed the beers and slammed the glasses onto the table. With that, Shelton made a promise to Rodríguez: If Che was truly working in Bolivia, he would not escape alive.

"It ends here," Shelton said.

Even with so much evidence to the contrary, the CIA still refused to acknowledge that Che Guevara might be alive in Bolivia. Che was the face of worldwide revolutionary movements, and CIA analysts just couldn't see him risking it all in a backwater country like Bolivia. It just wasn't his style.

Sure, rumors were rife. The Bolivians had documents and letters they'd found in an isolated camp. All the evidence pointed in one direction. But it all added up to smoke and ashes. No one had actually seen the man. No one could confirm anything.

The invisible guerrilla still managed to cast a long shadow.

At the August Latin American Solidarity Organization conference in Cuba, Che was named honorary chairman. Guevara's name was invoked so many times it was like he was in the room. Delegates from the confederation of twenty-seven Latin Communist and progressive movements sat through one of Fidel Castro's marathon speeches, wherein he promised to exert more influence in the hemisphere. Around him hung gigantic banners blazoned with Che's image. The conference soon turned into a pep rally for revolution. Delegates pledged to "strengthen the bond of militant solidarity among the Latin American anti-imperialist fighters and to draw up basic bonds for the development of the continental revolution." The Bolivian Communist Party representative Aldo Flores told the audience that Che's fighters were simply doing their patriotic duty in opposing U.S. advisors and materials sent to aid "oppressive forces" in Bolivia.

Black activist Stokely Carmichael stirred up the crowd when he promised "we are moving toward guerrilla warfare within the United States, since there is no other way to obtain our homes, our lands, and our rights." Praising Che, Carmichael echoed the guerrilla leader when he declared that "when the U.S. has fifty Vietnams inside and fifty outside, that will mean the death of imperialism."

When the meeting closed, the group declared Che Guevara "The Citizen of Latin America."

The conference caught the notice of CIA director Helms, who passed along an August 8 agency report to President Johnson. The analysis of the Bolivian military was stark and scathing. The Samaipata raid had made a deep impression.

The report said that all five nations on Bolivia's borders shared U.S. doubts about the Bolivian military's ability to stop the guerrillas. If the guerrillas succeeded in overthrowing Barrientos, Argentina and Paraguay agreed to consider military intervention.

The CIA said that the insurgency seemed "more sophisticated and professional than similar efforts elsewhere in Latin America," and the LASO conference provided propaganda assistance. Because of the "alleged presence of Che Guevara" and the capture of Debray, the CIA predicted that the insurgency would remain in the "public eye." "It could become a focus for the continuing polemical debate in the communist world over the wisdom of political versus militant revolutionary action."

The report said Bolivian guerrillas stood in contrast to pro-Castro guerrillas in Venezuela, Guatemala, and Colombia, in their ability to seize the initiative in encounters with the military. The guerrillas were "well-trained and disciplined" and "well-schooled" in Che's insurgency techniques—whether or not he was with them. Analysts attributed the guerrrillas' success to "totally inept" Bolivian counterinsurgency operations and noted Barrientos's need for a quick, decisive victory.

They also speculated that the Bolivian army posts tended to alienate the populations around them, terrorizing local inhabitants, molesting women, "and opening themselves to unfavorable comparison with the well-disciplined guerrillas."

In the end, the report concluded that the Bolivians were quickly losing ground. "Should the guerrillas continue succeeding in Bolivia, their experiences and methods are certain to be emulated in other Latin American countries."

On a Sunday night in late August, Mario Salazar was getting ready for the dance. Every weekend, the Bolivian men gathered around a small band in the La Esperanza plaza. When the right music started up, they paired up and danced the Cueca, a traditional Bolivian folk dance.

It looked a bit like square dancing to the Americans—the partners wheeled and turned around one another, and all the pairs moved together in a simple choreography round the plaza, with white handkerchiefs fluttering like doves from every right hand. The partners never touched each other, but maintained contact through facial expressions and mirrored movements.

It was a mating dance, and very seductive when the beat was slow. And in La Esperanza, when the soldiers danced, they danced with one another. The Bolivian trainees were forbidden any contact with local women.

To Shelton's crew, it was a little weird. Where they came from, men didn't dance with men, not to mention wave around their hand-kerchiefs.

But Salazar didn't care what they thought. Dancing was another way of relaxing after a long week of training. "We couldn't have contact with the women in the village. That was forbidden. We were isolated. For us, this made us feel like we were home," he recalled.

Salazar was happy in La Esperanza. These had been the best months of his life, the most purposeful. He got up each morning and ran to start training. The most important part, to him, was the growing camaraderie with his fellow soldiers. When a Ranger fell in the field, they all rushed to pick him up. When someone had a bad day shooting, others volunteered to stay afterward to help him out.

Life in the camp was hermetic and intense, sometimes tragic. In July, one of the men was killed when a gun went off accidentally in the barracks. A few weeks later, a Bolivian sergeant took his platoon out for mortar training on a Sunday afternoon, without clearing the exercise with his peers. A mortar fell short of its target, killing the sergeant and injuring several of his men. Because none of the officers knew an exercise was going on, the explosion brought the whole camp running.

Hapka and the medical team led the way, starting emergency tri-age and IV lines. They worked feverishly to stabilize men who were bleeding profusely. Soldiers loaded the wounded onto a truck, which sped off to a Santa Cruz hospital. But when the injured soldiers ar-rived, there was no doctor on duty. One soldier died there, but the others survived.

The accident pointed out just how serious the training was, Sala-zar recalled.

"This was not like the regular army training. In the past, soldiers trained, but knew they would go home. Here you knew there was a chance you would never go home. You could be in combat. You could die."

The soldiers knew they were all in this together, that they would be called upon to save their nation from the insurgents. They shared a sense of machismo—they were heroes-to-be. At the same time, they were homesick farm boys. At night, when they weren't on maneuvers, the men lay in their bunks in the dark and talked about their villages and families. Family ties were strong, and the rhythms of village life were bred in the bones of most of the soldiers.

That's why they danced—or why they didn't. Salazar's friend Luis was from a small village outside Vallegrande. Salazar asked him if he was going along to the Cueca that night. Luis said no, he was too tired.

Salazar sat down on the end of his friend's bunk and gave him a shove. "What's up, man?"

"Well," Luis said, "when I'm dancing, I think of my wife. She's home all alone and I wonder if I will ever see her again. I wonder if I will ever hold her in my arms. So if I go to the dance, I will feel bad. I'll start thinking about her. It's better I stay here."

Salazar smiled.

"I don't have a wife, but I understand. I think of my mother a lot. This dance, this keeps me busy. It keeps me from thinking about them. It takes my mind off everything. That's why I'm going."

"I know we're here because we have to go and fight. But I also want to see my wife again. I wonder if it's worth it," Luis said and sighed.

Salazar didn't have an answer. But he understood Luis's fear. No one knew what would happen once they left La Esperanza. If they fought the guerrillas, some of them would probably die. Soldiers on both sides were dying.

Salazar walked to the square, lost in thoughts of home. He had written, but he hadn't heard back from them. He tried to put it out of his mind—no one at home felt very comfortable writing things. But Luis had reminded him of home, and for a moment, he felt lonely.

He spotted Prado standing outside the casino, a sort of club for village leaders.

Prado hailed him. "How are you doing, my friend?"

They had become friendly during training. Prado liked the way the young soldier handled himself in the field. For Salazar, Prado represented everything that was right with the Bolivian military.

They walked together to the plaza. Salazar told Prado he was anxious to get in the field to find the guerrillas. The officer said it wouldn't be long now; in just a few weeks they'd be finished with La Esperanza and out there on the hunt. Then they would know if all the training had paid off—if they were indeed ready. But no one would have to ask Salazar if he was ready. He would go tonight, if they told him to. Even if it meant missing the dance.

Nighttime training was critical. Rangers might have to move under cover of darkness, through dense jungles, deep water, uphill and down. Ability to move in the night is a tactical advantage in battle; it enables a unit to stay a step ahead of the enemy.

As their training progressed, the men spent more of their nights on maneuvers.

It was Chapa's turn to ride along with C Company. They were conducting a night attack. He knew the drill.

There was no moonlight. Clouds hid the stars.

Chapa ordered the men to move out. The soldiers scrambled as quietly as they could down the trail in the dark, straining to see the winding path. They moved toward a thicket of trees along the edge of the training fields. Chapa was especially careful at night. You never knew what was hiding out there. Sometimes a bird or animal would suddenly shriek from the darkness alongside and scare the shit out of everyone.

Chapa had a good sixth sense for night maneuvers. His eyes were wide open and he watched every step. He saw the man in front of him duck his head under a low-hanging tree branch, and as he passed below it, Chapa felt something heavy strike his forehead. *What the hell?* he thought. A hot tingle shot down his arms and legs. He felt incredibly weak—his knees buckled. Salazar was just behind him and saw Chapa collapse to the ground. He sounded the alarm.

"He's down. Something's wrong. We need a medic," Salazar shouted to the other soldiers. He sent several men running back to camp. They ran as fast as they could up the dark pathway. Out of breath, they could barely get the words out.

"Chapa . . . not feeling good . . . fainted," one of the soldiers said.

Shelton stayed calm. He grabbed Hapka, the medic, and told the others they would need help. The Special Forces team bolted down to the tree line.

They found Chapa flat on the ground. He could barely move. He was dazed, fading in and out of consciousness. "We need to get him out of here," Shelton said.

They carried Chapa back to the first-aid station. Hapka and Peterson began working. They cut off Chapa's clothes and closely examined his face, body, legs—the only injury they found was a large bump on his forehead. Chapa was mumbling that his skin was on fire. He was tingling all over. His arms and legs were beginning to swell. They hadn't found any fang marks, but the symptoms said snakebite.

The area was infested with venomous tree vipers. Chapa was

in for a fight, the medics said. Hapka treated him for anaphylactic shock, injecting cortisone between his fingers and toes. Nothing seemed to work. They had to get Chapa to a hospital, the medic said.

But how?

It was nighttime. The road to Santa Cruz was all but closed after dark, and the trip would take more than two hours, if they were lucky. Hapka radioed Fort Gulick and asked for the group surgeon to be called in. It took a while. In the meantime the Green Berets huddled around Chapa, taking turns applying cold, wet towels to his body while they waited for the call back.

Chapa was like a brother to most of them. He was from Alamo, Texas. He had joined the army in 1953, when he was twenty years old.

Chapa did everything the right way, and he was a natural teacher—he excelled in marksmanship. In La Esperanza, he stayed late with the conscripts, patiently showing them the correct way to level a gun, line up the sights, and squeeze off a shot. He was also the one who'd given the recruits their how-to at the trench latrine.

The men in C Company were ordered back to quarters, but they were a long way from sleepy. They drifted back outside to wait for news.

The night was cool, and many villagers worked late, enjoying the break from the heat. Word spread quickly among them—one of the American soldiers was badly hurt. Villagers gathered outside the first-aid station. The Roca family sent one of the boys to see if the victim might be Graham, and when he returned with the answer they wanted, they peppered him with more questions.

"But which soldier was hurt?" they asked, all at once. "What happened to him? Will he live?" The family finally gathered up their things and headed up to the sugar mill to find out for themselves.

The word then passed through the crowd: "snakebite." Tree viper. Everyone knew how deadly tree vipers were. They blended into the scenery and struck without warning. So many villagers, lots of them children, had been killed and injured over the years by snakes that they all carried machetes with them for protection.

Finally the surgeon called back from Panama. The crowd fell silent as the medic shouted down the line. Yes, they'd treated him for shock. Yes, they'd injected cortisone. Cold compresses, pressure . . . Yes, yes, yes.

The surgeon ran out of suggestions. The medics had already tried everything. What they were doing was all they could do.

Hapka sighed. They had to find a way to save Chapa, but Hapka had reached the bottom of his medical bag. If they were in a hospital, he could give him antivenom. But there were no hospitals out here. They couldn't do anything but pray.

So the soldiers huddled around Chapa, each man making whatever prayer he knew. Shelton held out hope. Chapa was a tough bastard. The hours dragged on. The sergeant's skin took on a bruised look as the poison spread.

Valderomas stood in the dark outside. His neighbor told him the news and ended with the words "I don't think he's going to live." Valderomas peeked in the first-aid window and saw that it was Chapa—a happy man who always said "good day" when he passed. What a shame. Valderomas felt a little tingle, remembering how a snakebite felt. And then he remembered: The healer, Manosanta Humerundo.

When a snake bit Valderomas years ago, his father had called in Manosanta—the Holy Hand—a folk healer from a neighboring village. He was sure the old man was still alive.

The sun was rising. Valderomas didn't wait another minute. He took off at a fast walk, fast as he could go with dignity, down a grassy path, brushing back tree limbs and trailing vines. When he was clear of the village, he broke into a run.

A few minutes later, the holy man listened to Valderomas panting out his story. He was used to people showing up at his house without warning. He put some items into a black leather bag, locked the door behind him, and walked back to the camp with Valderomas.

They approached the first-aid station, and the old man knocked gently at the doorsill.

"I can help the soldier," he said. Shelton and the others were doubtful. Manosanta was tall, with dark brown skin. The flowing brown robe and white beads around his neck would have fit in at a hippy commune.

The villagers spoke up: Manosanta was a medicine man. He knew all the ancient remedies, and when they were sick they depended on his help. He was an honorable man, they said. Please, let him look at Chapa.

Shelton glanced at Hapka and nodded his head yes. They had nothing to lose.

Manosanta examined Chapa. The man was unconscious; his breath came in ragged, shallow gasps. The medicine man noticed the wound on Chapa's forehead—a mark he'd had seen many times before. It was a snakebite, he said. He knew the cure. Manosanta asked them to find a piece of raw meat. The soldiers scrambled to the supply shed, and from some deep hiding place a steak was produced. The medicine man laid the slab of meat on Chapa's forehead and bound it on with a bandage. He whispered a prayer, then turned to the soldiers.

"He will live," he said. "Just keep the meat on the wound; it will absorb the poison."

He stepped into the dawn and headed home.

The Americans were skeptical. A steak? Really?

But nothing else had worked.

Within a few minutes, Chapa seemed to breathe more easily. The swelling went down. The purplish bruises stopped spreading. Chapa woke up about an hour later, confused but feeling much better. They could tell he was going to make it. His friends told him to rest, and warned him not to look in a mirror.

When he went back to sleep, they removed the steak. They didn't want Chapa to think that the Special Forces medics had used voodoo medicine to cure him. "That was our little secret," Peterson said.

A few days later, Chapa was back in the fields, helping the soldiers train. Valderomas smiled when they passed each other in the village. *The healer did his job*, Valderomas thought.

He was glad he had played a small role in saving Chapa's life. He was a good man. The soldiers meant no harm. And even though they still kept him up at night, Valderomas stopped complaining.

CHAPTER 16

Yado del Yeso

A white apron hung in the trees, blowing softly in the breeze.

The cloud-like white stood out in the scrubby brush of the Bolivian countryside. From cover, Captain Mario Vargas Salinas could see the guerrillas—first one, now almost a half dozen—wading in the dark water of the Rio Grande. Swollen from the rainy season, the river cut through the valley, its swift current pushing against them as they crossed.

Vargas had his men set up in perfect position on the opposite bank. Alerted to the crossing point by a farmer, they had marched hours to get in position. Now they only had to wait a few more seconds.

Patience, Vargas thought. *Patience.*

In a farmhouse in the distance, Honorato Rojas tried to busy his hands while he waited for the bursts of gunfire. Only after would he feel safe. The day before, a guerrilla band had visited here. They asked him what place was best to cross the river. The Rio Grande was not wide, but it was deep in places. The fast currents made it dangerous unless it was done at the right time and place.

Rojas had helped the guerrillas earlier in the year. He kept a country store nearby, and the men bought supplies from him. A man who called himself Inti told Rojas that he was the leader. Inti persuaded Rojas to give him information about other families in the neighborhood. Rojas cooperated, and the guerrillas went away. He was surprised to see them again, asking about the river.

Rojas told the guerrillas he would take a look at the fords and find the safest spot for them to cross. Instead, he double-crossed them.

Rojas knew Bolivian soldiers were in the area, too. So after the guerrillas left, he sent his twelve-year-old son to look for them. The first soldier the boy found was Private Fidel Rea, who was fishing in a stream on his off-duty afternoon. The boy relayed his father's message: Three guerrillas were at his farm and he needed help. Rea knew this was important. He left his fishing tackle and sprinted all the way back to his post with the news. The day was waning, but Vargas did not wait to act. He marched his men ten miles to Rojas's farm. By the time they arrived, it was the middle of the night. They waited.

At dawn, Vargas spotted a woman walking down a dirt path with several small children in tow. It was Rojas's wife. She confirmed the story about the guerrillas and told Vargas it was safe to come down—the men had left.

Vargas went in the house and talked to Rojas, then devised a plan. The guerrillas were to return to Rojas's house that day, Rojas didn't know when. When they did, he would show them the exact spot to ford the river. He would do it by displaying a white apron at the crossing point. When the guerrillas spotted the signal, they would know "the coast is clear."

Now Vargas could see the apron hanging in the brush. It had been months since the first ambush in the Nancahuazu River canyon. At times, it seemed he'd been chasing ghosts; his troops were always one step behind. But if Rojas was right, Vargas would finally be in the right place at the right time. He would get a chance to pay the guerrillas back for all of their success.

It had been twelve hours since they arrived, and some of his soldiers were getting antsy. Hell, he was getting antsy. All of them were stiff and tired. Suddenly, the guerrillas appeared out of the brush and waded into the water.

Vargas took a deep breath as he watched the first one, chest-deep with his rifle over his head, cross the midpoint in the river. To his astonishment, none of the guerrillas provided security on the opposite bank. That was basic tactics—in the water they were vulnerable. One by one, the ragged men followed the leader into the water, trusting Rojas and the apron signal . . . but men? Vargas couldn't be sure, but from this distance one of them had a feminine shape.

The Bolivian soldiers watched and waited. The other nine were in the water when the first insurgent reached the opposite bank. The first guerrilla was barely on shore when Vargas cried out. The Bolivians opened fire. The lead man fired back, killing one soldier before he was cut down. His body slid down the muddy bank. The guerrillas trapped in the water had no chance. Vargas watched as the bullets turned the muddy river red. The barrage cut the guerrillas down in seconds. Several were swept downriver.

But two wounded and dazed guerrillas—both Bolivians—were fished out of the water: Freddy Maymura, a Japanese-Bolivian medical student, and Jose Carillo, a wild-eyed youth who insisted he was a student, not a fighter. Both men were rail-thin, with thick hair and beards. Vargas's unit regrouped. A squad of soldiers approached Vargas.

"We want one," one of the soldiers said.

The lead guerrilla had killed one of their patrol. They wanted revenge. Vargas glimpsed the prisoners. Carillo kept his head down. Maymura, the doctor, was defiant. He looked at the soldiers and refused to back down.

Both the men were injured, but Maymura was the logical choice. He had a deep chest wound—his shirt was soaked in blood. Meanwhile, Carillo continued to squirm on the ground, forcing his legs underneath Vargas. He begged for his life.

Vargas nodded toward Maymura.

The soldiers marched past Vargas and sprayed Maymura's body with bullets. For the moment, the other prisoner was spared. Despite the bullet wound in his arm, the soldiers marched him twenty miles to their headquarters in Vallegrande. The man was elated to be alive. He said his "camp name" was Paco.

Rojas ventured outside after the gunfire died down. He crept slowly to the riverbank and looked to where the noise had been. He was nervous—what if the guerrillas had won? But when Rojas saw the Bolivian soldiers leaving with a prisoner, he knew the guerrillas' fate.

When Major Saucedo, the Eighth Division intelligence officer, learned of the ambush, Rodríguez was the first person he called.

"We got Paco," Saucedo said.

It was exactly what Rodríguez wanted to hear.

CHAPTER 17

Paco

Rodríguez followed Saucedo down the tiled halls of Nuestra Señora de Malta Hospital in Vallegrande.

The pair had arrived the morning of September 3 on an olive-drab C-47 cargo plane. They were there for one reason: Paco, the survivor of the ambush. Rodríguez had never met the student, but he had an inch-thick file on him. Paco had been in custody for three days. He was recovering from a gunshot wound in his arm.

Paco's hospital room was crowded with Bolivian soldiers with guns at the ready. Paco was slumped in a chair, his arm heavily bandaged. His hair was long and dirty. A Fu Manchu mustache covered his lip, and patches of wispy beard covered his chin and cheeks.

Paco didn't look like he needed six guards. He looked like he needed a shave and a clean shirt. He was a sorry sight, and a potential gold mine of information about the guerrillas.

"We need to get this guy released to us," Rodríguez said to Saucedo. "Can you help me?"

Saucedo agreed.

The Bolivian Third Tactical Command headquarters was in an elegant colonial house nearby. The commander, Lieutenant Colonel Andres Selich, was there, chatting with a visitor from La Paz, General David Lafuenta. They introduced one another—Lafuenta had seen Rodríguez somewhere before, at a social event.

Selich was enjoying his moment in the spotlight. For the past three days he had paraded Paco around as his officers had their photos taken with "the notorious insurgent." Paco was his victory; one of the army's first real successes, and the colonel was reluctant to give up his trophy.

"We already told the press that the prisoner is badly wounded and is not expected to survive. Besides, I don't think we can get any more out of him," Selich told the intelligence men. He looked to Lafuenta for guidance. "General, just give me the word and I'll execute him."

Rodríguez nudged Saucedo. "Move in," the Cuban whispered. "Ask for the prisoner."

Saucedo tried, but Selich refused. Selich outranked Saucedo, so there was little the major could do. Rodríguez played his trump. He slid the card signed by Barrientos out of his pocket. Lafuenta noticed.

"*Mi general,*" Rodríguez said to him, "give me and Major Saucedo an opportunity with this prisoner. I assure you the information he will give us will be invaluable. And if, afterward, you don't agree with our assessment, I'll never ask you for another prisoner again. But, sir, please let us have this one."

Lafuenta remembered where he'd seen Rodríguez before—in La Esperanza, at a visit from U.S. General Porter, the SOUTHCOM commander. The Bolivian general knew Rodríguez was part of the

U.S. government, but his exact role wasn't clear. Lafuenta paused, then turned to the colonel.

"Give the prisoner to this young man," he said.

Selich glowered at Rodríguez. A Bolivian officer wrote the order on the back of a brown paper bag, and Selich signed it. Rodríguez trotted back to the hospital. The last plane for Santa Cruz was leaving within the hour, and if he didn't get Paco on it, there was no way he would ever get the prisoner to safety.

The Bolivian soldiers didn't want to give him up and they weren't going to make it easy. The paperwork must be prepared, Selich's officers said. They promised to send Paco back to Santa Cruz on a truck the next day. Rodríguez knew that if he let them do that, Paco would "try to escape" and the soldiers would shoot him.

So Saucedo and Rodríguez rushed Paco out of the hospital and shoved him into the back of a jeep. They raced to the airstrip, where the propellers were turning on the C-47. A Bolivian major stopped them at the gangway. The plane was full of reporters, he said. There was no way a nonmilitary passenger would be allowed on board.

"Look," Rodríguez said, "we have instructions from General Lafuenta to bring this guy with us, and that's exactly what we're going to do."

The major tried to argue, but Rodríguez ignored him. He snatched Paco's tattered jacket out of the jeep, threw it over the guerrilla's head, and shoved him toward the hatch of the plane. Rodríguez forced Paco up the ramp.

The reporters heading back to Santa Cruz were crammed into the seats along the fuselage. Rodríguez kept his hand on Paco's good arm as he pushed the guerrilla up the aisle toward the front compartment, with Saucedo right behind. The reporters watched the trio, curious about the barefoot man covered by the jacket.

Rodríguez and Saucedo didn't stop for questions.

Safely up front behind the curtain, Paco collapsed in one of the seats. He wept and muttered to himself. Saucedo got a bottle of Coca-Cola and some cookies from the flight crew and handed them to Paco. The guerrilla tore them open and ate ravenously, his hands trembling.

"You're going to kill me," Paco repeated between sobs.

"No," Rodríguez said. "I'm not."

Paco cried some more, whining between bites and gulps.

"I never wanted to be a guerrilla," he said. "I never wanted to fight. And now you're going to kill me. Soon as we get to where we're going. I know it."

"We need you alive," Rodríguez told Paco.

The plane landed in Santa Cruz. Rodríguez and Saucedo waited until the journalists were gone. Then they took Paco in a car to Eighth Division headquarters. They followed a winding route, to throw them off, and Paco never stopped crying. At the headquarters building Rodríguez found a plain room with a single bunk, handed the prisoner some soap, and pointed to the shower room. While Paco cleaned up, soldiers barred the bedroom windows and doors with wood. When it was finished, Paco was ushered inside. Rodríguez could tell that when the young guerrilla saw his "cell," he knew he wasn't going to die, at least not yet. The CIA and the Bolivian officer had kept their promise.

Breaking Paco would take time, but Rodríguez was an expert.

Rodríguez hired a nurse to treat Paco's wound. Flies had got to the hole while it was fresh, and now it was infested with maggots. It was disgusting, but the worms ate rotting flesh and staved off gangrene. They probably saved Paco's life. As discussions proceeded over the next few days, Rodríguez watched hundreds of the little rice-like bodies moving in and out of the wound.

Paco slept in a regular bunk bed. He wore clean clothes and comfortable new shoes. Rodríguez brought him a stack of magazines and newspapers to fill the empty hours, and a barber came to cut his hair and shave his scruffy beard. Rodríguez was determined to talk with Paco like a man, but first he had to make him look like one.

The two talked for hours every day. On either side of a simple table, Rodríguez and Paco shared their stories. Rodríguez talked about Cuba. He told Paco how Castro had ruined his country, ushering in inequality and forcing many Cubans into exile.

"I am an exile," Rodríguez told Paco. "Your Communism destroyed my country. It destroyed families like mine, and made us seek shelter far from home."

Paco listened, rapt.

And when Paco told his story, Rodríguez listened just as closely.

Unlike Che and the other fighters, Paco wasn't really a hard-line Communist. His real name was José Castillo Chavez. He was born in 1937 and started going to Communist Party meetings in 1958. His membership in the party wasn't cemented until 1967, when his uncle, Bolivian Communist Party leader Moises Guevara, offered him "a revolutionary education" in Moscow and Havana. The young man was delighted at the prospect. But first he would have to escape Bolivia through the countryside, so his passport wouldn't show he'd left.

Instead of being smuggled across the border, his handlers delivered Paco to a base camp in the jungle, where other recruits joined him. Paco tried to explain that he wasn't a fighter and had only come for the education. Nato and Antonio, his squad leaders, ignored his complaints. They gave him a backpack, a canteen, a hammock, and a Mauser rifle with 120 rounds. They decided to call him "Paco."

"You're a guerrilla soldier now," Nato told him.

Rodríguez smiled at the story. "You didn't have a lot of choices," he said.

It didn't take long for Paco to learn that the group's leader, Ramon, was Che Guevara. Paco was starstruck at first, but that faded fast as Che's fighter-training regimen kicked into gear. Paco struggled to keep up with the days-long marches in the mountains. The guerrillas carried all their gear and sometimes had to race up the mountains as fast as they could. It was the way Che hardened up his fighters. He was a brutal taskmaster, and he'd seen the method succeed. This was how they'd done it in Cuba, when they were stuck in the Sierra Maestra—and just look at the glory they'd achieved.

Paco obviously admired Communism, but he felt used by the Communists. Rodríguez was determined to jam a wedge between the belief and the experience.

Rodríguez was warm and friendly. He asked about Paco's family. He offered to get a message to Paco's parents, to assure them he was all right. Rodríguez handed Paco a pen and paper and made sure the letter was mailed. Soon, Rodríguez and Paco had built enough rapport that Paco talked about his daily life in Che's guerrilla force.

Even while he worked with Paco, Rodríguez mined another rich vein of inside information on the rebel force. His name was "Braulio," and he was dead, killed in the river at Yado del Yeso. His real name was Israel Reyes Zayas. He was a Cuban lieutenant, and a dedicated diarist. Between conversations with Paco, Rodríguez read the diary—a handwritten book of revelations.

According to Braulio, the guerrilla war was poorly organized, badly planned, and poorly manned. The fighters in his unit were weak and sick from hunger. Supplies were scanty and of poor quality. But most amazing of all, Braulio's force had absolutely no communication with Che's unit. Before it was ambushed, his unit had been wandering through the mountains. The two halves of Che's dreaded rebel army had lost each other. They wandered around the jungle for months looking for each other.

All this talk about hundreds of disciplined guerrillas poised to make a run at La Paz? Horseshit, pure and simple, Rodríguez realized. The world had been scared for nothing. What the hell was Che doing out there? Rodríguez just shook his head in disbelief. It was unreal.

He used insights gleaned from the diary to work on Paco. It was a delicate dance, built on the illusion of a friendship. Paco thought Rodríguez was in his corner, protecting him, so he continued to talk. The more Paco talked, the more details emerged. Details would lead them to the guerrillas, and to Che.

Rodríguez's interrogation plan worked, with only one hitch— one afternoon a U.S. Special Forces officer in Santa Cruz decided to "have a talk" with Paco. The prisoner didn't know the man, and he wasn't as forthcoming as he was with Rodríguez. Sensing that Paco was lying, the officer threatened him and dunked his head underwater.

When he learned about the unauthorized visit, Rodríguez was livid. He apologized to Paco, promised it would never happen again. Then he made it clear to the guards that no one was allowed to speak to Paco without Rodríguez's direct clearance.

Soon, Paco was feeling like himself again.

"Tell me about the camps," Rodríguez said. He wanted a clear picture of the factions within the groups. According to Braulio, there was friction between the foreigners and the Bolivians. He wanted to hear it from Paco.

Paco started with Tania, an East German agent named Tamara

Bunke Bider. Tania worked for the KGB and brought Debray and Bustos to the camp. She set up the urban support network that was broken up by the Bolivians after her Jeep was discovered.

"She wrote all of the nasty things anyone said about her in a notebook," Paco said. "She then took the notebook to Che. Tania and Joaquin, the leader of the rear guard, argued about who sacrificed more for the revolution. The arguments always ended with Tania in tears."

Rodríguez smiled and listened. He soaked up the details. Between conversations with Paco, Rodríguez cross-referenced his story with Braulio's diary.

"She couldn't keep up on the marches. She fell back frequently," Paco said. "She slowed the whole group down."

Tania was Che's radio operator. She got messages at noon, 1 P.M. and later at 8 P.M., Paco said. Paco's memory for detail was prodigious. The more Rodríguez talked to Paco, the more he figured out the man had a knack for retaining information. He would have been a great intelligence agent. He recited the names of places he'd passed through six months before, and the addresses and names of sixteen different people involved in the movement.

"What happened to Tania?" Rodríguez asked.

"She was killed in the ambush," he said.

"Are you sure?" Rodríguez asked Paco. "We didn't find her body."

"She got sucked under the river," Paco said. "She's probably wedged between some rocks not far from the crossing point."

After the meeting, Rodríguez shared his information with Saucedo. Four days later, Bolivian soldiers, in the exact place Paco had indicated, discovered Tania's body. Unlike the other guerrillas, who were buried in a mass, unmarked grave, Barrientos ordered that Tania have a proper Christian burial.

One story that intrigued Rodríguez: how two fellow Bolivian guerrillas deserted early in the campaign.

"Vicente and Pastor were sent to check traps for food," Paco told him. "They took off and they never returned."

"How do you know they deserted?" Rodríguez asked.

"Moises Guevara was concerned when they didn't come back by early afternoon. He went to check their backpacks," Paco said. "He found a note from Vicente."

Paco remembered exactly what was written.

"'I am not leaving because I am a coward, but because I am profoundly preoccupied and worried about my little children. As soon as I can take care of my problems at home I am going to return. It is a matter of economics. My children do not have anything to eat.'"

Three days after the desertions, Che arrived in the camp with his entourage, including Pombo, a veteran of the Sierra Maestra. Pombo was Che's right-hand man, his bodyguard in Cuba and in Africa.

"Then what happened?" Rodríguez asked.

"Tania was in the camp kitchen, and when she saw Che she kissed him and shook his hand," Paco said. "Che was angry there were so many people in the camp. He wanted to know why the guerrillas weren't more spread out at other camps."

To Paco, this was just the daily soap opera of being in Che's dysfunctional guerrilla family. But for Rodríguez, it was a window into the soul of the movement. He urged Paco to continue.

"El Chino told Che about the desertions, and that Marcos, the camp commander, retreated because the army was getting too close and he didn't want to fight. Che was pissed off. He ordered the guerrillas to go back to their camps the next day and not give them up without a fight."

Rodríguez checked his notes. This happened in March, about six months ago. It was around the time the Bolivians were first hit by Che and his guerrillas.

Paco said Che's people cooked a meal in the kitchen and Che sent for Marcos. When Marcos arrived, there was a vicious argument. Che called Marcos "a piece of shit and a coward."

Marcos was a high-ranking Cuban named Antonio Sanchez Diaz, commander of the First Revolutionary Regiment in Havana and a member of the Central Committee of the Cuban Communist Party. Rodríguez already knew about Che's fight with Marcos— Braulio had written about it. At first, Rodríguez didn't understand the entry, but Paco was filling in the details for him.

Paco said Marcos protested, saying he was "as much *comandante*" as Che. The men looked like they were going to fight, but Marcos finally backed down.

Paco was later assigned to the rear guard, a group led by Joaquin, a Cuba veteran named *Comandante* Juan Vitalio Acuna Nunez. He took away Paco's gun, but he still had to carry the ammunition.

That night Che gathered the guerrillas together for an hour-long speech.

Che told them the Cubans had volunteered to come to Bolivia because it was their duty to assist Latin America in fighting North American imperialism. He said it was going to be a long fight—a war that would last a decade. The Cubans would stay in Bolivia "until you can walk by yourselves." Then they would spread revolution to other nations.

Rodríguez knew the speech. It was the typical Communist bullshit parroted by guerrilla leaders all over Latin America. But then came the key information: Because Vicente and Pastor had deserted, Che demoted Marcos from *comandante* to soldier. He placed him in the rear guard, under Joaquin's command.

He promoted Miguel, a Sierra Maestra veteran named Captain Manuel Hernandez, to head the vanguard.

It was obvious to Rodríguez that Che didn't trust the Bolivians. When several other Bolivian guerrillas deserted as well, Che put Cubans and Tania in charge of the operation. On their home ground, Bolivians were more concerned with providing for their families than his Communist revolution.

One of the biggest coups in Rodríguez's investigation was Paco's explanation of guerrilla logistics. Paco explained that Che operated in three groups—vanguard, center, and rear guard. Each unit was about a half mile apart from the rest. The vanguard had six to eight people. In the center was Che and the main force. The rest were in the rear. That way, if there was an ambush, the vanguard or the rear guard would be hit first. Both units would protect the center.

By the end of his time with Paco, Rodríguez had a twenty-page debriefing report for the Bolivians detailing everything he had learned, from how the guerrillas operated to the friction points between Che and his commanders.

All they needed now was a lead.

CHAPTER 18

"Go get him."

Training was winding down. The Rangers were ready. Shelton had been watching for weeks, looking for little things. Were the units in sync during maneuvers? Were the snipers hitting the targets? Did the field artillery units coordinate among themselves?

To Shelton, the answer was yes.

The Bolivian high command hadn't decided where or when the Rangers would be deployed. That didn't matter. Shelton knew they were ready. That's all anyone could ask for.

Their fourth month of training had begun with two weeks of field exercise in the wilderness outside Santa Cruz. The battalion had put its training to work, maneuvering the Rangers through terrain similar to what they'd find in the operations area. They'd made it as hard and realistic as possible so the soldiers could stay alive while they tracked down Che.

It was downright elaborate in places. At one point, the Special Forces team set up a mock village to teach the soldiers how to properly clear buildings—a bit like a fun house, with blank guns. Groups of three or four Rangers moved inside and cleared each room of lurking "guerrillas" before heading to the next one. Some of the soldiers dressed up like women and popped out of rooms without warning. The message was: Shoot the soldiers you find, but not women. Only men, and only if they have weapons.

There was unfinished business in La Esperanza. Most of the framing was done at the school project, but wrangling continued over funding. Shelton badgered the U.S. embassy—and Henderson—until the roof and the windows were paid for. That was a battle won, but the war continued: He had to push his bosses to get anything done. At one point in the program, Shelton and his deputy, Captain Fricke, were summoned to Panama to explain to the SOUTHCOM brass why they had requested so many costly supplies. Didn't Shelton know there were lots of other projects going on, in other countries?

The major was quiet for a moment. He looked General Porter in the eye.

"You wouldn't want to lose that battalion, now, would you, General?" Shelton asked. Porter backed down. Supplies continued to flow freely to La Esperanza. Sure, Shelton was a hotshot, but the general respected his candor, and his utter dedication to his mission. Shelton had promised himself at the beginning that he would do things the right way in Bolivia—*his way.* He kept his promises.

He had a few more things on his to-do list. After the Rangers were deployed, his team was slated to train nine Bolivian infantry companies. That assignment would be a breeze compared to Ranger training. Shelton was confident his team would be home by Christmas.

For Shelton, the last few weeks had been a whirlwind of visiting dignitaries. General Porter had toured La Esperanza. He presented gold wristwatches to the outstanding Bolivian officers and silver ones to the best Rangers from each company. The Bolivians had big plans for the graduation ceremony. Vice President Adolfo Siles would speak, along with Colonel Joaquin Zenteno Anaya, the Eighth Division commander.

Shelton felt that the tide was turning in favor of the Bolivians. While he hadn't seen Rodríguez and Villoldo for weeks, he'd heard that key guerrillas had been killed or captured. Rodríguez and Villoldo were probably deep into interrogations now.

Che's role was no longer a mystery. The revolutionary was not only involved, but leading the guerrillas. Che must have an escape plan. If things got really dangerous, surely he had a way out? Why would he risk everything in a Bolivian jungle?

The dead revolutionaries rode into town facedown, lashed to the backs of mules. Rodríguez thought he'd never been so happy to see a corpse before—he'd rushed through the morning to get to tiny Pucara, driving up from Vallegrande in a jeep with Villoldo and Saucedo, shouting into field phones to the sergeant at the ambush scene: "Get the bodies to Pucara, we'll meet you there."

If Rodríguez could identify the dead men, they'd have a clear picture of Che's whereabouts, at least for the next few days. It was worth a shot.

But jeeps move faster than mules. Once they arrived, the wait began. He couldn't take any more coffee, so Rodríguez wandered the streets.

The village was cut into a mountainside, with lovely views over finger-like valleys pointing down to the Rio Grande. The steep hills were covered in thorny thickets, dense vegetation, and boulders. It was impossible terrain, Rodríguez thought. No wonder their "delivery" was taking so long.

At around four o'clock Second Lieutenant Eduardo Galindo and his platoon arrived with the bodies. The three intelligence men introduced themselves briefly, then got to work.

Soldiers undid the knots and laid the stiffening bodies in the dirt street. Rodríguez took out an ink pad, grasped the dead guerrillas by their wrists, and rolled their fingerprints onto a pad of paper. While Rodríguez shot photos of documents taken from the guerrilla's backpacks, Villoldo and Saucedo debriefed Galindo on the ambush.

The guerrillas had been walking along a dirt road in broad daylight, no cover. Galindo's men spotted them from the heights. He ordered them to set an ambush, but Galindo quickly realized that he was facing a conundrum. The guerrillas walked with a good distance between one another, so it was hard to hit the whole group. There wasn't much cover. The guerrillas would spot his men as they drew nearer. Galindo took his chance.

"After we opened fire, the guerrillas retreated," Galindo said. "I ordered my troops to advance." Some of the guerrillas fell. The rest turned and ran. We went all the way down to La Higuera, but the rest escaped into the canyons near the town."

The Bolivians recovered the bodies and brought them back to Pucara.

The trio thanked Galindo, patted the mules, and headed back to Vallegrande, where Rodríguez compared the prints to his files.

The dead guerrillas were Miguel, a Cuban, and two Bolivians—Coco and Julio.

Rodríguez flipped through several sheets of notes and scribbled his findings on a tablet.

In March, Che had promoted Miguel to commander of the vanguard. If Miguel's unit was in the area, Che was nearby. Rodríguez recalled the view from Pucara, the steep, thorny valleys cutting into the mountainside. He prayed Che was still stuck down there. Rodríguez was not a military strategist, but he knew what an opportunity looked like.

He gathered his notebooks and rushed to Eighth Division headquarters, ready to make his pitch to Zenteno. But Zenteno was busy. Rodríguez cooled his heels in the hallway. It was a classic case of "hurry up and wait," the second one of the day.

After what felt like hours, Zenteno invited Rodríguez into his office.

"Sir," Rodríguez said. "It's time to move the Rangers from La Esperanza to Vallegrande. Che is in the area."

Zenteno took a deep breath. President Barrientos had made several visits to town to check on operations, and Zenteno knew that if his men caught Che, the glory would be all his.

"How do you know that?" he asked Rodriguez.

"The bodies from the ambush this morning. One was Miguel. Miguel was in Che's vanguard," Rodríguez said. "That was Che's vanguard coming up the road."

There was a real sense of urgency: They needed the Rangers. Now.

"But Félix, they have not finished their Ranger training," Zenteno said. "They have another two weeks to go. I will move them as soon as they complete their cycle."

Rodríguez clenched his teeth and shook his head.

"In two weeks we have no idea where Che will be," Rodríguez said. "If we don't move the troops now, all the training in the world won't help them. Everything I've tried to do since I got here is coming to a head right now."

Using Paco's information, Rodríguez could predict where Che Guevara would next move his main guerrilla force. That caught Zenteno's attention.

"We know where he is now," Rodríguez said. "And the last two weeks of Ranger training is for getting diplomas and all that shit. They're ready now."

Then he said the words that Zenteno wanted to hear:

"I am certain we can deal the Communists a mortal blow. But only if you, sir, act decisively. Order the Second Ranger Battalion into combat now."

Noise, more noise, roused Valderomas from his bed. He stood by his window and saw the soldiers gathering, lining themselves up in front of the sugar mill. But unlike other mornings, they wore huge backpacks and carried duffel bags.

They were on their way out.

Valderomas heard from his neighbors that the Rangers were leaving for their first secret mission. Probably looking for the guerrillas, Valderomas thought. The Americans would stay behind, and other Bolivian soldiers would be arriving soon—but not so many. Maybe things would calm down now.

The night before, Valderomas had watched the Bolivian soldiers say good-bye to people in town. He spotted that tall American soldier with the sunglasses, holding hands with the Roca girl. The soldier had asked to marry her, everyone said. Valderomas doubted that would happen, but if it did, the girl would leave. He couldn't imagine an American settling in La Esperanza. La Esperanza was a poor village. It would always be a poor village.

Valderomas had made a little extra money selling the soldiers vegetables. Good things had happened for the village, too. The school project would be finished soon, maybe in time for the president to lift the "winter holiday" and send the children back to class.

Valderomas watched the Rangers climb onto the trucks and

head out of town. As he stared at the convoy receding in the distance, he felt a sense of sadness. Those were good men, he thought. How many of them would die out there?

They stood in formation under a crisp blue sky, tall and proud. The men of the Second Ranger Battalion wore olive-green uniforms and green berets. Their ceremony was held at Eighth Division headquarters in Santa Cruz and broadcast live on Bolivian National Radio. Vice President Siles and other Bolivian officials gave impassioned speeches. These were the Bolivian elite, they declared, their finest soldiers, off now to cleanse the land of the Communist scourge.

The vice president presented each man with a gold pin in the shape of condor wings, the word "Ranger" engraved below. The men beamed. Watching the ceremony unfold, Shelton couldn't help thinking about all they had accomplished in just a few months. *Enjoy yourselves today, men*, he thought.

Training is over. Reality starts tomorrow.

And only then would Shelton be able to gauge his success, if the men had truly grasped the program. He just wished he could be there with them in the field, to see them take the first steps—this was a lot like raising a child, he thought. There was nothing Shelton could do now except wait and see.

When the ceremony wound up, a smartly dressed officer broke ranks, stepped up to Shelton, and shook his hand—Prado. He looked every inch an officer, with stars on the collar of his neatly pressed tan uniform. He wore dark sunglasses and his green beret angled over his eye, just so. They'd put him in charge of Company B.

He and Shelton walked across the parade ground to the gates of the headquarters.

"It was an inspiring ceremony," Prado said.

"They did it up right," Shelton agreed. "Look at the men, and think of how far they have come. Remember the first day they showed up?"

Prado smiled. "We didn't look like soldiers, did we?"

"Prado, you always looked like a soldier. They didn't. But I'll give them this: They always tried their best. They always worked hard. We had to cover a lot of things over a short period. But they got it."

There was a moment of silence. Prado looked up to Shelton. The major treated even the lowest-ranking men with respect. He listened when others talked. He never seemed to raise his voice—Shelton was calm and collected. If he could command like Shelton, Prado thought, he'd have the respect of the men in his company.

"I'm leaving today," Prado said. "I'm headed to the operations area. I wanted to say good-bye."

Shelton stopped and turned. "Gary, I'm sure you're going to do well. Any army would be glad to have you."

He was headed back to La Esperanza to train infantry, Shelton said, but he would miss the Rangers. This had been the most important mission of his army career. His team had grown to care for the Bolivian soldiers. When the Americans finally returned home in a few months, they would always remember their time in La Esperanza.

"You take care of your family, Gary," Shelton said. "Be safe. And go get him."

PART THREE

RED ZONE

Che Guevara's Capture

October 8, 1967

El Churo Canyon

Bolivia

700 km

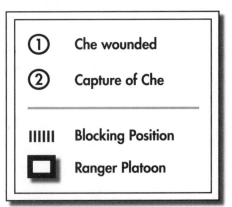

① Che wounded

② Capture of Che

||||| Blocking Position

▬ Ranger Platoon

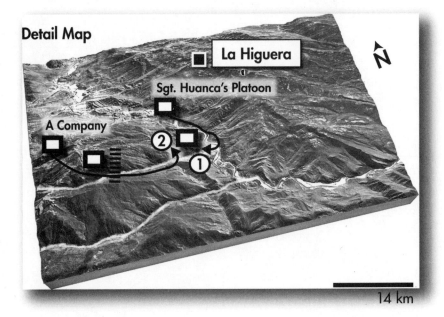

Detail Map

La Higuera

Sgt. Huanca's Platoon

A Company

② ①

14 km

CHAPTER 19

"We will destroy these men."

The last week of September, the Rangers packed themselves into open-topped transport trucks used to carry sugarcane, and traveled down eighty miles of rutted roads from Santa Cruz to Vallegrande. It was a market town of about six thousand people, with the usual narrow cobblestone streets, hole-in-the-wall shops, and outdoor markets where farmers sold their garden produce. It was a place where people worked hard all week and went to church on Sundays.

The tenor in town had changed over the last few months as it became a way station for international journalists and Bolivian Army troops. The locals had grown used to seeing military trucks and jeeps parked on the streets. They'd heard that Che and his army were nearby, but having more soldiers in town only added to the anxiety. No one trusted the government's assurances and warnings. In the spring, Bolivian commanders had told them hundreds of fighters were in the canyons just outside the city. They'd spent the summer wondering when Vallegrande would be attacked. Now the soldiers said the guerrillas were on the run. Which one was it?

Mario Salazar was just happy to get to Vallegrande in one piece. As the convoy rolled down the cobblestones into town, Salazar waved at the people lining the streets. He could sense from the smiles and waves that some were happy to see the Rangers. Salazar loved the attention. He and the men felt like they were part of something special.

The trip down had been a singsong of boasting, a review on what they'd do when the time came to kill the guerrillas. Methods were thrown up and shot down in turn: String them up? Shoot them? Grenades, machine guns, mortars—each weapon was considered in turn. Some of them may have been scared inside, but today, with C Company, they were macho men. Salazar stared at the mountains in the distance—he couldn't wait to get into a firefight. The Rangers were ready for action.

Captain Prado, commander of B Company, was feeling similar emotions. He had been preparing for this moment his entire life. He'd grown up with his father's stories of the Chaco War and knew about the brutal battles, attacks, and casualties. Even in that losing war there were victories. This war, today, was Gary Prado's war. He was not going to lose.

Training was over. Prado and his men were prepared, both mentally and physically.

The guerrillas were trapped along the Rio Grande, just outside Vallegrande.

Once everyone arrived, Prado and the other company officers were summoned to a briefing with Colonel Zenteno. The mood was grim. Zenteno wasted no time. They all knew there had been skirmishes in the area and that the guerrillas had occupied the village of Alto Seco. The guerrillas had been there for less than twenty-four hours, but they had terrorized the town.

First, they cut the telegraph line linking Alto Seco to Vallegrande. Then the guerrillas rounded up all the men inside the school. The men expected violence, but what they got was a guerrilla recruiting pitch.

"You may believe that we are crazy to fight the way we're fighting," one of the guerrillas said. "You call us bandits, but we are fighting for you, for the working class, for workers who earn very little while the military has high salaries. You work for them, but tell me what do they do for you? You don't have water here, you don't have electricity, the telegraph isn't working. You are abandoned like all Bolivians. That's why we're fighting."

The speech was met with silence, the villagers told the army. The guerrillas left the next morning.

Then, Zenteno continued, three of the guerrillas were killed in a skirmish on a dirt road between the villages of Pucara and La Higuera. Intelligence had identified them—and concluded that Che Guevara was traveling with this band. That's why the Rangers were deployed so quickly from La Esperanza. The hunt was on. There was no time to waste. Trucks were requisitioned to move the first squads closer to the area.

Zenteno turned to the A Company commander. "I want you in the operations area tonight."

Captain Celso Torrelio Villa was struck dumb for a moment, then told Zenteno that not all his men and weapons had arrived in Vallegrande.

Prado interrupted. "My company is ready, sir," he blurted.

Zenteno nodded. "Very well, Captain Prado. You go in first."

For the next few hours the men loaded weapons, ammunition,

food, and medical supplies. As time approached to roll out, Prado gathered his men around him.

"The guerrillas were spotted near La Higuera. Three of them are dead. We know who they were, and we know they were traveling with Che," he told them. "You are on the most important mission of your lives."

Some of his men were scared. They looked at the ground to avoid eye contact. Prado felt anxious, too, but he couldn't let it show. That was one of Shelton's lessons: The officer sets the tone. If Prado was confident, his men would follow confidently.

"We are Rangers," he told his men, "the best-trained, best-armed—the elite of the Bolivian military. The enemy is on the run. We have the upper hand." He turned and spat on the ground. "We will destroy these men."

It was another long drive. The road ended in Pucara. Prado hired a guide to lead them the rest of the way to Vado del Oro, a fork on the Rio Grande where they could cut off the guerrillas' escape route. They loaded the contents of the trucks onto their backs and followed the guide along a footpath into the mountainous jungle. They marched until sundown, set up a patrol base, and waited for morning. They nursed cuts from razor-sharp grass and cacti. But sleep came easy that night.

The morning brought more of the same. At the head of San Antonio Canyon a man named Francisco Rivas told them his dogs had barked much of the night in the direction they were heading, and his dogs only barked at strangers. B Company searched the area. An hour later, a ragged man emerged from the trees, gasping for breath. He was one of Che's soldiers, he said. His name was Camba. He wanted to surrender.

The prisoner was filthy, with long greasy hair, a scraggly beard, and a wild-animal look in his eyes. To Prado, the man looked pitiful. He decided to put him to use. Once his soldiers were assembled again, Prado pointed to the man. "Look at this guy," Prado said. "Pathetic. A soldier of Che Guevara. Are you afraid of these guys? Look how they are. Are you still afraid?"

It was posturing. Prado felt a little embarrassed, but he thought it would give his troops a boost. The point was not lost on the men: They still did not know exactly how many troops Che had, but if they all looked like Camba, there was little to fear.

Camba was taken back to Vallegrande, where Major Miguel Ayoroa, the battalion commander, interrogated him with Captain Raul Lopez Leyton, the battalion intelligence officer.

Camba's real name was Orlando Jimenez Bazan, and he was from the Bolivian village of Beni. He said he'd trained in Cuba in 1962 and was recruited by one of Che's men. They'd been wandering the valleys near La Higuera for days, he said, and if he did not eat soon he would die. He had deserted. He didn't know where the rest of the group was headed, and he didn't give a damn what became of them. He didn't want any part of Che.

For Camba the revolution was over. He was lucky—he lived. He was tried by the military and sentenced to thirty years in prison. Camba was pardoned in 1970 and returned to his village.

Barrientos was ecstatic.

The tables had turned. His troops had Che trapped like a rat in the jungle. It was just a matter of time before the bastard was captured and brought to justice. It was an astonishing turn of events. Just a month earlier, everyone was predicting Barrientos's downfall. They were taking bets on which of his generals would lose patience first and seize power.

They underestimated me, Barrientos thought. All they had to do was look at his life. He'd clawed his way up from the tough streets of Cochabama to the presidential palace, and that didn't happen by accident—not in a country that admired daring and machismo. Che and the Communists talked a good game. They may have landed the first blow, but they'd taken on Barrientos. He wasn't just the most powerful man in Bolivia, he was a survivor. Now he was back in control. Che would soon be his. Nothing would be more satisfying.

Che was here in Bolivia, there was no longer any doubt. The interrogations, the documents, the goddam cigar butt even—everything pointed to Che being trapped. The guerrillas didn't appear to have an endgame. No one was coming to their rescue—not even the Cubans. At this point Che's guerrilla army wasn't fighting for revolution, it was fighting to survive. Che was probably desperately trying to find a way to escape, to just see another day.

Newspapers were beginning to hone in on that point. The *New York Times* asked if this was "Che Guevara's last stand." The story recounted the guerrillas' success: "In the early encounters with the Bolivian army patrols, who must rank among the worst-trained troops in the world, the guerrillas were murderously efficient; they expertly cut off escape routes, used their automatic weapons well, and showed a total command of tactics." The article said Samaipata was the rebel's "boldest stroke of the campaign." But in August, things began to change. "The guerrillas' supplies became short. The Bolivian Army began concentrating on containment rather than armed contact." Now the "dashing Che Guevara" is trapped in a canyon . . . mosquito-bitten and scorched by the sun."

Even the United States was beginning to praise Bolivia's army. After the ambush that killed Tania, Rostow told President Johnson in a memo: "The Bolivian armed forces finally scored their first victory—and it seems to have been a big one." It should do much to "boost morale" in the Bolivian Army. He added that the Rangers—the unit trained by the Green Berets—was headed to the battle zone.

To capitalize on the victory, a triumphant Barrientos attended Tania's funeral in Vallegrande. He went to the home of Honorato Rojas, the farmer who had betrayed Che's men, to shake the hand of a patriot. He put a price on Che's head, offering 50,000 bolivianos (4,200 U.S. dollars) to anyone who captured the rebel leader. Newspapers and radio stations carried Barrientos's statement, and airplanes dropped leaflets announcing the offer throughout the guerrilla area.

Barrientos wasn't the only one strutting. Ovando predicted publicly that Che would soon be captured. But until then, none of the high command would rest. It was one thing to predict victory. It was another to make sure it happened.

Mario Salazar sat down and took off his boots. C Company had been hiking all day in the mountains, trying to find guerrillas. The other companies, including Prado's, searched the arroyos nearby, but the only thing any of them got was blistered feet and aching backs.

The men were feeling the weight. Each carried a weapon and forty pounds of his own supplies. Several carried more: food, first-aid kits, ammunition, and camp supplies. Salazar wondered if the four bags of rice on his back would kill him before the guerrillas ever took a shot.

The worst was the hillsides, where the path dissolved into loose dirt and rocks. Their top-heavy rucksacks made it easy to fall. Everyone's hands and knees were scraped raw.

Salazar realized this was even more difficult than training in La Esperanza. There, they had always known they would be headed back to the barracks, where they'd sleep in a dry, safe room. Now they had to stay alert, not just for biting, stinging plants and animals. The guerrillas were right here, somewhere.

Salazar still wanted to see action. His fellows told him to be careful what he wished for. Yes, they were elites. Yes, they could handle Che. But no one wanted to die. Bad shit happens in firefights.

With the sun setting over the mountains, the men prepared a patrol base for the night. Salazar was one of the soldiers pulling security on the perimeter of the encampment. It was a bright starlit night—not a cloud in the sky—but it was getting a little cool. Salazar stared at the stars and wondered about his life. Would he make it out of here alive? When this was all over—and if he made it out safely—he'd go home and find a nice girl and start a family. And one day when his boy was old enough, he would tell him how he'd hunted Che in the mountains.

Still, Salazar prayed that no son of his would ever have to carry a gun, or wonder if a rebel might start shooting any minute. Salazar didn't mind so much fighting. If he did a good enough job, maybe his son wouldn't have to fight at all.

The days dragged on.

The Rangers' burdens lightened as the rations and supplies were consumed. But soon the food ran low, then ran out entirely. They started cutting edible plants and boiling them together with whatever kind of meat they could trap. Zenteno sent Villoldo into "the red zone" for a status report on the Rangers, and the CIA man was dismayed at the supply situation. As soon as he returned to Pucara, Villoldo let Zenteno have it. The Rangers were in desperate need, he said. Zenteno didn't seem to hear him. "General Ovando is thinking about requesting dry rations from Argentina," Zenteno said. "If we can't get supplies, we'll just have to pull back."

Villoldo knew they couldn't pull back now. Not with the Rangers so close to getting Che. Instead of waiting for Ovando to start filling out request forms, Villoldo decided to head back the next day to Santa Cruz to see if the CIA could help resupply the Rangers.

CHAPTER 20

Che

For Prado, it had been the same routine for nearly two weeks. His men were stationed at makeshift bases in three villages: La Higuera, Abra del Picacho, and Loma Larga. They got up early, consulted the maps, and spent the day conducting sweeps along the north and south banks of the Rio Grande. Soon they shifted their attention to the narrow canyons that fed streams into the big river.

By the end of each day, Prado's men were physically exhausted and anxious. They never had any idea if the day's hike would end in an ambush. Intelligence sent the same messages: Che's army was in tatters. No one knew if he had received any new troops.

In the jungles, anything was possible. Prado's soldiers had closed off the obvious entry point, but that didn't mean new recruits weren't flooding into the operations area some other way. That wasn't entirely out of the question.

October 8 looked to be much the same as the previous weeks. Dawn broke over El Churo Canyon, a steep godforsaken place with thickets of thorny bushes. Roosters crowed. The white mist rising from the canyon stream looked like dancing ghosts.

About 6:30 A.M. a campesino approached Second Lieutenant Carlos Perez at his patrol base in the hilltop village of La Higuera. Perez was the commander of the First Section of A Company. Pedro Peña was a farmer. Like many of the campesinos in the area, he was on the lookout for any strange men. The campesino had heard the radio reports and seen the Bolivian soldiers. He'd heard about the reward.

He told Perez that shortly after midnight, as he was irrigating his small potato field near a stream that ran through El Churo Canyon, he'd spotted a group of about seventeen men walking slowly along the riverbank. They set up a camp along the edge of the water.

Peña waited until dawn to go to La Higuera to inform the army.

Perez thanked the campesino, and immediately told Second Lieutenant Eduardo Huerta. They had to act quickly. Huerta took some men and headed down to the canyon. Following protocol, Perez immediately called Prado, the B Company commander.

He told Prado what the campesino had said, and asked the captain to bring mortars and light machine guns to help reinforce his operation.

This was the call Prado had been waiting for. As in a game of chess, the captain had been trying to figure out Che's next move. If he were Che, where would he go? What would he do?

Prado knew that if he were in a tight spot, he would move in the dark along the stream in the bottom of the canyon. You made the best time that way, and your pursuers weren't out looking for you. For the guerrillas, moving in the day would be suicidal. They could be spotted by air, or soldiers stationed on the high ground overlooking the stream.

Prado and his men arrived at the high ground near El Churo

Canyon. He made contact with Perez and Huerta and assumed command of the operation.

Prado knew the area well. He had been studying the landscape for weeks. El Churo Canyon was only about 330 yards long. At the southern end it merged with La Tusca Canyon and fed into San Antonio Canyon—the two upper canyons like the arms on a letter Y. Because the guerrillas had probably moved since the campesino saw them, Prado ordered Perez's men to enter through the upper part of El Churo, while the third section of B Company, under the command of Sergeant Bernardino Huanca, would do the same on the upper part of La Tusca. If they were still inside the canyons, the guerrillas would flee downstream, where Prado set up the command post and blocking position at the confluence.

Everything was ready by twelve-thirty. Prado stayed at the command post at the bottom while the troops swept down from the hills above. He didn't have time to think about his next move. Gunfire erupted almost immediately from the north end of El Churo.

Two of Perez's men fell. Prado ordered Huanca to speed up the search of La Tusca. He had his men train their machine guns and mortars at the confluence of El Churo and La Tusca. Prado was certain the guerrillas would appear any moment.

Moments later, the canyon erupted with a cacophony of machines guns and exploding mortars. There weren't many guerrillas, but they were armed. They quickly retreated back into the canyon, hidden by the dense vegetation. They were trapped. There was no way out.

Prado's men were in the perfect position. The slopes were steep and rose to open fields where the guerrillas could be seen if they fled. To reinforce the blocking position, Prado ordered two squads from A Company to the confluence to await Huanca's section, which was still moving slowly in La Tusca.

Prado's eyes were fixed on the confluence. He was confident the guerrillas would try again to break through. It was the only way out. The guerrillas again tried to penetrate through the narrow ravine, but were forced back into the brush.

Prado's heart was racing. His battlefield fear faded. He was cool and decisive. He grabbed the PRC-10 radio and called back to his base at Abra del Picacho. He described the situation to Second Lieutenant Tomas Totti, who radioed the Eighth Division headquarters in Vallegrande. They were under fire and needed a helicopter to evacuate the casualties. This was the news the commanders were waiting for—and they didn't want the guerrillas to get away. They dispatched two T-6 airplanes armed with machine guns and bombs, designed to support ground troops. Within a few minutes, the planes were overhead and asking for instructions: They wanted to know where to drop the bombs.

But Prado held them off. They couldn't drop bombs because his men were too close to the guerrillas—the Rangers could be killed alongside the guerrillas. He ordered the planes back to Vallegrande. Soon an evacuation helicopter arrived at the scene. The pilot was going to land at the command post, but Prado told him the guerrillas could hit the helicopter as it landed. Prado had no idea what kind of weapons the guerrillas had.

During the chaos, Huanca had concluded his search of La Tusca Canyon without finding a thing.

"What should I do?" he asked, his voice crackling over the radio.

"Move into the lower part of El Churo," Prado responded.

Prado wanted Huanca to continue on upward, to link up with Perez's section and clear out El Churo.

Huanca moved quickly to the front of his troops—he was an aggressive soldier. As the point man, he faced the most danger. His men hurried to keep pace. If the guerrillas were still in the canyon,

Huanca was going to find them. They ran straight into a volley of fire. His men fell back—one was killed, two more were wounded. They were too close now, and the enemy knew their position. Snatching a grenade, Huanca rushed toward the volley, firing his automatic and throwing the hand grenades. He killed two of the guerrillas and drove the rest deeper into the canyon. Huanca quickly consolidated his men and radioed Prado to report his casualties.

Prado acknowledged the call and jumped back on the radio to Vallegrande: "I have soldiers dead and wounded. Send me a medical person to take care of the wounded."

While Prado was talking, two of Prado's men spotted a pair of guerrillas moving toward the command post, their weapons at the ready. They let the men advance and, when they were a few feet away, ordered them to surrender.

The guerrillas lowered the weapons. One of the Rangers shouted to Prado:

"Captain. Captain. There are two here. We have caught them."

Prado scurried up the hill with Private Alejandro Ortiz and found two members of the guerrilla band. They were gaunt, covered in dirt, and showing signs of great fatigue.

Prado could tell the first was undoubtedly a foreigner. He had an impressive gaze, clear eyes, and a thick wild beard. He wore a jacket with a hood, a shirt with no buttons. Barely hanging on to his feet was a pair of homemade moccasins. In his right hand was a carbine. The other man was short and dark, with long hair and a little goatee.

As soon as Prado saw them, he ordered them to drop their weapons.

"Who are you?" Prado asked the taller man.

"I am Che Guevara," he answered in a low voice.

Prado was certain of his identify before he had asked the question. The distinctive shape of his face and beard made him an instantly recognizable figure to anyone who had seen his photographs. Now it was confirmed. Prado's heart raced, but he maintained his composure. He addressed the other man like it was no big deal.

"How about you?"

"I'm Willy," he replied.

"Are you Bolivian?"

"Yes."

"What is your real name?" Prado asked.

"Simon Cuba."

Prado turned back to the bigger man. Maybe it was someone who looked like Che, sent to throw them off his tracks. There was only one way to prove it. Prado asked Guevara to show him his left hand. The long scar was there beneath the dirt, right where the intelligence reports said it would be. There was no doubt this was Che.

Prado ordered his men to take the guerrillas' equipment. Ortiz collected everything Che was carrying: a pack, two knapsacks, a pistol at his waist, and five hard-boiled eggs he had been saving to eat. Another soldier picked up Willy's pack.

"They destroyed my weapon," Che said.

Prado noticed that his carbine had had its barrel perforated from a hit. "When was that?" Prado asked.

"When your machine guns began to fire. I'm also wounded."

Prado looked for the wound, but it was hard to find.

"I suppose you're not going to kill me now. I mean more to you alive than dead. We have always healed prisoners."

What arrogance, Prado thought. Even here, in the worst moment of his life, Che thought he was above it all, that somehow he would be able to walk away with no consequences. He'd invaded the country and tried to start a revolution that would topple the Bolivian government and impose Communist rule, and he felt superior enough to compare his forces and techniques to the Bolivians'.

No, Prado had no intention of shooting his prisoners. That's not what a good soldier does. That would violate every military principle—everything Prado had been raised to believe about the rules of engagement.

"We'll fix you up," Prado said. "Where is your wound?"

Che rolled up his pants and showed Prado his right leg. He had a bullet entry mark on his calf, with no exit mark. It was bleeding very little and the bone did not appear to have been touched.

Prado ordered his soldiers to take the guerrillas back to the command post.

"Can you walk?" Prado asked Che.

"If I have to," he replied, leaning a bit on Willy.

At the command post, Prado ordered the prisoners' feet and hands tied with their own belts. The pair sat down against a tree. Two of Prado's men stood guard, watching the prisoners' every move.

Prado turned his attention back to the ravine—he knew there were other guerrillas out there. It couldn't just be Che and Willy.

"Don't bother, Captain, this thing is all over," Che said.

Then Che—the picture of confidence, the icon of the revolutionary movement—hung his head.

Prado felt sorry for Che. He didn't want to, but for a moment, Prado identified with what Che was feeling. He looked so demoralized. Che knew his war was over, his hopes and illusions destroyed. So many people had died in this failed campaign. Now Che himself faced an uncertain future.

And for once, Che had nothing to say.

* * *

Leaving the prisoners under guard at the command post, Prado radioed Totti at the base. He told him to transmit the following message to Vallegrande:

"I have Papa Cansado and Willy. Papa slightly wounded. Combat goes on. Captain Prado."

"Papa" was the code name the Bolivian military gave to Che. "Cansado" means "tired," but on this mission it meant "in custody, wounded." When Vallegrande confirmed, Prado returned to the canyon to continue combing the area. Prado suspected the guerrillas would try to mount another attack, especially when they discovered Che was captured.

But within minutes, Prado heard Totti's voice crackle over his radio. Commanders were urgently requesting that Prado confirm Che's capture. Apparently the news had been received with skepticism, Prado thought. He lost patience. He replied that it was most certainly Che and that he had neither time nor any reason to make up stories.

Then Prado bolted into the canyon, followed closely by the medic Tito Sanchez, who was trying to reach a wounded soldier. When they reached Huanca's position, Prado was able to gauge the terrain and the situation close-up. Directly in front of him were rugged, well-protected grounds from which his soldiers' movements could be easily monitored. Not a good place to be.

When Huanca began advancing again to find the guerrillas, Prado and Sanchez spotted a wounded Ranger. Sabino Cossio was lying on his back; his uniform was pockmarked with bullet holes and soaked with blood. He was having difficulty breathing—each breath sounded like it might be his last. Although the Green Berets had trained Sanchez as a medic, he had few supplies. He just stood there with a dazed look on his face, panicking. Prado stared at him.

"You take care of him," the commander ordered.

Sanchez reached into his supplies, but couldn't find any bandages or dressings. Prado knew he had to get help quickly for the wounded soldier. He returned to the command post to call for more assistance, but as soon as he reached his position, Huanca radioed Prado and told him Cossio was dead.

Prado stopped.

For a moment, he was overcome with sadness. He knew death was part of being a soldier. You knew a bullet could end your life at any moment. But as a commander, he felt responsible. Sanchez came out of the canyon, his uniform bloody, his face contorted, and his eyes full of tears.

"Cossio died, Captain. There was nothing I could do."

Prado tried to calm him down. He told him not to lose hope. He reminded Sanchez that despite the loss of life, the mission had been a success. It seemed to work. The medic looked at Prado and said: "This is going to be over, Captain. That bum who was the head has fallen."

Under the tree nearby, Che was listening.

"The revolution has no head, comrade."

Maybe it was the tone. Maybe it was the hubris. Whatever the reason, Prado snapped. "Maybe the revolution you advocate has no head, but our problems end with you."

At that moment, a Bolivian soldier emerged from the canyon bleeding. It was Valentin Choque. He had two wounds, one in the upper part of his neck and the other in his back. Neither appeared serious. Sanchez reached into Che's backpack and removed a shirt to tear apart for bandages.

"Do you want me to treat him, Captain?" Che asked quickly.

"Are you by any chance a doctor?"

Che responded that he was a revolutionary first, "but I know medicine."

"No, let it go," Prado said.

Then Willy spoke up: "Captain, doesn't it seem cruel to you, having a wounded man tied up?"

He was referring to Che.

Prado knew Willy was right. So he ordered the men in charge of security to untie the prisoners' hands. Che asked if he could sip water from his canteen.

But Prado was wary about letting Che use his own canteen. He was worried that Che might be carrying poison and try to take his life. So Prado gave him his own canteen. After Che drank from it, he passed it to Willy.

"Can I have a cigarette?" Che asked.

Prado offered him one, but Che refused. They were Pacifics—a mild brand. He said he preferred strong tobacco. One of the soldiers had Astorias. Che smoked one of those.

Prado turned his attention back to the canyon. The guerrillas launched another attack, but Huanca's men returned fire, and the guerrillas fell back. Somehow the guerrillas found a break in the encirclement that allowed them to move some distance away. After another search, Prado's men couldn't find them.

At dusk, El Churo Canyon was clear. Prado withdrew his men to La Higuera, leaving behind a few troops to block the exits. The town was only a little over a mile distant.

After scaling the steep path, they were met by Major Ayoroa, who had come from Pucara when he heard the big news. He was hopping with excitement and peppered Prado with questions. Ayoroa peered at Che and couldn't believe it. It was really him. He was no ghost after all. And he looked nothing like the major had envisioned. He was emaciated, draped in tattered fatigues; he was a scarecrow, a hobo. Ayoroa and other Bolivian commanders knew they would all be up for promotions. They already were hard at work embellishing whatever role they had in the operation. As President Kennedy uttered after assuming responsibility for the Bay of Pigs fiasco: "Victory has a thousand fathers, but defeat is an orphan." All the fathers congratulated themselves that day.

Prado, though, was worried about the guerrillas still loose out there. The prisoner was his responsibility, and he had to get him safely delivered to La Higuera. Too many people were celebrating too soon. No one seemed to wonder if the guerrillas might launch an attack to free their leader.

The entry into La Higuera became a procession. Dozens of villagers lined the streets. The Rangers carried the bodies of their three fallen companions, followed by the wounded on three more stretchers. The dead guerrillas were dragged down the road by the collars of their shirts, and behind them walked Che and Willy, surrounded by a security detail. The dusty, tired Rangers followed in their turn. They were tired, but joyous. They had captured Che. The conflict was nearing its end.

The parade wound up at a tiny, one-room schoolhouse in the middle of the village. A partition divided the building into two classrooms, and a single window let in a shaft of sunlight. It was more a barn than a school. There were three thick wooden doors and a brown tiled roof that leaked when it rained.

Inside were a few chairs and a wooden bench. The floor was muddy. Prado placed Che in one room and Willy in the other, and the bodies of two dead guerrillas near the door. Guards surrounded the schoolhouse with orders to shoot to kill.

Prado set up his new command post at the telegraph operator's house. He sent a complete report of the day's events to division headquarters. He told them about the dead and wounded.

"Presume more casualties inside canyon. Due to late hour and difficult terrain, impossible to effect search and recovery over sharpshooters' resistance. Will continue operation tomorrow."

He requested a helicopter to La Higuera to evacuate the wounded and asked for more M-1 ammunition.

Then Prado undertook a detailed inventory of all the items in Che's backpack:

Two notebooks, containing Che's diary (one corresponding to November–December 1966 and the other to January–October 1967)
A notebook with addresses and instructions
Two notebooks with copies of messages received and sent
Two small codebooks
Twenty maps of different areas, updated by Che
Two books on socialism
One destroyed M-1 carbine
One 9-mm pistol with one clip
Twelve undeveloped rolls of 35-mm film
A small bag containing money (Bolivian pesos and dollars)

Prado sent the report to headquarters. A few minutes later, at 10 P.M., he received an urgent message from Colonel Zenteno in Vallegrande: Keep Che alive until he arrived by helicopter first thing in the morning.

CHAPTER 21

Papa Cansado

Rodríguez was rigging a homemade antenna for the PRC-10 radio on a Bolivian Air Force PT-6 turbo propeller plane when Prado's voice crackled over the speaker.

"Papa Cansado," he heard among the chatter.

At first, Rodríguez wasn't sure what he had heard.

"Papa Cansado," there it was again.

Since arriving in Vallegrande with the Rangers, Rodríguez had hung around the Eighth Division headquarters with Colonel Zenteno. When he wasn't working on the intelligence coming in from the field, he was at the airfield with the antennas and the PRC-10 radios. With one of Rodríguez's homemade antennas installed, a pilot could use the portable radio in his cockpit to communicate with soldiers on the ground below.

"Papa Cansado."

Rodríguez knew the codes, and almost instantly he knew what

the voice meant: "Papa" was Che, and "Cansado," or tired, meant he was captured and wounded.

They had captured Che.

The excitement hit him like a wave. At first, Rodríguez didn't believe that a bunch of green Rangers could have captured such a seasoned guerrilla in so little time. Maybe it was a mistake, a joke.

Rodríguez hustled back to headquarters. He could see the excitement in the Bolivian officers when he entered the building. But that enthusiasm soon turned to confusion. Had Prado's men really captured Che?

"We don't know for sure," Major Serrate, the division's operations officer, told Rodríguez when he arrived. "Come with me. Let's go see."

Serrate and Rodríguez returned to the tarmac. Two PT-6s with PRC-10 radios were ready and waiting. The propeller was spinning as Rodríguez climbed into one of the waiting planes, and Serrate climbed into the back of the lead aircraft. Rodríguez was barely belted in when the planes shot down the runway and climbed high into the crystal blue sky.

Just as the landing gear retracted, Rodríguez saw white smoke start to fill the cockpit. "What's wrong?" he shouted to the pilot in the seat in front of him.

"A short," the pilot shouted back. "A short in the electrical system."

Up front, Rodríguez watched as the pilot went through his checks and started to work on the plane's circuit breakers. Finally, the smoke thinned out. Since the plane was flying without problems, they continued. Turning north, they followed Serrate's plane. During the flight, the pilot realized that the firing mechanism for the rockets attached to the wings and the plane's .50-caliber machine guns were inoperable. If the soldiers on the ground needed support, the plane couldn't provide it.

But because of the radio installed by Rodríguez, they could talk with the soldiers on the ground. And for Rodríguez, that was the only reason he was racing over the jungles toward La Higuera.

Staring out the window, Rodríguez watched the jungle pass beneath the plane. For three months he'd tracked Che and his guerrillas through this hard terrain. They owed this all to Paco and his fabulous memory, Rodríguez thought. He hoped to God that "Papa" was Che and not just another bearded guerrilla in fatigues.

As the plane banked over the jungle near La Higuera, Rodríguez heard another radio message.

"Papa—*el extranjero*," the radio operator on the ground said. ("Papa is a foreigner.")

It was Che that Prado's Rangers had captured.

The planes circled over the valley for a while longer. Without guns to support the Rangers, the pilot started to buzz the treetops. Rodríguez held on in the back as the pilot dove toward the trees. The plane made a shrieking sound as it raced toward the ground. Then the pilot pulled back. The roar had to echo up and down the valleys and spook the guerrillas, who were running from the Rangers' air support. But the move was also a symbolic gesture, the pilot's tribute to the Rangers below.

After the bone-jarring dive, Rodríguez's plane headed back to Vallegrande. At the airfield, Rodríguez and Serrate met with Zenteno and confirmed Che's capture. Prado had sent an update with more information about Che.

"Not only did we capture him," Serrate said. "We recovered a lot of documents, including a journal."

Zenteno immediately ordered Selich, the commander who had

interrogated Paco, to La Higuera to question Che and seize the documents. Returning to the safe house, Rodríguez was disappointed that Selich had got the assignment. The Bolivian had shown poor judgment with Paco. But Rodríguez was only an advisor. He knew he couldn't interfere with Bolivian Army orders. But he had another plan.

Villoldo, meanwhile, was stuck. Hours before Che's capture, he and his CIA contact had decided to meet halfway between Vallegrande and Santa Cruz to pick up some money to buy supplies for the Rangers. He was on his way back when he heard about the battle over the command radio. Racing back to Vallegrande, Villoldo was shocked to hear the news. He was disappointed. He wanted more than anything to interrogate Che, and now he wasn't sure he would get the chance.

While Villoldo sped back to Vallegrande, Rodríguez put his plan in motion. Grabbing two bottles of high-end Ballantine's Scotch, he joined the other officers for dinner at the Vallegrande Hotel, where Zenteno was staying. Rodríguez had purchased the bottles a few days before in Santa Cruz, for just such an occasion. He wanted to celebrate in style.

Rodríguez sat with Zenteno and the others and toasted their victory. But in the back of his mind, Rodríguez wanted to be in La Higuera. He wanted to get face-to-face with Che before anything happened to the revolutionary. There was no doubt that Che might not survive for long, especially in Selich's custody—the officer had been ready to shoot Paco before Rodríguez took him in hand. Rodríguez knew he had to get to La Higuera if he was going to have any chance of getting Che out alive.

After a couple of rounds of whiskey, Rodríguez asked Zenteno a question.

"*Mi* Colonel, would you permit me to accompany you tomorrow morning to La Higuera to speak with the prisoner Ernesto Che Guevara?"

The other officers at the table all wanted to go as well. Zenteno took a few moments to consider the request. The helicopter could only accommodate two passengers and the pilot.

Finally, Zenteno rose. He stood straight and addressed the table. He told the officers that he knew they all wanted to go with him to La Higuera.

"But Félix has been tremendously helpful to us, and I want to thank him for all the cooperation he has shown us over these months," Zenteno said. "I also know how important it is for him to come face-to-face with one of the very Communists who forced him out of his country. How much it will mean to him to see with his own eyes Che Guevara. And so, if you don't oppose, I will take him with me tomorrow to La Higuera."

The officers were silent. Then, one rose and agreed that Félix should go. The others shouted their agreement, too.

Zenteno lifted his glass.

"To Bolivia," he said. "And to the return of peace for our country."

CHAPTER 22

"The revolution is not an adventure."

Prado watched his men celebrate. The camp in La Higuera was in a festive mood. Soldiers chatted and feasted and congratulated one another. It had cost the lives of three Rangers, but Che had been captured. In their minds, that meant the war was over. Without Che, there was no revolution in Bolivia.

Prado should have been celebrating, too. After all, it was his unit that captured Che. He should have been happy. Instead, Prado was uneasy. He decided to pay a visit to the schoolhouse.

The security guards in front of the building waved him through. First, Prado looked briefly in on Willy, who was fast asleep on a bench. Then he went to the room where Che was being held. A candle burned, illuminating the little space. Che was seated against the wall, his eyes closed. Totti was there, guarding the guerrilla leader. The bandage around Che's calf was spotted with blood. Che opened his eyes and saw Prado.

The Bolivian officer pulled out his pack of Pacific cigarettes and offered them to Che. This time, Che did not refuse. He took two, unrolled them, and placed the tobacco in the bowl of an old pipe he'd carried throughout the Bolivian campaign.

Prado wanted to hate Che for everything he had done—he was responsible for killing three men today, men Prado knew personally. He was responsible for stirring a revolution in Bolivia, and God-knew-what horrors he'd overseen in Cuba. But even sitting there in rags, there was still something charismatic about the man.

"How are you feeling?" Prado asked.

Che said he was feeling some pain. "That's inevitable, right?" Che said.

"I'm sorry we don't have a doctor with us," Prado said. "In any case, the helicopter will come first thing in the morning and you will be taken to Vallegrande. They will take better care of you there."

Che thanked Prado. They made some small talk, but Prado was curious about one thing: Why did Che pick Bolivia? Why did he want to start a revolution in one of the poorest nations in South America?

"I'd like to know firsthand the reason for this exploit of yours, which is so foolish, so senseless," Prado said.

"Maybe from your point of view," the revolutionary cut in.

Prado sat on a bench and lit a cigarette. He offered one to Totti, who plopped down next to Prado. The room filled with tobacco smoke.

"I have the impression that you made a mistake from the start by choosing Bolivia for your adventure," Prado said.

But Che stopped him.

"The revolution is not an adventure."

And Che reminded Prado of Bolivia's proud beginnings. Didn't the war of South American Independence start in Bolivia? he said, referring to Simón Bolívar, who fought colonial armies in Bolivia,

Venezuela, Colombia, and Ecuador in the 1800s. "Aren't you Bolivians proud to have been the first?"

But maybe it was a mistake to have chosen Bolivia, Che conceded, but the choice was not all his to make. The revolution needed a South American launching point. When they floated the idea, the most enthusiastic response came from Bolivians.

"What happened?" Prado asked. As far as Prado could tell, there were not many Bolivians among the guerrillas. Che shrugged his shoulders.

"Do you think we are going to solve problems this way," Prado went on, "with gunfire? As a result of this encounter, I have three dead and four wounded, whom I had learned to love and respect in the time we were together. I ask you: What am I going to say to their parents, when I talk about them and why they died?"

"For the fatherland . . . fulfilling their duty," Che said sarcastically.

"That sounds poetic, and you know it," Prado snarled. "That's why you're saying it in that tone. Give me a realistic answer."

But then Che said something that incensed Prado. He said Prado's background prevented him from truly understanding the campesinos and their troubles.

"It is you, sir, who does not understand. You don't understand Bolivia," the captain snapped. He reminded Che that Bolivia had a revolution in 1952. As a result, Indians were given rights. The military was temporarily disbanded. That revolution forced the ruling class to concede some of their power to the people. Prado ticked off a list of changes: land reform, universal suffrage—real changes you still can see, Prado said.

Che told Prado he understood. He was riding his motorcycle around Bolivia during that period, and he remembered the announcements and celebrations.

Prado shook his head. "But what you don't know, for example, is that I was educated at the military college after the revolution, with another mentality, with more sense of the people and the fatherland. Our army is part of the people."

"But it oppresses the people," Che said.

"The campesinos that looked at you so indifferently today? They show affection for my soldiers. Do they seem oppressed to you? Right now, they are out there cooking dinner for us."

The campesinos didn't understand what was going on in South America because of their poor education and lack of opportunity, the revolutionary said. "Their ignorance, the backwardness they are kept in, doesn't allow them to understand what is happening on this continent. Their liberation is on the way," Che told Prado.

Now Prado was angry.

"I was brought up in these valleys, these mountains. I had to walk two leagues from Guadalupe to Vallegrande to go to school together with the children of the campesinos. I have come across schoolmates here, friends of mine from childhood, and they are all willing to help us, to help the army. Those bonds are stronger than these ideas you bring in from the outside."

But Che was relentless. He told Prado that all Latin Americans were in a struggle against imperialism that "can no longer be stopped." He warned that there would be many deaths in that revolution and that eventually Prado and the soldiers in many Latin American countries would have to decide "whether you are on the side of your people or in the service of imperialism."

They continued to debate until a soldier barged into the room and told Prado that Major Ayoroa and Lieutenant Colonel Selich needed to talk to him.

"I'll be back later to continue our talk."

"I'll be here, Captain, I'll be here," Che said.

Prado walked to the command post, in the telegraph operator's house. Ayoroa and Selich were anxious. They wanted to go through Che's things, they said, but they needed to have Prado present in order to get started. They thumbed through his diaries. Che was a disciplined writer. He never missed a day. Entries were never longer than a page or two; sometimes it was just a few sentences. He simply summed up what had happened that day. Prado, Ayoroa, and Selich checked the diaries for dates that had been important during the guerrilla campaign. They read Che's comments on ambushes and skirmishes. They quickly realized the diaries' significance. In his last few entries, Che wrote about being trapped in the valleys. His last entry was dated October 7:

Today marks eleven months since our guerrilla inauguration. The day went by without complications, bucolically, until 12:30 p.m., when an old woman tending her goats entered the canyon where we were camped and had to be taken prisoner. The woman gave us no reliable information about the soldiers, simply repeating that she knew nothing, and that it had been quite a while since she had last gone there. All she gave us was information about the roads. From what the old woman told us, we gather that we are now about one league from Higueras, one from Jaguey and about two leagues from Pucara. At 5:30 p.m., Inti, Aniceto and Pablito went to the old woman's house. One of her daughters is bedridden and another is a half dwarf. They gave her 50 pesos and asked her to keep quiet, but held out little hope she would do so, despite her promises.

The 17 of us set out under a waning moon. The march was very tiring and we left many traces in the canyon where we had been. There were no houses nearby, just a few potato patches irrigated by ditches leading from the stream. At 2 a.m. we stopped to rest, since it was useless to continue. Chino is becoming a real burden when it is necessary to walk at night.

The army made a strange announcement about the presence of 250 men in Serrano, who are there to cut off the escape of those who are surrounded, 37 in number. They gave the area of our refuge as between Acero and Oro rivers. The item appears to be diversionary.

Altitude = 2,000 meters.

That was it. The next day Che was captured. When they were finished examining the materials, Prado, Ayoroa, and Selich returned to Che's room.

"How are you feeling?" Ayoroa asked.

"Fine," Che replied.

Ayoroa told Che that he would be taken to Vallegrande in the morning. Unlike the other two, Selich showed his disdain for Che.

"You'll have to look your best," Selich said. "There are a lot of people who will want to take your picture. How about if we shave you first?"

He leaned down to pull Che's beard.

Che stared straight into the officer's eyes. He calmly raised his right hand and pushed Selich's hand away. Selich moved back and laughed.

"Your parade is over," Selich said. "Now we're playing the tune. Don't forget it."

With that, Selich left the room.

There was an uneasy silence. Prado didn't like the way Che had been treated. He was a prisoner, helpless. Taunting him was wrong.

Ayoroa felt the same way. He continued questioning Che. "How many men are still available for combat?" he asked.

"I don't know," Che replied.

"Where were you going to meet? What was the rallying point?" Ayoroa said.

Che said they didn't have one. They were lost, surrounded by soldiers. "We had no place to go."

"So why did you come to La Higuera in the daylight?" Ayoroa was referring to the day they entered the village.

Che just shook his head.

"Who cares why? Have any more of my men fallen?"

"There are probably some inside the canyon that we haven't been able to find. We'll just look for them tomorrow. Why do you ask?"

Che took a deep breath.

"They were good people. I'm concerned about them, that's all."

"We'll keep you posted," Ayoroa said. "You should rest now. We'll see you tomorrow."

It was midnight. Prado and Ayoroa walked back through the narrow streets. The town was quiet now, with occasional merry outbursts from the military camp. In one area a group of soldiers were singing around a campfire. Battle cries and rival cheers between A and B companies were heard every so often. On the way, they met Second Lieutenant Huerta. He couldn't sleep. The three decided to check the security perimeters. It was about midnight, cold, with stars shining high over the mountains. Prado wondered what Rosario was doing tonight. He wished she was here, to hear him describe every detail of the day, to help him make sense of it. But he had to stay focused on the here and now.

At every checkpoint, the soldiers were alert and aware of their responsibilities. Satisfied, Prado told the men he was headed back to the command post to get a few hours of sleep.

There was too much on his mind. Prado replayed the day over and over—the firefight, the dead soldiers, and, of course, Che. At about 3 A.M. Prado rose to make the rounds one more time. He walked by the security checkpoints. Everything was in order. No matter where he ambled in this village, the road always seemed to lead back to the schoolhouse.

Finally, he just gave up and went inside. Perez was standing guard. Che was sleeping, but he opened his eyes when he heard Prado come into the room.

"Can't sleep, Captain?" Che asked.

"It's not easy after all that has happened. What about you? You're not sleeping either."

"No. I've forgotten what it's like to sleep soundly," Che said.

"Now you have an advantage. You don't have to think about your safety or the danger of being overtaken by the troops," Prado said.

"I don't know which is worse. There's also the uncertainty." He paused for a moment. "What do you think they'll do with me? They said over the radio that if the Eighth Division captured me they would try me in Santa Cruz, and if it were the Fourth, in Camiri."

"I don't know. I guess it will be in Santa Cruz," Prado said.

Che asked Prado about Zenteno, the division commander. Prado assured him he was a gentleman. Che paused for a moment and looked into Prado's eyes.

"You're unique, Captain. Your officers mentioned some things to me," he said, his voice trailing off. "Don't take it wrong, we had some time to talk. They appreciate you. That's obvious."

Prado was stunned. Che was praising him. He didn't know how to respond.

"Thanks. Can I do anything else for you, Commander?"

"Maybe a little coffee. That would be a big help."

"Try to rest," said Prado, before leaving the room. "Tomorrow begins another phase."

CHAPTER 23

Operation 500 and 600

Rodríguez arrived at the airfield early the next morning and checked his equipment.

He had a powerful RS-48 field radio with an antenna and battery. He carried two cameras—a Pentax 35mm and a tiny Minox. With his Bolivian uniform and cap, he looked like the other officers gathered at the airfield.

It was the morning of October 9, 1967. Rodríguez couldn't wait to reach La Higuera. He had been tracking the revolutionary for so long that it didn't seem real. Now Che was within his grasp, and if things went according to plan, he would soon be face-to-face with the most feared revolutionary in the world.

At dawn, Rodríguez wrote a long message to his CIA contact in La Paz. In it, he updated his superiors on the capture of Che and urged them to act quickly to protect Che's life. He encouraged the CIA station chief to work his channels immediately. But Rodríguez didn't have a lot of hope. The Bolivians had been killing prisoners.

A few months earlier, Ambassador Henderson had stepped in and pressed the Bolivian high command to spare Debray's life. It worked, but Rodríguez doubted the same would happen for Che.

When Zenteno showed up, Rodríguez climbed into the back of the helicopter. The colonel sat in the front next to the pilot—Major Jaime Nino de Guzman. A minute later, Guzman gripped the throttle and the helicopter shot into the sky. Banking to the north, Guzman set a course for La Higuera.

No one spoke as the helicopter flew over the mountains and jungles. Rodríguez was lost in his own thoughts. He checked his watch as the helicopter started its approach. It was 7:30 A.M. Several Bolivian soldiers stood waiting for their arrival. As the whine of the engine faded, Rodríguez heard mortar and gunfire nearby. He knew the Bolivian soldiers were still pursuing members of Che's guerrilla band. Maybe they were having some luck.

Prado was among the officers in the landing zone. When the bird landed, Zenteno and Rodríguez jumped out, and Lieutenant Colonel Selich and two wounded soldiers boarded the helicopter. Moments later, they were whisked away to Vallegrande. Shuttle flights between the two points would continue all day.

Prado told Zenteno and Rodríguez that Che was resting inside the village schoolhouse. Che's belongings were inside the command post at the telegraph office.

Prado wasted no time. He led Zenteno and his entourage to the command post in the center of La Higuera. Rodríguez followed a few steps behind. There wasn't much room for a village up here on the hilltop, he thought, but the views were spectacular. The stone houses were small, and a single dirt road ran from the town square all the way to Vallegrande.

As they walked, Prado asked what would happen to Che. The

colonel said he'd received no instructions. That decision would come from Barrientos himself.

Once at the command post, Prado showed Zenteno and Rodríguez a haversack filled with documents. Zenteno took a cursory look. He knew there would be time to examine the documents later. As for Che? No one really knew. So Zenteno said he wanted to head to the schoolhouse and confront Che in person. But as Rodríguez thumbed through the notebooks, he realized he had hit the mother lode. There were photographs, microfilm, and a list of "accommodation addresses" in Paris, Mexico, and Uruguay. Guerrillas sent messages to the addresses. Essentially, Che could send a letter to Castro and the recipient at the address would forward it on.

Rodríguez also found two codebooks. The numerical codes were printed on tissue paper and used one time and thrown away. One set was in black ink, for transmitting, and the second was in red ink, for receiving.

Putting the codebooks aside, Rodríguez flipped open a big German-made diary. Inside were pages of notes and entries written in Che's hand. The stylish cursive chronicled the entire revolutionary campaign in Bolivia. It was unbelievable, Rodríguez thought. He'd kept a diary. Now they could backtrack his daily movements.

The bag also contained several Guevara family snapshots, and a black mask and medicine for his asthma.

Rodríguez didn't have time to carefully go through all the materials. That would come later. He returned them to the bag and followed Zenteno to the schoolhouse. Prado pointed to the door on the far left. Che lay inside on the dirt floor. His arms were tied tightly behind his back and rope bound his feet together. Nearby were the expanding corpses of two Cuban officers who had followed Che to Bolivia: Antonio and Arturo.

Rodríguez noticed Che's leg wound right away. Blood was oozing from the gash. For Rodríguez, this should have been a moment of celebration. Even after all his years working toward this moment, all he could feel was pity. Che was a filthy beaten dog. He looked like a beggar.

"Why did you choose to come to Bolivia?" Zenteno asked Che. The guerrilla ignored him.

"How did you enter my country?"

Che didn't respond.

"Why do you fight against my government?"

The question was again met with silence. Rodríguez could hear Che breathing, his cheek pressed against the dirt floor.

After a few more questions, Zenteno was exasperated.

"The least you could do is answer my questions," Zenteno said. "After all, you are a foreigner and you have invaded my country."

Zenteno motioned for Rodríguez to follow him outside. As the two men stood in front of the school, Zenteno expressed his frustration. Che could fly all over the world giving great speeches about *la revolución*. Yet on a dirt floor—with his life at stake—he was speechless. He was a damn mute.

Rodríguez, meanwhile, had to suppress his urge for revenge. His pity had morphed to anger. He had to keep reminding himself he was there as a representative of the U.S. government—not as an exiled Cuban freedom fighter. In his head, Rodríguez started to make a list of what needed to be done. The first thing was the documents.

"*Mi* Colonel, I'd like to photograph all of the captured documents," Rodríguez said to Zenteno.

Zenteno agreed. He warned Rodríguez to take care of business quickly because Barrientos was anxious to see them. For the moment, Zenteno said he'd had enough of Che. He was heading out to

El Churo Canyon with Prado to watch the troops hunt down the remnants of Che's guerrillas.

When they left, Rodríguez picked up the documents and raced to the telegraph operator's house, the only place in the village with a telephone. On a sunlit table outdoors, he unpacked the RS-48 radio and started to spread out the captured documents.

Rodríguez started the painstaking camera work. He had to hustle. He didn't know how long he would have, and this stuff was dynamite.

The president was a bundle of nerves. Now that Che had been captured, he had to decide what to do with him. Barrientos called an emergency meeting with General Ovando, Air Force general Jorge Belmonte Ardile, and a few of his closest advisors.

In Barrientos's mind, there were only two choices: prison or death. There was no way they were going to send Che to Cuba. That was out of the question.

Although very few people knew that Che was in custody, the pressure had started to mount. Ovando, Belmonte, and members of the Bolivian high command had been taking a late lunch at a La Paz country club when they received the message: Che had been captured. They rushed out, catching the attention of Ernest Nance, the U.S. Defense Intelligence Agency attaché to the embassy in La Paz. When Nance found out why they had left so quickly, he sent a message to Washington saying: "This is the first notification to the world of the capture of Che Guevara." It was Sunday, and Nance was unsure whether anyone would get the message. Still, he tracked down Ovando and Belmonte and urged them to spare Che. They promised him nothing.

At the meeting in the presidential palace, Barrientos asked his commanders for their advice. One by one, they said putting Che on trial would be a disaster. Look what happened when they arrested Debray. It brought on an international shit storm. Governments lobbied Bolivia to spare Debray's life. The story attracted international attention. It was a public relations nightmare. All because an insignificant Marxist like Debray came to Bolivia for a taste of the revolutionary life. Imagine what would happen if they put Che on trial?

Ovando reminded Barrientos that Bolivia had no death penalty. With a trial, the most they could give Che was thirty years in prison. "Where do we keep Che for thirty years?" Ovando asked. There wasn't a prison in Bolivia secure enough to hold him. He would have to be kept under armed guard twenty-four hours a day. Che-inspired revolutionaries would storm the prison. Hell, Cuba might send troops to try to rescue him. They had no choice but to execute him, Ovando argued.

Barrientos listened intently. He would have the final say. But the more he pondered Che's fate, the angrier he became. This revolutionary had killed innocent Bolivian soldiers. He had tried to incite a revolution that would have killed thousands. Executing Che would send a clear message: Don't fuck with Bolivia. Barrientos remembered the promise he made to the CIA's Villoldo: It ends here.

Death it would be.

Rodríguez snapped pictures like a photographer at a fashion show. He wanted to make sure that he copied every page of the diary. He heard bursts of gunfire in the distance. Nearby, two more guerrillas were brought into town. One had been shot in the face and was in considerable pain. The other one was dead. Both were placed by Rodríguez's table and later moved to the schoolhouse.

Around 10 A.M., a Bolivian soldier interrupted Rodríguez.

"Phone call," he said. "Headquarters, Vallegrande. They want to talk to the highest ranking officer," the soldier said.

Rodríguez looked around. Zenteno was still out at the command post, coordinating the battle. Rodríguez held the rank of captain and at that moment was the most senior officer present. Rodríguez grabbed the phone.

"Captain Ramos," he said, using his alias.

"Ramos. You are authorized by the Superior Command to conduct Operation 500 and 600," said the voice on the phone.

Rodríguez knew the code. 500 was the numerical code for Che. And 600 meant dead. The Bolivians wanted to execute Che. Rodríguez swallowed hard.

"Can you repeat your message?" Rodríguez said.

"You are authorized to conduct Operation 500 and 600."

If the Bolivians wanted Che alive, the message would have been 500 and 700. Che was short by one hundred. But Rodríguez also knew the United States wanted to smuggle Che to Panama for interrogation. It was of supreme importance to the intelligence officers at CIA headquarters in Langley, Virginia.

Shit, Rodríguez thought.

He was in a quandary, a deep fucking hole. Rodríguez said nothing. He hung up the phone. He went back to shooting photos while his mind raced through his options.

Zenteno returned an hour later. Rodríguez stopped his work, grabbed the colonel, and passed along the order, and then asked Zenteno to reconsider.

"My instructions from the United States government are to keep him alive under any circumstances," he said.

But Rodríguez had used up his credits the night before when he asked for a ride to La Higuera. This time, the commander just shook his head no.

"Félix, we have worked very closely, and we are grateful for all the help you have given us," Zenteno said. "But don't ask me to do this. If I don't comply with my orders to execute Che, I will be disobeying my own president."

Zenteno needed to get back to Vallegrande. He glanced at his watch and then turned his attention back to Rodríguez.

"I know how much harm he has done to your country," he said. But there was nothing he could do. It was eleven. The helicopter would continue flying between La Higuera and Vallegrande, evacuating the dead and wounded and resupplying the troops with food and ammunition, until it wasn't needed anymore.

"At two P.M., I will send back the helicopter," Zenteno said. "I would like your word of honor that at that time you will personally bring back the dead body of Che Guevara to Vallegrande."

There was nothing Rodríguez could do. It was easy to give an order to keep Che alive—just look at the guys sitting behind the desks at Langley. Out here, oh God. This was a different story.

Zenteno could tell Rodríguez was struggling. He gave him some options. "The manner in which you deal with Che is up to you. You can do it yourself if you want, as I know how much harm he has brought to your country."

Rodríguez understood that Zenteno was only following orders. But Rodríguez had to follow his orders, too—and they were to keep Che alive. He tried one more time. He asked Zenteno to get them to try to change their minds. "But if you cannot get the counterorder, I give you my word as a man that at two P.M., I will bring you back the dead body of Che Guevara."

Zenteno embraced Rodríguez, then headed to the field where the helicopter waited.

Standing by the table scattered with Che's diary and codebooks, Rodríguez took a deep breath. For a moment, he considered trying to break Che out and smuggle him to La Paz. There was only one phone in town. He could cut the line, severing communications with Vallegrande. And when the helicopter came back for Che, he would lie and tell the pilot they really wanted Che alive. Once back at Vallegrande, it would be harder to kill him.

But Rodríguez remembered how wily this man was, his hands stained red with the blood of Cubans, how Castro had been jailed, too, and returned to destroy Cuba. He knew Che was more dangerous than a viper as long as he remained alive. Ideas ping-ponged through Rodríguez's brain, but each one ended with the same conclusion. He had exhausted his ability to change the order through regular channels, and even if at the moment he was dressed like a Bolivian officer, he was just a CIA advisor, an outsider. He had no choice. This was their country. These were their rules.

If I have to do it, I will put him in front of a firing squad and execute him the same way he assassinated so many of my friends at La Cabana Fortress, Rodríguez thought.

But suddenly, as if someone could read his mind, gunfire erupted from the schoolhouse. Racing to the left door, he shoved it open and saw Che still alive on the dirt floor. In the room next door stood a soldier holding a smoking rifle. Willy was lying over a small table, the last seconds of his life slowly ticking away. The soldier looked at Rodríguez. His eyes were wide with fear.

"*Mi capitan*, he tried to escape," the soldier said.

Rodríguez knew better. The soldier was making sure there were no prisoners. Like Willy, Che was leaving La Higuera a dead man. But before Che died, Rodríguez wanted to talk with him.

Rodríguez stepped back into Che's room. There was an uneasy silence. He didn't have to say a word about the gunfire. Che knew what had just happened.

Rodríguez stared at Che again and tried to reconcile the man in front of him with the dashing revolutionary depicted in hundreds of newspapers, books, and magazines. He had studied the pictures of Che in China and Moscow. In those photos, he was handsome, chic in his guerrilla fatigues. He could have had anything in the world—flashy clothes, money, fast cars, and beautiful women. Instead, he opted for life on the run, fighting, plotting, killing. But look at him now. Was it worth it?

Rodríguez stood above Che just as the guerrilla leader had done to Nestor Pino, one of Rodríguez's fellow Cuban patriots after the Bay of Pigs. Pino, a company commander in the paratrooper battalion, had been captured and beaten by Castro's men. Lying in a fetal position, he tried to protect himself as blows cascaded down on him. Then they stopped suddenly. Standing over him, with polished black boots, was Che.

"We're going to kill you all," Che told Pino.

Luckily, Pino survived the beating, and he later recounted the story to Rodríguez. Now the roles were reversed. Che was lying at Rodríguez's feet.

"Che Guevara, I want to talk to you," Rodríguez said.

"Nobody interrogates me," Che said, still clinging to the last shreds of his command.

"*Comandante*," Rodríguez said, giving full rein to his native Cuban accent. "I didn't come to interrogate you. Our ideals are different. But I admire you. You used to be a minister of state in Cuba. Now look at you. You are like this because you believe in your ideals. Even though I believe they are mistaken, I have come to talk to you."

"Would you untie me? May I sit?" Che asked, eyeing Rodríguez.

"Of course. Take the ropes from Commander Guevara," Rodríguez told the soldier standing in the door. The man looked at him incredulously, but he followed orders. Che groaned as the ropes were loosened. The soldier helped Che onto the wooden bench.

"Do you have any tobacco for my pipe?" Che asked.

Rodríguez got a cigarette from one of the Bolivian soldiers and gave it to Che, who stripped the paper, stuffed the tobacco into the pipe, lit it, and inhaled.

Rodríguez pressed Che about his operations and plans. The guerrilla leader begged off.

"You know I cannot answer that," he said.

Rodríguez changed tactics. He knew the clock was ticking—the helicopter would return at 2 P.M., and Rodríguez would have no more chance of winning Che over. So Rodríguez stuck to simple, broad questions about the revolutionary's philosophy. The guerrilla leader opened up.

"*Comandate*, of all the possible countries in the region, why did you pick Bolivia to export your revolution?"

Che took a draw off his pipe and paused for a second. It was the same question Prado had asked him.

"We considered other places," Che said. He rattled off names: Venezuela, Central America, Dominican Republic. But in each spot, the United States had reacted quickly to counter the threat. "We figured that by picking a country so far from the U.S., it wouldn't appear to present an immediate threat," Che said.

He took another puff and admitted to Rodríguez that he had been looking for a poor country.

One more thing, he continued, Bolivia shared boundaries with five countries. "If we are successful in Bolivia, then we can move into other places—Argentina, Chile, Brazil, Peru, Paraguay," he said.

Rodríguez asked why the Bolivians didn't offer any support. Che made up excuses, including that the campesinos wanted a "*co-*

mandante Boliviano," not a Cuban, "even though I am an expert in these matters."

Cuba quickly became a topic. Rodríguez wanted to take Che to task over his country's faltering economy. It was in shambles, thanks in part to Che's leadership of the Cuban National Bank. Che blamed the poor economic conditions on the U.S. boycott. "But you helped cause that," Rodríguez responded. "You, a doctor, were made president of the Cuban National Bank. What does a doctor know about economics?"

The revolutionary chuckled. "Do you know how I became president of the Cuban National Bank?" Che asked.

"No," Rodríguez said, shaking his head.

"I'll tell you a funny story. We were sitting in a meeting one day, and Fidel came in and asked for a dedicated *economista*. I misheard him. I thought he was asking for a dedicated *communista*, so I raised my hand. And that's why Fidel selected me as head of the Cuban economy."

To Rodríguez, it wasn't funny. Too many people in Cuba were suffering under the harsh Communist regime. Not only were they living in a police state, they had little food or medicine. They had become totally dependent on foreign aid—most of it from the Soviet Union.

Rodríguez and Che talked for an hour and a half. They discussed politics and life.

But when Rodríguez heard the helicopter approaching the village, he excused himself and went outside. He looked at his watch. It was still too early. He had promised Zenteno he would deliver Che by 2 P.M. and it wasn't even 1 P.M.

After the helicopter landed, the pilot, Nino de Guzman, walked over to Rodríguez and handed him a camera. He said Saucedo, the intelligence officer, wanted a picture of Che as a souvenir. Like a sportsman, he wanted to remember the hunt.

Rodríguez helped Che limp outside. De Guzman gave Rodríguez the camera, which was set correctly. But Rodríguez didn't want to get Saucedo in trouble, so he changed the speed and aperture, so the picture would never come out. Rodríguez pointed the camera and snapped a photo of Che with Nino de Guzman.

Rodríguez then set the exposure on his camera to get an accurate picture for himself and gave it to Nino de Guzman.

"Watch the little birdie," Rodríguez said, standing next to Che.

Che smiled, but quickly turned grim when Nino de Guzman hit the shutter. It was almost the same scowl he had worn in the Hotel Copacabana in La Paz, when "Adolfo Mena Gonzales" snapped his own portrait, a long time before.

Back inside the schoolhouse, Rodríguez continued their conversation, asking Che about the firing squads at La Cabana.

"We only put to death foreigners," Che said. "Imperialistic agents and spies who had been sent by the CIA."

The irony was not lost on Rodríguez, who called Che on it immediately.

"You're not a Bolivian," Rodríguez said. "You are a foreigner. You have invaded sovereign Bolivian territory."

Che was defiant, saying Rodríguez couldn't possibly understand the reasons for revolution. Che pointed to his bloody leg. "I'm spilling blood here in Bolivia." Then he pointed to the corpses in the room with him. One was Antonio.

"Look at this one," Che said. "In Cuba, he had everything he wanted. And yet he came here to die like this. To die because he believed in his ideals."

Now it was Che's turn to call out Rodríguez. It was obvious

both men were fighting a proxy war in Bolivia, and neither one cared much for the fate of the South American country. Theirs was a bigger fight.

It was democracy versus communism.

It was good versus evil.

It was the United States versus the Soviet Union and China.

In the fall of 1967, it was a fight being waged all over the world.

"You are not Bolivian," Che said. "You know too much about Cuba and me."

"No, I am not," Rodríguez said. "Where do you think I am from?"

Che didn't hesitate. "I believe that you work for the intelligence service of the United States."

Now it was Rodríguez's turn to smile.

"You're right, *comandante*," Rodríguez said. He told Che that he was Cuban. That he had been a member of the 2506 Brigade. In fact, he was a member of the infiltration teams that operated inside Cuba before the invasion at the Bay of Pigs.

"What's your name?" Che said.

"Félix. Just Félix, *comandante*," Rodríguez said.

Rodríguez wanted to say more, but he held back. No, what good would it do at this point? Rodríguez knew he needed to get back to the table and continue copying the documents. As he left the room, he told Che he would return.

At the table, Rodríguez continued snapping pictures of the papers. He stopped when the village's schoolteacher approached him.

"When are you going to shoot him?" she asked.

"Señora, why do you say that?" Rodríguez asked.

She told Rodríguez she saw him take a photo with Che. But the radio was reporting that the guerrilla leader had already died from combat wounds.

Shit, he thought. With news reports of Che's demise already broadcasting, he could no longer stall the inevitable. It was time.

Before Zenteno had left La Higuera, he had asked for two volunteers to execute the prisoners. Warrant Officer Mario Teran and Sergeant Huanca, whose actions in battle had led to Che's capture the day before, stepped forward. The plan was simple: Huanca and Teran would simultaneously enter the separate classrooms. Huanca would shoot Willy; Teran would kill Che. But Willy was already dead. Only Che was left.

Walking back down the hill to the schoolhouse, Rodríguez went into the classroom where Che was still sitting on the little bench. Rodríguez stood in front of him. Teran, meanwhile, was waiting outside the door.

"*Comandante*," Rodríguez said. "I have done everything in my power, but orders have come from the Supreme Bolivian Command."

Che's face turned pale. He knew at that moment that death stood at the door.

"It is better like this, Félix," Che said. "I should never have been captured alive."

"If I can, is there anything you want me to tell your family?"

Che replied: "Tell my wife to get remarried and try to be happy."

Che approached Rodríguez. They shook hands and then embraced. Che was a man—a man facing his end with dignity. Rodríguez didn't hate him anymore.

Rodríguez released Che and walked outside. He stepped over to Teran and gave the Bolivian his instructions. "Don't shoot from here up," Rodríguez said, pointing above his neck. "This man was supposed to die from combat wounds. Don't shoot at the face."

"*Sí, mi capitan*," Teran said.

Rodríguez walked fast up the hill to finish photographing the documents, putting as much distance as possible between himself and the schoolhouse. No, he didn't want to see it. As a soldier he'd never killed a prisoner in cold blood.

A few minutes after he reached his table, Rodríguez heard a short burst of fire. He looked down at his watch and recorded the time: 1:10 P.M.

After a firefight and sweep of the canyon, Prado and his men headed back to La Higuera to regroup. He was proud of his soldiers. They didn't panic during the skirmish. They had lived up to their billing as an elite fighting unit. He was thrilled that Zenteno had watched them in action.

As Prado approached the village, Ayoroa greeted him, but something was wrong. Ayoroa blurted out the news: Che had just been executed on the "highest orders."

Prado was stunned. That wasn't what he'd been expecting. Prado picked up his pace, moving faster and faster, until he arrived at the schoolhouse. He rushed inside and saw the body. He knew Che was dead, but nothing could have prepared him for this. The body was riddled with bullets. Blood was spattered on the floor and walls. The schoolroom was a slaughterhouse, and it now was filling up with spectators.

Prado examined Che's face. His eyes were open, staring into his own. Prado shook his head in disgust. Just hours ago, Che was here, discussing imperialism and Bolivia. Now this was all that remained of him, a face gray and distorted. Prado was outraged. It's one thing to kill in combat. That's what soldiers do. But this was flat-out murder. Killing a prisoner in cold blood violated everything Prado had been taught about treating prisoners with respect.

Prado didn't like what Che stood for, or what he had done to his country. But that didn't mean they had to use the same brutal tactics he did. That's why they had courts. That's why they had courts-martial.

Without warning, one of the officers in the room struck Che in the face above his eyebrow, opening up a small gash. Some soldiers put their feet on the body.

"You son of a bitch," one soldier screamed at the lifeless figure on the ground. "You have killed so many of my soldiers."

Rodríguez and Prado looked on. Neither man felt the need to desecrate the corpse.

To prevent further deformation of Che's face, Prado took his handkerchief and placed it around the guerrilla leader's lower jaw. Then he tied a knot in the handkerchief at the top of Che's head. Someone remarked that Che looked as if he had a toothache. Nobody laughed at the joke. Rodríguez called for a bucket of water. Kneeling next to Che's body on the muddy floor, he cleaned the guerrilla's face.

Time was short. Rodríguez dashed to the telegraph office and shot off a short message to the CIA station in La Paz about Che's execution. His boss, John Tilton, wasn't there, but surely someone would get the message and pass it along. Rodríguez had done everything he could. The news was on its way to Langley and the White House. He gathered his things and headed back to the school. The two o'clock helicopter was landing.

A group of soldiers arrived with it and loaded Che's body onto a canvas stretcher. They carried it to the airstrip and secured it to the helicopter's landing skid. As he was helping tie the rope, Rodríguez's hand slipped under Che's body. When he pulled it out, it was covered in blood. Rodríguez wiped it on his pants.

He clambered into the back of the helicopter and waited for it to take off. But the helicopter stood still, its rotors turning. Rodríguez spotted a mule trotting up the road, a priest on its back. The old man stopped short of the spinning rotors and scuttled, head bowed, over to the body. He made the sign of the cross and gave a benediction. Rodríguez was amazed at the irony. A hardened Communist and atheist was receiving the last rites.

The helicopter lifted off for Vallegrande. Prado watched it go, and pondered the empty feeling in his chest. The image of Che's torn body would stay with him for years.

CHAPTER 24

End Game

Rodríguez's head rang with helicopter din as he stared at the tangle of jungle below. Perched on the narrow bench behind the pilot, he shifted his weight to balance out the helicopter's flight path. Che's body was tied like a package on the right landing skid. Rodríguez hoped they'd fastened it tight enough. The last thing they needed was for the corpse to plummet into the forest. It was going to be hard enough explaining how Che died.

Rodríguez remembered what the schoolteacher had told him: Official radio broadcasts claimed that Che was killed in battle. Killed in battle? How the hell were they going to pull this off? Journalists would soon be crawling over La Higuera like cockroaches. They would uncover the truth in no time. Rodríguez didn't know how the Bolivian government was going to cover its ass.

Rodríguez took a deep breath. With Che dead, this was the first time since he'd arrived in Bolivia that he had time to reflect. He was twenty-six years old, but he had fought the Communists for almost a decade. Now he was bringing back one of the ultimate prizes. His three months of hard labor had borne strange fruit.

Crammed inside the helicopter, Rodríguez had a hard time keeping his thoughts on the job. His wife and two young children didn't know where he was, or when he would come home. Rosa wasn't naive; she had a good idea of what he was doing. But Rodríguez wondered if he would ever be able to tell his kids the whole story. It couldn't be easy for them, having a dad who disappeared and reappeared for months at a time.

He loved those kids. But deep down, Rodríguez knew he would always be a soldier. He had fought Castro and the spread of Communism for most of his life. Che's death was just one small victory in a longer war. Rodríguez would go where he had to in order to fight it.

The jungle soon melted into mountain as the helicopter approached Vallegrande. Rodríguez hoped they would land near the barracks and not at the airport, where there would undoubtedly be a crowd.

"Landing soon?" he asked Guzman.

He nodded his head yes. "But not where you thought," he screamed over the rotor. "They ordered us straight to Vallegrande Airport."

Since the hunt for Che started, Vallegrande had been teeming with journalists. What Rodríguez didn't know was that two stories had already been published in Bolivian newspapers about Che's capture. From the air, Rodríguez spotted the airfield. It was mobbed—at least two thousand people. Reporters and photographers pushed as near as they could to the landing zone.

Rodríguez's mission was still secret. None of the Bolivians knew his real name. Rodríguez didn't want to be photographed with the body. There were already rumors that the CIA was helping the Bolivians. Rodríguez didn't want to give them confirmation.

The helicopter descended at 5 P.M. The mob surged forward to catch a glimpse of the body. The craft settled onto the pavement, and the crowd took a step back—no one wanted to get hit by the rotor. Time to escape. Tugging his Bolivian army cap down over his eyes, Rodríguez exited the left side of the helicopter. The crowd moved toward the body on the right landing skid. Moving as quickly as possible, Rodríguez disappeared into the crowd. To onlookers, he was just another Bolivian officer.

Villoldo waited on the other side of the chopper. He'd returned to Vallegrande earlier that day and met with Zenteno. They discussed how to handle the press, and now he had to help dispose of the guerrilla leader's body. When the helicopter landed, Villoldo and the Bolivian soldiers untied the stretcher and loaded it into an old gray ambulance. It was whisked down the narrow dirt and cobblestone streets to Neustra Señora de Malta Hospital.

Instead of taking him inside the main building, the soldiers carried Che to a laundry room, a small structure on the hospital grounds. The building was open on one side and housed a long concrete basin with a spigot and hose. The staff started work on Che's body. They removed his jacket and shirt, opened an incision in his neck to drain the tissue fluid, then washed down the body.

Drs. Moises Abraham and Jose Martinez Caso examined the body and took notes on a small pad. Villoldo stood in the back and watched. In his green army fatigues, he blended in with the other officers.

Che had gunshot wounds in both collarbones, with a compound fracture in the right one. Three bullets had peppered his rib cage, another had struck his left breast. The shots smashed into his lungs.

Slugs were found in his vertebrae. The autopsy report listed eight wounds in all. The doctors determined that Che had died from "chest wounds and consequent hemorrhage."

Villoldo stared at the body. He thought about the thousands of other bodies washed and blessed and buried, all the lives this man had stolen and destroyed. Che was responsible for so many deaths. But most of all, Villoldo thought about his father's body, the way it had looked curled up on the guest-room bed. This man had hurt his family. And now it was Villoldo who'd helped put an end to his deranged revolution.

With the examination complete, the army permitted journalists and the thousands of curious Bolivians waiting outside a glimpse of Che, the mysterious guerrilla leader who had terrorized the nation for months.

Quiet, stern campesinos filed past the makeshift bier. Flashlights danced along the walls and floor as they shuffled inside the laundry room. Once inside, the flashlights eventually stopped on the gaunt figure with the thick beard. Che looked remarkably Christ-like in death. His chest was bare, his wounds fully displayed. His hair was matted, his mouth slightly opened, and his dark eyes stared into oblivion. Even the Bolivian soldiers who had hunted him for so long were spooked. They paused to stare at the dead revolutionary until the guards ordered them to keep moving.

Hours later, when the crowd thinned, the soldiers blocked off the room.

Then the doctors did the unthinkable—they cut off both of Che's hands. Castro could deny Che's death, they said. This way they had proof that Che was really gone. Prints were lifted from Che's amputated hands, which were then placed in jars of formaldehyde for safekeeping.

Now they would have to find a way to get rid of the rest of the body.

Rodríguez could see the lights of Santa Cruz in the distance. It had been a long night. Hell, the last twenty-four hours had been a blur.

After he left the helicopter, Rodríguez searched the crowd for Serrate, the operations officer, and Saucedo, the intelligence officer. The trio embraced. Rodríguez told them about his conversations with Che. They listened intently to the story and congratulated Rodríguez. Che was dead. The mission was a success. They could all move on.

On the walk back to the safe house he shared with Villoldo, Rodríguez felt an odd sensation grip his chest. He wheezed as his lungs tightened—he could draw a deep breath in but couldn't seem to push it out. Asthma. He'd never had an asthma attack before. Che had asthma. And every attack ever after took Rodríguez back to that day, to his "end of mission" moment of strange panic.

He couldn't relax yet. Rodríguez had to get the film with the Che materials to the CIA. He was tired, but he couldn't take a chance of his cameras falling into the wrong hands—they were pure gold, spywise, and Bolivia hosted almost as many spooks as journalists. The Soviet agents tailed the Americans, the Americans kept tabs on the Soviets, and the Chinese followed everyone.

Rodríguez jumped in his car and headed north to Santa Cruz Airport, hoping adrenaline would kick in soon. He boarded a flight to La Paz and from the airport took a cab to a hotel. There a CIA officer finally greeted him.

"Here," Rodríguez said, handing the man his briefcase with all of the film inside.

"No, no, no," the CIA officer said. "We're going to take you to a place where you can talk to John Tilton. But first you have to shake your surveillance."

Damn, Rodríguez thought. He wasn't in the mood for spy games.

"You see anybody following you, put your briefcase on the left side and you shake them," the CIA man said. "When you shake the surveillance, then you put it on the right side and we'll pick you up."

Sure enough, when Rodríguez left the hotel, he picked up his tail, a Chinese. He'd been in Santa Cruz for too long; he wasn't used to the thin air of La Paz. His lungs burned as he walked a zigzag route into the marketplace labyrinth. He needed to shed his tail and pick up his ride.

Rodríguez headed for the thickest crowds, increasing his pace to a slow jog. He ducked into a carpet shop stacked with rugs and pillows. He ducked down as if to tie his shoe, and saw the Chinese man trot past the shop entrance, his brow furrowed in consternation. Moments later, Rodríguez emerged from the market the same way he'd gone in. He switched his briefcase to his right side. A Volkswagen glided to a stop at the curb. The whole thing was a training mission, he found out later, testing to see if he followed directions. Rodríguez sat wheezing in the passenger seat as the car whisked him to a safe house.

Debriefing took several days. Rodríguez gave the agency a detailed account of the guerrilla leader's capture and execution, and accounts of his conversations with Che. He explained the contents of the diary—how important they were to the Che puzzle. He briefed the CIA officials on what Che did in Bolivia, his movements and critical tactical mistakes. When Rodríguez was done, he said his good-byes and headed home to Miami.

* * *

It was midnight in Vallegrande. Villoldo changed out of his usual fatigues, pulled on a gray sweater and a pair of jeans, slid his 9mm Smith & Wesson pistol into his pants. Che's body had lain in the laundry for two days now. It was time to put him away.

Che's brother, Roberto Guevara, was expected the next day.

Villoldo left his jeep at the safe house and walked the route to Señora de Malta Hospital. He passed outside the Hotel Teresita, where dozens of foreign journalists were holed up, drinking Bolivian beer. The streets were empty. Clouds blocked the moon.

At the hospital gates, Villoldo met the truck driver and the Bolivian soldier sent to provide security. The hospital caretaker waved them through. They loaded the ripening bodies of Che and two dead guerrillas—Willy and Chino—into the truck and covered them with canvas. For this load, Villoldo didn't want anyone to see the cargo.

With the bodies secured, the three men climbed into the truck. Villoldo noticed that the driver's hands were shaking. The soldier sat in the middle. Villoldo rode shotgun.

They headed toward the Eighth Division Engineer Battalion headquarters at the airport. Just past the headquarters building they turned right onto a pockmarked dirt road. A new runway was under construction, and other parts of the airport were being refurbished or repaired. They rolled past a bulldozer and toward the east gate, an older part of the airport complex.

"Turn off your headlights," Villoldo ordered the driver as the truck passed the gate. "Head toward the airstrip slowly."

Villoldo scanned the landscape until he spotted a "natural depression" where they had buried the bodies of Che's vanguard just a few weeks earlier.

"Stop," Villoldo said. He climbed out of the truck.

The depression was about twenty-five feet from the runway. Right beside it was a new excavation. Villoldo stepped to the edge of the hole that was eighteen feet deep and about thirty feet wide.

He walked back to the truck. A light rain started to fall. He could feel the temperature dropping. Villoldo was glad he'd worn the sweater. The others were not so lucky. They shivered with cold and nerves.

"Back up to the edge," Villoldo told the driver.

Then he ordered the soldier to get the bulldozer parked by the gate. When the soldier reached the tractor, the operator was already waiting inside. He started the engine and followed the soldier. It was time.

They tossed the bodies into the pit. The bulldozer covered them. Che's Bolivian campaign was finished, buried in the wet darkness.

Rain pelted down. The field was becoming muddy. The three men decided to get out of there while the truck could still move, get this over with.

No one marked the grave.

CHAPTER 25

Aftermath

Che's death was a moment of glory and triumph for the Bolivian high command. Barrientos emerged stronger than ever. To the public—especially the campesinos—he had taken decisive action and had rid the world of a Communist thug. Barrientos built on that, later saying, "Che died because he came to kill."

The president offered no apologies. He accepted full responsibility for Che's death, and issued a warning, too: "We will again crush any intent to subjugate our fatherland."

When Ovando arrived in Vallegrande with his fellow commanders, journalists from all over the world besieged him. He did not comment about details, but proclaimed: "The guerrillas have been liquidated in Bolivia." He conceded there were still members of Che's guerrilla band on the loose, but they "will be destroyed in the next few hours." Later that day, he released a statement touting the armed forces, proclaiming the campaign was nearly over:

"Well-organized positions in the rugged mountain ranges surrounded by thick jungle still continue firing on Bolivian troops, who will finally show the world that Bolivia is a sovereign nation, able to fight on its own for its development and its liberty."

Commanders relayed the happy news to troops in the field. Mario Salazar, who had seen no action since being deployed, was a bit disappointed. He wanted to fight the guerrillas. That's why he joined the army in the first place.

His chance came at sundown on October 14. Salazar spotted a campfire in the jungle, down along a Rio Grande tributary. Around it were four men, remnants of Che's army.

Salazar immediately reported them to his commander. Second Lieutenant Guillermo Aguirre Palma elected to wait until dawn to move. With the first beams of morning, C Company troops surrounded the men and shot them dead.

While the Bolivian high command was praising the operation that killed Che, the world began questioning the narrative of how he had died. At first, the government said Che was wounded in a fierce battle outside La Higuera and died a short time later. In a public statement on October 9, Colonel Zenteno embellished the story. He said that after Che was wounded, he told the soldiers: "I am Che Guevara. I have failed." Then he lapsed into a coma and died. Ovando repeated Zenteno's story—including the quote.

A day later, though, Ovando said that Che had actually died at 1:30 P.M. on Oct. 9—nearly a day after the battle. To many, that was implausible. How could Che have lived so long with so many wounds? Zenteno quickly changed his story to support Ovando's.

But journalists kept uncovering new details that contradicted official accounts.

One *New York Times* story said that Che was "executed by the army after the surrender." Jose Martinez Caso, a doctor who'd examined Che's body in Vallegrande, told journalists that soldiers at the scene told him Che was taken alive.

The government also made contradictory statements about Che's remains. One statement said Che was buried in a "safe place." Ovando later said the body had been cremated. And when Che's brother, Roberto Guevara, visited Vallegrande to take the remains back to Argentina, he was not allowed to see the body. At first, Bolivian officials refused to meet with him. But even after talking with Ovando, Roberto left Bolivia with no answers, and no body.

There was still another concern.

Gruesome photographs showed up in Bolivian newspapers. Snapshots illustrated each step of Che's Via Dolorosa. The first photos showed a ragged man in curious homemade shoes, alive in the La Higuera schoolhouse. Then followed a series of death photographs: in the schoolroom just after the execution, on the ground like a hunting trophy with gun-toting Bolivian soldiers grinning alongside, and finally displayed in a laundry room.

The entire episode frustrated and embarrassed U.S. officials. While Bolivia celebrated Che's death, the White House was in the dark. Rodríguez had been there in La Higuera and had duly reported events as they unfolded. But communications broke down somewhere between the CIA, the State Department, and the White House.

Ambassador Henderson—who had prided himself on being in the loop—said he didn't know Che had been captured until after his death was announced. He personally countermanded a proposal to send embassy observers with Ovando the following day, when Ovando visited Vallegrande. He wanted the United States to stay in the background.

On October 9, Walt Rostow, the president's assistant for national security affairs, told Johnson in a memo that they had unconfirmed reports that Che was dead. But a day later, William Bowdler, the State Department's executive liaison officer for Latin America, reported to Rostow that there was still uncertainty about whether Che had been killed—despite newspaper and radio accounts and nationwide celebrations. Incredibly, CIA director Richard Helms wrote a memo to Rostow on October 11 asking if he knew anything about Che's death.

You are aware of the published accounts concerning the death of Ernesto 'Che' Guevara which were based in essence on the Bolivian Army press conference on 10 October attributing Guevara's death to battle wounds sustained in the clash between the army and the guerrillas on 8 October 1967. Guevara was said to be in a coma when captured and to have died shortly thereafter, the heat of battle having prevented early or effective treatment by Bolivian soldiers.

On the same day, Rostow sent President Johnson a memorandum saying, "This morning we are about 99 percent sure that 'Che' Guevara is dead." He said Che was taken alive and that General Ovando ordered him shot.

I regard this as stupid, but it is understandable from a Bolivian standpoint, given the problems which the sparing of the French communist and Castro courier Regis Debray has caused them.

Rostow continued that Che's death carried "these significant implications":

It marks the passing of another of the aggressive, romantic rev-olutionaries like Sukarno, Nkrumah, Ben Bella and reinforced this trend.

In the Latin American context, it will have a strong impact in discouraging would-be guerrillas.

It shows the soundness of our 'preventative medicine' as-sistance to countries facing incipient insurgency. It was the Bo-livian Second Ranger Battalion, trained by our Green Berets June–September that cornered and got him.

Two days later, Rostow sent the president another note, say-ing new intelligence information "removes any doubt that 'Che' Guevara is dead."

At SOUTHCOM, General Porter and his staff monitored devel-opments. When they learned Che was dead, they expressed disap-pointed relief. They understood why the Bolivians had executed Che. SOUTHCOM had to be realistic. If he had been taken to Panama for interrogation, it was highly unlikely that Che would have given up any information. He despised the United States. And if Che had lived, and been found in U.S. custody, imagine the worldwide protests. It would have added fuel to anti-American sen-timent all over the globe. In the end, things turned out well. Che had to die.

The CIA and the intelligence community were raking in details about Che's failed campaign. The information in his diary gave of-ficials a window into his entire Bolivian operation. On October 18, a CIA cable to Washington highlighted the errors leading to Che's defeat in Bolivia:

Che's presence at the guerrilla front precluded all hope of
saving him and others in the event of an ambush and

virtually condemned them to die or exist uselessly as
fugitives;

Che was dependent on the campesinos in the area for supplies
and recruits; neither of them was forthcoming;

Che was overconfident about the support of the Bolivian
Communist Party, which was inexperienced and divided in
Pro-Soviet and Pro-Chinese factions.

The cable downplayed the role of the Bolivian military in Che's
failed campaign. Che's defeat had more to do with his flawed leadership than any Bolivian military prowess.

In a memo to Secretary of State Dean Rusk, Thomas Hughes,
director of the State Department's Intelligence and Research Division, noted that Che's death was a "crippling—perhaps fatal—blow
to the Bolivian guerrilla movement and may prove a serious setback
for Fidel Castro's hopes to foment violent revolution in 'all or almost
all' Latin American countries." But he also included a warning
about Bolivia's future:

*"Guevara's death is a feather in the cap of Bolivian President
Rene Barrientos. It may signal the end of the guerrilla movements as a threat to stability. If so, the Bolivian military, which
is a major element of Barrientos' support, will enjoy a sense of
self-confidence and strength that it has long lacked. However,
victory could also stir political ambitions among army officers
who were directly involved in the anti-guerrilla campaign and
who may now see themselves as the saviors of the republic."*

Cuba was notably silent. On October 18—nine days after Che's
death—Castro addressed his nation. Before hundreds of thousands
of Cubans in Plaza de la Revolución, Castro eulogized Che. He told

dozens of anecdotes about his old friend and praised Che's lifelong struggle against imperialism.

He told the crowd there was proof that Che was "killed in cold blood."

"He was always characterized by his daring and by his scorn for danger on numerous occasions," Castro said. "Che's death deals a heavy blow to the revolutionary movement, but the movement will go forward."

He ended by warning that Che's murderers would be disappointed when they realized that "the art to which he dedicated his life and intelligence cannot die."

And so it was. As with his life, mystery and confusion surrounded Che's death. It would take years for the full story to be revealed. It would take even longer to find his grave.

For Prado, the last few weeks had been a blur. The day after Che was killed, Barrientos and Ovando arrived separately to congratulate the troops. They made speeches and praised the soldiers, saying it was one of the proudest days in the nation's history.

Prado was still disturbed by what had happened to Che. And he still had more work to do. The Rangers had to find the remaining handful of fugitive guerrillas.

With Che out of the picture, the country quickly lost interest in insurgent fighters. Life returned to normal.

Prado, the officer who'd captured Che, was a national hero. His superiors congratulated him and promised promotions. Prado didn't like all the attention. He was just doing his job.

Prado went back to La Esperanza, where Shelton in turn embraced him, congratulated him, fed him, and regaled him with questions about the mission.

"I knew you'd do it," Shelton said. "Gary, I'm proud of you."

Prado knew it was a big success for Shelton, too—and that the major wished he could've been in El Churo Canyon and La Higuera.

But La Esperanza had its comforts. The schoolhouse was almost finished: four brand-new classrooms and an office for the teacher. Training for the more experienced Bolivian troops was going well. The village was quieter now with all the Rangers gone.

The plan was running on schedule. They'd all be out of there by Christmas, Shelton said.

And by this time next year, Shelton wouldn't be "Major" anymore. He'd be "Mister."

Maybe it would save his marriage. He was leaving on a high note. His team took 650 men and, in a short time, turned them into the fighting force that captured Che Guevara.

"It's going to be tough leaving," Shelton said, "but it's time to go home."

It was time for Prado to go, too. They took a few pictures and promised to stay in touch. "I wish you the best, Major, with everything you do," Prado said.

"*Igualmente*, Gary," Shelton replied.

After Prado left, Shelton picked up his guitar and strummed a few chords before heading to Kiosko Hugo. He felt like celebrating.

EPILOGUE

Gary Prado Salmon sits behind a desk in his Santa Cruz home and listens patiently to another question about Che Guevara. For more than four decades he's been answering questions about the legendary revolutionary—usually today they are some version of the same questions asked by the last two generations of journalists. Prado was the Bolivian Army officer who captured Che.

When he's not doing interviews, Prado tries to avoid the subject. Che was just one page in his career. He went on from there, he says, he accomplished lots of other things besides that—you don't retire as an army general if you spend your career sitting still. But on this day, he opens up to two American journalists writing another book about Che Guevara.

"That was just a small part of my life," Prado insists. "But if you must know, Che failed miserably in Bolivia. But sometimes it doesn't seem that way."

Indeed, in the years since his death, Che has become a mythical figure. His famously fierce beret-wearing image glowers from T-shirts, posters, coffee mugs, and key rings, merchandise bought and sold by consumers who have no idea who Che was or what he stood for.

Forty-plus years after his tawdry death in a Bolivian backwater, Che Guevara is a pop star.

Nowhere is that more evident than Bolivia, the last country he terrorized. The soldiers who extinguished Che's rebellion are forgotten, and Bolivian souvenir vendors have taken up his myth. From the street markets in big cities like La Paz and Santa Cruz to snack bars in rural mountain villages, Che's image is flogged on T-shirts and wallets. The great revolutionary has become a capitalist commodity.

Pilgrims traverse the Ruta del Che (the Che Guevara Route), making stops along the way at towns like Samaipata, Camiri, and of course La Higuera, where Che was killed.

In La Higuera, an enormous concrete bust of Che casts a shadow on the schoolhouse where he was executed. La Higuera has become a shrine for Che admirers.

In Vallegrande, the Che Guevara Museum takes pride of place on the village plaza. Here are housed photographs and historical memorabilia from Che's Bolivia campaign, including graphic photos of his death. The hospital laundry room in Vallegrande, where Che's body was washed and displayed, is another tourist attraction, its walls a sounding board for revolutionary wannabes whose weapons are spray paint and markers. "Che Lives" is scrawled on the walls in cities and the countryside.

Each October, on the anniversary of his death, thousands travel to Vallegrande to celebrate Che's memory. Festivities include music and dancing, lectures and speeches, art exhibits and (of course) souvenirs.

Prado has no love for the long-dead guerrilla fighter, but his name is inextricably linked to Che's. In newspaper stories, Prado is identified as "the man who captured legendary revolutionary Ernesto 'Che' Guevara."

Prado would rather talk about his family, his military career, or even Bolivian history. But the conversation inevitably returns to Che. Prado was one of the last people to talk to the man.

"There were so many questions I wanted to ask him," he says.

So many questions remain, forty-five years later—many focus on what happened those two days in October 1967 when a wounded Che hobbled out of the jungle and into the shabby schoolhouse in La Higuera. What words did he say? How was he treated in La Higuera? Who ordered his execution?

Che Guevara is one of the twentieth century's most fascinating and influential figures. Like the graffiti on all those Bolivian walls, his theories on revolution are faded but still legible. His how-to books on revolution and guerrilla operations are dated but still relevant. He is held in high esteem in many parts of the world, especially in Latin America. Strange as it might seem in a Western world overrun with capitalism, some people still believe that joining together in mutually beneficial collectives might overcome poverty and promote a more just society.

Che is more than a T-shirt icon. He is a polarizing figure. To the left, he is a romantic revolutionary—a rebel with a cause. To the right, Che is a Communist thug who would take away their hard-earned goods and give them away to society's parasites.

When we decided to write about Che, we wanted to examine the role that Major Ralph "Pappy" Shelton's Special Forces team played in the Bolivia campaign. Most books about Che's Bolivia sojourn contain a few sentences about the Green Berets' mission, but we wanted to know more. We have written extensively about the military, especially Special Forces. Coauthor Kevin Maurer was embedded with Green Beret units in Afghanistan and has written several books about Special Forces missions.

But as we traveled through Bolivia and talked with dozens of people who were involved in the campaign or lived in the villages in the operations area, we discovered another important part of the story: the manhunt. For nearly seven months in 1967, fear gripped Bolivia while soldiers tracked the guerrillas. The Bolivians helped us understand what life was like during those months—how they believed that the nation might at any moment be overrun by Communist guerrillas. They followed every development of the manhunt in newspapers and on radio broadcasts, and like Americans who remember where they were when they heard about the September 11 terrorist attacks or President John F. Kennedy's assassination, many Bolivians remember Che's capture and death as a defining moment for them.

Looking back, it's easy to understand their fear. The United States had precious little intelligence about Che or his movements. The Bolivian high command stoked the chaos by claiming Che had hundreds of well-trained Cuban guerrillas. At the time, it made sense. Che's reputation as a skilled guerrilla leader preceded him. No one imagined that his "army" was so small, skinny, and scared or that he'd already committed a series of blunders that would seal his fate.

Che believed, with good reason, that Bolivia was ripe for revolution. Long considered to have South America's weakest military, Bolivia also had a history of coups. The government, especially under Barrientos, was unstable and weak.

For his operation Che picked a remote part of Bolivia with a treacherous landscape, making it difficult to maneuver.

The area in southeastern Bolivia was sparsely populated, and the people who lived there—the campesinos—were suspicious of outsiders. The early stages of a revolution depend on secrecy—mobilizing rural forces against the government. Yet the campesinos reported the guerrillas' every move to authorities. That's how Che's band was initially discovered.

If Che had picked another area to stage his revolution—one closer to the mines and urban networks of La Paz—he might have had a chance. There was real discontent in the country. Many were unhappy with Barrientos for seizing power. The unions battled the government over living and working conditions. Che could have capitalized on the mining massacre and the protests that followed. Instead, he was stuck in an unforgiving part of the country, with no way to get out his message.

The Bolivian military didn't know it, but Che scrambled from village to village to escape detection. He was more an on-the-lam fugitive than revolutionary commander.

In addition, a serious rift developed within the rebel band. The Bolivian Communists wanted to lead the revolution, but Che insisted the Cubans stay in control. At that point, many Bolivian Communists withdrew their support, leaving Che's army without a supply pipeline.

Even at the height of his fame, Che only led about fifty guerrillas. Many of them—driven by Che's relentless marching and desire to replicate the Cuban Revolution—had become so disillusioned with the campaign they were looking for ways to leave.

One of his most grave errors was dividing his thin guerrilla forces into two groups. For the final four months of the campaign the two groups constantly searched for each other. They never met again. In this way Che lost Joaquin, one of his most faithful men, a friend who had served with Che since the Sierra Maestra in 1958.

As a student of history, Prado still doesn't understand many of

Che's moves. They defy conventional military wisdom, he says. His bookcases are filled with hundreds of books about war and strategy. Prado is retired and now teaches history at a university.

He looks the part of a retired general with his thick mane of silver hair and neatly trimmed mustache. He spends most of his days at home.

Prado is confined to a wheelchair. In 1981, he was shot in the back while putting down a right-wing Falangist takeover attempt at an Occidental Petroleum site in Bolivia. It left him paralyzed below the waist.

It also gave him time to reflect on his life and to write a book about Che's campaign, called *The Defeat of Che Guevara: Military Response to Guerrilla Challenge in Bolivia*, in which he detailed his nation's military response to the guerrilla threat. The text includes his conversations with Che.

He understands why President René Barrientos Ortuno ordered Che Guevara's execution, but he wishes justice could have been dispensed by a Bolivian court. For years, he had to fight allegations that he played a role in Che's death.

"There have been so many rumors over the years. They are wrong. It's been frustrating," Prado says.

Che's defeat helped solidify Barrientos's government. But in April 1969, eighteen months after Che's death, the rotor on Barrientos's presidential helicopter snagged electricity cables running through a rural canyon. Barreintos was killed in the crash.

Vice President Luis Adolfo Siles stepped up, but like most governments in Bolivia, his tenure was short-lived. General Alfredo Ovando Candía seized power a few months later, but was himself deposed after a year.

He died in January 1982.

Of Che's band of guerrillas, only three made it out of Bolivia alive. On February 22, 1968, after crossing the Andes on foot, three Cuban and two Bolivian guerrillas reached the Chilean border. Chilean socialist senator Salvador Allende welcomed the refugees. The two Bolivian guerrillas decided to stay inside their country and were later killed by police.

Regis Debray, the French Marxist, was convicted on November 17, 1967, of having been part of Che's guerrillas. He was sentenced to thirty years in prison but set free in 1970 after an international campaign for his release. His celebrity supporters included Jean-Paul Sartre, André Malraux, General Charles de Gaulle, and Pope Paul VI.

Debray didn't give up his revolutionary ways. He sought refuge in Chile, where he interviewed Allende and wrote *The Chilean Revolution*. Debray returned to France in 1973 following the coup by Augusto Pinochet. He is alive and living in France.

Some paid a high price for helping Barrientos. In July 1969, in an act of vengeance, Communists gunned down Honorato Rojas, the farmer who betrayed Joaquin's lost patrol at Yado del Yeso.

For Major Ralph "Pappy" Shelton the Bolivian mission was the highlight of his military career.

Shelton left the army when he returned to Tennessee. He and Margaret eventually divorced. He later remarried.

Shelton went to school. He earned bachelor's and master's degrees from Memphis State University and later became an executive with the federal Office of Personnel Management in Memphis.

He taught twelve years of Junior Reserve Officers' Training Corps (JROTC) in the Memphis City schools and served five years as director of Operation Wilderness, a summer "boot camp" program modeled after Outward Bound. Shelton was elected a Sweetwater City commissioner from 2000 to 2006.

Like others, Shelton was contacted over the years to talk about the Bolivia mission. He collected photos, books, and clippings about the Rangers training program. It made him proud, he said—he called it "a classic Green Beret mission." The training techniques used in Bolivia are still in use today in Afghanistan.

"We did what we had to do," Shelton recalled. "We turned these boys into soldiers. The mission was a total success. You couldn't have planned or executed it any better."

Still, not many people knew the full extent of Shelton's role. In most history books about Che's Bolivian campaign, Shelton and the Green Beret mission are relegated to a few paragraphs. The focus is always on Che Guevara.

Shelton died in July 2010. He left behind family and friends and a community who fondly recalled the tough-as-nails commander who did things his way. The La Esperanza schoolhouse is still standing.

For years, many of the Special Forces soldiers who took part in the Bolivian mission couldn't speak of it because it was a classified exercise. But in time the restrictions expired, and documents have been released. Some of the men have opened up.

"We did a good thing," said Peterson, the medic. He said he still takes "great pride" in knowing he played a role in Che's capture.

All of Pappy Shelton's Special Forces soldiers, including Peterson, eventually left the army. One kept his promise to a village girl. After the mission was over, Sergeant Alvin Graham returned to Bolivia on leave and married Dorys Roca. Villagers in La Esperanza recalled the excitement.

"There was a big ceremony in the village when he came back," said Dioniso Valderomas, the farmer who kept a watchful eye on the soldiers so many years ago. "It was beautiful."

Graham took his bride with him to the base in Panama. He stayed in the army until 1970, then became a high school teacher in

Phoenix, Arizona. Dorys Roca became a U.S. citizen in 1971. She never returned to La Esperanza.

Today, the village is much the way it was in 1967. The sugar mill and the outbuildings used for the mission stand vacant on the edge of town. Stories of that time have been passed down. Dozens of villagers fondly recall the guitar-playing major who brought the town together that summer over at Kiosko Hugo. La Esperanza is quiet these days. There are no markers to let the curious know that in 1967 a Special Forces team trained Bolivian conscripts in this sleepy village. It's hard to imagine that anyone from outside really cares.

"We know what happened. It was an important time for the village," said Valderomas, whose four children are grown and live nearby.

For Mario Salazar, his days in La Esperanza were among the best of his life. After the Che campaign he stayed in the military for a few years, then left as a sergeant. He returned to his village, got married, and had two children. He worked hard as a farmer and laborer and supported his family.

"I have no regrets," he said.

One windy September day he escorted us to La Esperanza. It was the first time he had been back in decades. His face lit up when we pulled into the village square. Salazar bounded out of the car and looked around. "It's the same," he said.

As he walked, he pointed out familiar places, including the spot where they held the dances. At times, tears would well in the corners of his eyes. This whole place reminded him of his lost youth.

Back in Santa Cruz, he ordered a Bolivian pale ale. He lifted his mug and said "*salud*" before taking a long swig. He licked his lips and placed his glass down, then turned serious.

"No one in this country appreciates what we did," he said. "It's all about Che. But we killed Che. We brought him down. Even in death, he got all the glory. When you think about it, we got no credit."

Once home in Miami, Rodríguez and Villoldo continued their CIA careers.

Rodríguez became an American citizen in 1969. He flew hundreds of helicopter missions in Vietnam. He trained provincial reconnaissance units for the Phoenix Program, a counterinsurgency group later accused of torturing and murdering suspected South Vietnamese Communists.

In the 1980s, Rodríguez was a key player in the Iran-Contra affair—a complicated scheme to trade arms to Iran in exchange for U.S. hostages held at the U.S. embassy in Tehran. Part of the proceeds from the arms sales was diverted to fund the "Contras," anti-Communist guerrillas in Nicaragua.

When the plot came to light, it created a scandal in Washington. Congressional hearings were held to determine whether President Ronald Reagan's administration knew about the plan.

Rodríguez is retired now. He is president of the Brigade 2506 Veterans Association and chairman of the board for the Bay of Pigs Museum and Library in Miami.

We arrived on a fall morning to meet Rodríguez at the museum. Tucked into a Little Havana neighborhood, it looks more like a house than a memorial to those lost.

Inside, the walls were lined with mementos. Glass cases were filled with photos of the soldiers training and documents about the mission. Weapons and other memorabilia were on display in tribute to the more than one hundred men killed during the failed invasion.

Coming from his office, Rodríguez met us in the hall. His skin was still bronze and his gray hair perfect. He moved quietly like a cat as he ushered us into his office. He had reluctantly agreed to meet with us after several emails. Like Prado, he has talked about the mission many times and published a book about his long career in the CIA.

Sitting there, Rodríguez recalled his time in Bolivia, the planning and the gathering of intelligence. It was a chess game, he said, trying to figure out Che's next move.

He still regrets not doing more to save Che's life.

Villoldo worked for the CIA in Latin America and the Caribbean before leaving in 1988. He is now a businessman with fishing, banking, and development companies. Villoldo never stopped fighting Castro, ultimately winning one more victory in 2009: A federal judge awarded Villoldo over $1 billion in damages against the Cuban government for the suicide of his father. Cuba still has not paid the fine. The lawsuit was more symbolic than anything else. It's unlikely that Cuba will ever pay the judgment.

Despite their successful partnership in Bolivia, Villoldo and Rodríguez no longer speak to one another.

"Unfortunately in the last few years Villoldo started claiming that he was the boss of the operation and I was his radio operator," Rodríguez said. "Our boss was the American case officer."

He paused for a moment.

"It is sad. Villoldo and I were very good friends and I have fond memories of our tour in Bolivia," Rodríguez said.

To this day Che remains a worldwide icon for radical change. His romantic image, heightened by his early, violent death and the power of international media, allowed his appeal to transcend ideological lines.

And it's that romantic figure that is portrayed in books and movies.

Writer Christopher Hitchens said, "Che's iconic status was assured because he failed. His story was one of defeat and isolation, and that's why it is so seductive. Had he lived, the myth of Che would have long ago died."

Maybe. The way one faces death tells a lot about the man. When Che saw his executioner enter the schoolhouse, he didn't flinch. He told the soldier, "I know you've come to kill me. Shoot, coward! You are only going to kill a man!" The executioner did. Che died alone in a hail of bullets. Even staunch anticommunists admired the way he faced death—unapologetic and defiant to the end.

Che's diary, a day-by-day recording of the Bolivian campaign, has only added to the legend. He was a prolific writer—friends said he always had a pad and a pen and was disciplined enough to write every day. After his death, the diary was smuggled to Cuba, where it became a publishing sensation. Che's writing has a clarity that belies his campaign. On September 10, his entry started this way: "A bad day. It began promising, but then, as a result of the poor state of the trail, the animals began to put up a struggle. Finally the mule refused to go any further and we had to leave it on the side." He continued: "I swam across the river with the mule, but lost my shoes in the process. I am now wearing sandals, and do not particularly enjoy it." He ended the day by saying: "I forgot to highlight an event. Today, after more than six months, I bathed. This constitutes a record that several others are already approaching."

In the end, Che's legacy harkens back to a different time, when the ideological struggle was between democracy and communism. Now the lines are less clear. Capitalism trumps democracy at home, and the "outside" threat comes from religious zealots willing to fly airplanes into buildings or blow themselves up at checkpoints.

One of the final mysteries of Che's demise took thirty years to unravel: Where was Che's body?

In 1995 retired Bolivian general Mario Vargas revealed to Jon

Lee Anderson, author of *Che Guevara: A Revolutionary Life*, that Guevara's body was interred near a Vallegrande airstrip.

The result was a multinational search that lasted more than a year. In July 1997 a team of Cuban geologists and Argentine forensic anthropologists discovered the remains of seven bodies in two mass graves, including one man with amputated hands.

On October 17, 1997, Guevara's remains, with those of six of his fellow combatants, were laid to rest with military honors in a specially built mausoleum in the Cuban city of Santa Clara, where he led a decisive military victory of the Cuban Revolution.

Miles away in Havana, a seventeen-ton, five-story steel profile of Che covers the facade of the Interior Ministry headquarters in Revolution Plaza.

His monumental image now is a backdrop to Fidel's speeches, the icon of the Cuban capital.

The man who served Cuba as a general, banker, hero, and a martyr of revolution now serves a most capitalistic function.

He is a logo.

Why the Hunt for Che Matters Today

Ahmed flashed his yellow toothy grin and nodded toward a baseball hat on the table of the operations center.

With his thick black beard and scrawny body, Ahmed looked like a mop top on a stick figure clothed in camouflage. As he waited for me to say the word in Pashtu, his eyebrow climbed up his forehead. If it got any higher, it would hit the back of his collar.

I smiled and said "hat" in Pashtu. He followed by pronouncing the word in English.

He was pleased because he was winning. He was close to beating the "gray one" in our game of wit, intellect, and clash of culture.

We were essentially playing "Show and Tell," but in our version of this game, Special Forces and Afghan soldiers would compete to see who could describe the objects chosen by the opposing team and translate the words into either English or Pashtu. Whoever got the most translated out of twenty objects won a case of Gatorade or energy drinks.

The game, which started as an icebreaker when my team first arrived, became so popular that before long I was bombarded by Afghans walking past my truck, pointing to weapon magazines, pencils, bread, cups, knives, or any object that they thought they could stump me on while betting a piece of chewing gum or candy. The game was an exercise in rapport building that generated not only cultural understanding but also friendships while expanding vocabulary and providing English training for the Afghans.

It eventually grew to provide any opportunity or excuse to have a large meal together to play the game for the right to be base champion for the week. At one point it became so popular that other Afghan units were coming to our firebase to play. Some Afghan units tried to smuggle in ringers from other bases.

The game, like Pappy Shelton's guitar in Bolivia, is solid proof that no matter the situation you can build rapport with people who came from opposite ends of the earth by combining camaraderie, good food, different cultures, and a war against a common enemy.

United States Special Forces teams are strategic assets. There are many "Special Operations" forces—but only one Special Forces. Any unit can be helicoptered onto an objective to fight for an hour or two but not every unit has the diverse skill sets to build or destroy an entire country. Training and building armies are one of the fundamentals that make Special Forces unique.

Even today, Special Forces soldiers are doing and using the same time-honored skills that Shelton and his team did in 1967. As you read this, Special Forces teams on almost every continent in the world are performing the same mission Shelton's team accomplished in Bolivia.

What Shelton did in Bolivia was classic FID or Foreign Internal Defense and has been emulated by every Special Forces team leader since, with varying degrees of success. Since the units were created more than fifty years ago, the Special Forces teams have successfully trained soldiers to fight tyranny and oppression in Vietnam, Colombia, and Afghanistan to name just a few.

Green Berets trained in the language and culture of the host country is working by, with, and through native soldiers to carry out American policy. In this case, as are in most involving Special Forces, the men in this story were of the highest quality and caliber capable of executing a highly sensitive and classified operation for both the Bolivian and American governments.

But what separates Shelton's mission and makes it so impressive was that, unlike Afghanistan today, Shelton's Green Berets couldn't go with the Bolivians. They had to trust their training and hope the Rangers could execute under pressure. And they did, but their success was put in place months before when Shelton, guitar in tow, started building the rapport that would forge the lifelong friendships.

Special Forces personnel are extremely sensitive to the political implications and national interests that their actions, decisions, and mission accomplishments affect. A clear understanding of the population is the key terrain that defines a mission's success or failure. Take Shelton's relationship with Prado. I had a similar experience in Afghanistan.

Shinsha was my Afghan counterpart during my 2006 deployment. He had an avid interest in all things American as I did for things Afghan. He would come by my room to visit and we would sit and drink strong black or green tea called "chai" for hours talking about our families, where we would visit after the war, and our beloved Buzkashi. Buzkashi means "goat grabbing," and is essentially like a violent combination of polo and the rodeo. It is especially associated with the northern Uzbek and Tajik tribes in Afghanistan, and it is considered to be the national sport of Afghanistan.

Shinsha had fought the Taliban and Al Qaeda fighters since 1995 and the Soviets before that. He was a man who commanded and deserved respect. I knew that his friendship and support would allow my team to accomplish our mission. On one particular evening I had already spent the entire day in Kandahar City drinking chai with the provincial governor and was in no mood for any more. Knowing that I would be up all night anyway, I decided to introduce Shinsha to the wonderful world of espresso. Not long after his arrival, we began making the syrupy black concoction on my tiny machine. His expression after the first cup was like that of realizing he had been missing something awesome his whole life. He grew such an affinity for the teacup-sized liquid that he would sneak over to my room several times a week to get a shot of the boiling hot rocket fuel before going out on patrol.

After realizing that he would be going on leave soon to visit his family and see his son who would be playing in the upcoming season of buzkashi, I presented him with the best gift I had, my silver espresso maker and a large yellow coffee container of ground espresso. He nearly broke my ribs as he swooped the bag from my hand and headed north to Kabul. Nearly a month later Shinsha showed up at my door holding a large object wrapped in a wool blanket. Knowing I would never get to go to Kabul and physically see the game together with him, Shinsha had brought a saddle he had made for me. I had to promise that one day when the war was over, I would return to Afghanistan, if we were still alive, and play the great game of buzkashi with my old warrior and friend.

If the FID effort is a success, it essentially prevents the requirement for larger scale commitments of American military forces. By training the Second Bolivian Ranger Battalion to conduct basic combat operation and counterinsurgency, the United States would be able to assist Bolivia in building a partner and capabilities to deal with current and future internal threats.

Plans can be made, men organized and equipped but the actual culmination of training and the ultimate conduct of any mission and its success or failure ultimately rests squarely on the shoulders of the men responsible for executing it. The selection of a United States Special Forces team to train the newly established Bolivian Second Ranger Battalion was the right decision at the right time to deal with the growing threat. What made this mission work was the experience and maturity of the Special Forces team members and their commander.

Shelton was the kind of leader men aspire to be, past, present, and future, including myself. I had the honor of speaking with Pappy two years ago. I was in complete admiration of his selfless service to this country and his dedication to his team and their mission. Shelton was not willing to compromise his mission or his men for the sake of climbing the ladder or willing to make himself look good to get promoted. He was an old-school veteran of multiple conflicts who forced himself to master the basics and was driven to give himself the tools to succeed wherever his country sent him. To Pappy, the mission and the men came in that order, and he would do whatever was needed on the battlefield to ensure mission success, even if it meant going around, under, over, or through people who were obstacles.

Missions like this and men like Shelton should be celebrated and honored by those who have earned and worn the Green Beret because every day we are following in their footsteps.

Major Rusty Bradley
Fort Bragg, North Carolina
November 2012

ACKNOWLEDGMENTS

This book was two years in the making.

We started and stopped many times before finally getting to work, but as with all books, the author is just a member of a bigger team. We want to thank a number of people who helped us along the way, including the historians before us who found and archived the necessary documents and accounts to tell this story.

We would like to thank Félix Rodríguez for allowing us to interview him for hours in Miami and then bombard him with follow-up questions. A special thanks to Gary Prado, who opened his home to us and helped us track down his unit mates in Bolivia. Prado's book, as well as Rodríguez's book, provided a wealth of information and only highlighted the stories told in the interviews.

There was no better guide and companion on a trip through the backcountry of Bolivia than Noah Friedman-Rudovsky. Without Noah, we'd have been as lost as Che. Thanks also to Judy Royal for the interview transcripts and the U.S. Army Special Operations Command Public Affairs Office, especially Carol Darby, for trying to dislodge some of their archived information. The professionals in that office truly serve the soldiers of that command.

Special thanks to Julie Reed and Rebekah Scott. Reed, an incredible researcher, helped track down critical documents. Scott provided insightful guidance and wisdom along the way.

We'd like to express our gratitude to our wives—Suzyn Weiss and Jessica Maurer. We spent many weekends and long nights working on the book. Without your patience, love, and understanding, we could not have written the book.

Finally, none of our books exist without our agent, Scott Miller of Trident Media Group, who recognized the importance of this story, and thank you also to Penguin Group, especially Robin Barletta, for all the editorial support. Our editor, Natalee Rosenstein, continues to help refine our manuscripts and make them better. A writer's best friend is a good editor, and Natalee has been that for us.

AUTHORS' NOTE

This is the story of a group of extraordinary men who hunted down and captured one of the most feared revolutionaries of the late twentieth century.

The events depicted in this book are based on extensive interviews with key members of the team of Green Berets tasked with training the Bolivian Rangers for the hunt, the Ranger officer who captured Ernesto "Che" Guevara, and the CIA operative sent to gather intelligence for the Bolivian unit.

We reviewed thousands of pages of documents and photos from the National Archives and private collections. We also examined hundreds of news stories from the *New York Times*, the *Washington Post*, and the Associated Press, among other media outlets. Many of the key characters in the story have written their own biographies, which were used to offer the reader an internal monologue or to help reconstruct conversations.

The narrative is intended to tell the story of how Che was captured and executed through the eyes of the American trainers. In lieu of adding footnotes that we felt would bog down the narrative flow of the book, we've included a detailed bibliography in the back for future reading.

As with many popular histories, people are familiar with the story, but few know the behind-the-scenes details. The hunt for Che, in some ways, reads like a 1960s spy novel. And the best part is the story is all true.

REFERENCES

BOOKS

Anderson, John Lee. *Che Guevara. A Revolutionary Life.* New York: Grove Press, 1997.

Castaneda, Jorge G. Companero. *The Life and Death of Che Guevara.* New York: Alfred A. Knopf, 1997.

Castro, Fidel. *Che. A Memoir.* New York: Ocean Press, 2005.

Debray, Regis. *Revolution in the Revolution.* 1st edition. New York: Grove Press, 1967.

Escalante, Fabian. *The Secret War: CIA Covert Operations Against Cuba 1959–1962.* New York: Ocean Press, 1995.

Farcau, Bruce. *The Chaco War: Bolivia and Paraguay, 1932–1935.* Westport, CT: Praeger Publishers, 1996.

Fontova, Humberto. *Exposing the Real Che Guevara: And the Useful Idiots Who Idolize Him.* Reprint edition. New York: Sentinel Trade, 2008.

Gotkowitz, Laura. *A Revolution for Our Rights: Indigenous Struggles for Land and Justice in Bolivia, 1880–1952.* Durham, NC: Duke University Press, 2008.

Guevara, Che. *The Bolivian Diary of Ernesto Che Guevara.* 1st edition. New York: Pathfinder Press, 1994.

———. *Guerrilla Warfare.* 3rd edition. Wilmington, DE: Scholarly Resources, Inc., 1997.

———. *The Motorcycle Diaries: Notes on a Latin American Journey.* Sal Val, 2003.

Harris, Richard. *Death of a Revolutionary. Che Guevara's Last Mission.* New York: W. W. Norton & Company Ltd., 2007.

John, Sandor S. *Bolivia's Radical Tradition: Permanent Revolution in the Andes.* Reprint edition. Tucson, AZ: University of Arizona Press, 2012.

Klein, Herbert S. *A Concise History of Bolivia.* 2nd edition. Cambridge University Press, 2011.

Rasenberge, Jim. *The Brilliant Disaster: JFK, Castro, and America's Doomed Invasion of Cuba's Bay of Pigs.* Reprint edition. New York: Scribner, 2012.

REFERENCES

Rodríguez, Félix, and John Weisman. *Shadow Warrior: The CIA Hero of* a *Hundred Unknown Battles*. 1st edition. New York: Simon & Schuster, 1989.

Ryan, Butterfield Henry. *The Fall of Che Guevara: A Story of Soldiers, Spies and Diplomats*. New York: Oxford University Press, 1998.

Salmon, Gary Prado. *The Defeat of Che Guevara. Military Response to Guerrilla Challenge in Bolivia*. Westport, CT: Praeger Publishers, 1990.

Villoldo, Gustavo. *Che Guevara. The End of a Myth*. Rodes Printing, 1999.

ARCHIVES AND DOCUMENTS

After Action Report of MTT BL-404-67x.

Anti-Government Activity in Bolivia. CIA report, August 21, 1964.

Bolivian Demonstrations Most Serious in Fourteen Years. CIA report, October 30, 1964.

Bolivian Government Imposes Strict Control Over Opposition. CIA report, September 25, 1964.

Bolivian Junta Leader Prepares to Be Elected President. CIA report, January 15, 1965.

Bolivian Junta Moves to Win Public Support. CIA report, November 20, 1964.

Bolivian Junta Still In Control. CIA report, November 13, 1964.

Bolivian Power Struggle Threatens New Violence. CIA report, March 26, 1965.

Castro's Excesses Alienating Other Latin American Countries. CIA report, November 19, 1959.

Increasing Difficulties of the Bolivian Government. CIA report, May 14, 1965.

Kornbluh, Peter. *The Death of Che Guevara Declassified*. National Security Archive Electronic Briefing Book No. 5, 1997.

Lyndon Baines Johnson Library, Austin, Texas.

Memorandum of Understanding Concerning the Activation, Organization and Training of the 2nd Ranger Battalion, 1967.

National Archives and Records Administration, Washington, D.C. This archive includes CIA, U.S. Army, Defense Department, and military intelligence files related to Ernesto "Che" Guevara's guerrilla war in Bolivia and the U.S. government's response.

National Security Archive, Washington, D.C.

Pressure Growing for Bolivian Junta Chief's Resignation. CIA report, March 19, 1965.

Situation and Prospects in Cuba. CIA report, August 5, 1964.

The Che Guevara Diary. CIA report, December, 1967.

The Crisis USSR/Cuba. CIA report, October 26, 1962.

The Fall of Che Guevara and the Changing Face of the Cuban Revolution. CIA report, October 18, 1965.

The Situation in Bolivia. CIA report, September 14, 1967.

Threats to Barrientos Regime in Bolivia. CIA report, May 28, 1965.

Turmoil in Bolivia. CIA report, November 6, 1964.

Waghelstein, John D. *A Theory of Revolutionary Warfare and Its Application to the Bolivian Adventure of Che Guevara.* Master's thesis. Cornell University, 1973.

PERIODICALS

"Bolivia: Operation Cynthia." *Time,* July 1967.

"Bolivia: The Case of Regis Debray." *Time,* September 1, 1967.

"Bolivia: Unwitting Betrayal." *Time,* November, 1967.

"Cuba: Come Out, Come Out Wherever You Are." *Time,* June 1965.

"Latin America: Elusive Guerrilla." *Time,* September 29, 1967.

"Latin America: End of a Legend." *Time,* October 20, 1967.

Moyano Martin, Dolores. "A Memoir of the Young Guevara." *New York Times Magazine,* August 18, 1968.

Ray, Michele. "The Execution of Che by the CIA." *Ramparts,* March 6, 1968.

Shelton, Ralph. "Advice for Advisers." *Infantry Magazine* 54 (July/August 1964).

St. George, Andrew. "How the U.S. Got Che." *True,* April 1969.

Veritas: Journal of Army Special Operations History, PB-31-05-2. Vol. 4, no. 4 (2008).

Waghelstein, John. "Che's Bolivian Adventure." *Military Review* 59, August 1979.

NEWSPAPERS

Associated Press

Miami Herald

New York Times

Reuters

Times (London)

United Press International

Washington Post

INDEX